Dream Mail

Secret Letters
for
Your Soul

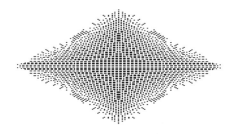

DREAM MAIL

Secret Letters for Your Soul

by

KATYA WALTER, Ph.D.

Read Your Dreams

Dream messages are sent in nightly letters.
This book shows you how to read them.

Kairos Center

4608 Finley Drive
Austin, Texas 78731
Phone: 1-800-624-4697
FAX: 512-453-8378

⬚ Colophon is a trademark of the Kairos Center

Dream Mail: Secret Letters for Your Soul

Editor: Jan Huebsch
Cover design by Kairos Center

Published in 1995

Library of Congress Cataloging-in-Publication Data
Walter, Katya C.
Dream Mail: secret letters for your soul / Katya Walter, Ph.D.
320 p.   22.5 cm.   "A Kairos Center Book"
Includes annotated table of contents, bibliography,
    & illustrations

1. Dreams—dream symbols, dream analysis
2. Science and Religion—interface of science & spirituality
3. Literature—fairy tales, folk wisdom
4. Philosophy—Plato, Taoism, Chinese thought,
5. Psychology—Jung, archetypes, complexes, ego, dreams
6. Mysticism—I Ching, synchronicity systems, dreams, chakras
7. Title

BF 1091.W83 1995   DDC — dc 20   95-75232
                                                   CIP
ISBN 1-884178-18-9 PBK
ISBN 1-884178-19-7 HBK

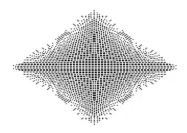

Contents: Dreams & Days

Thanks

Thanks to all those who helped me write this book, and especially to the Austin Arts Umbrella project for a cultural contract with the city of Austin, Texas, that helped me to bring this book to print.

Quotations

I have kept records of a large number of my own dreams which for one reason or another I had not been able to interpret completely at the time or had left entirely uninterpreted. And now, between one and two years later, I have attempted to interpret some of them.... These attempts have been successful in every instance; indeed the interpretation may be said to have proceeded more easily.... A possible explanation of this is that in the meantime I have overcome some of the internal resistances which previously obstructed me.

Sigmund Freud
The Interpretation of Dreams, page 560

The unconscious is not a demoniacal monster, but a natural entity which, as far as moral sense, aesthetic taste, and intellectual judgment go, is completely neutral. It only becomes dangerous when our conscious attitude to it is hopelessly wrong. To the degree that we repress it, its danger increases. But the moment the patient begins to assimilate contents that were previously unconscious, its danger diminishes.

Carl Jung
Collected Works 16, paragraph 329

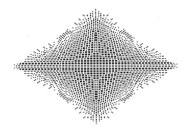

Preface

In the dark I was lying awake, thankful yet again for the gift of a dream. It was about a dog named Happy, my childhood pet, long dead and forgotten, but now suddenly leading me to new happiness. As I thought it over, this dream's simple promise delighted me.

What a gift they are, I thought, these dreams. Yet some people don't know how to open these letters from the unconscious. They don't know how, in James Hillman's happy phrase, to befriend the dream.

Dreaming can be trained, shaped and harvested in a way that the more rigid structures of reality cannot. Creative dreaming can change the quality of your life more completely than any amount of will power can change your job or your spouse or your special hobby. It changes your very being and the events that you encounter daily.

Yet many people don't know how to interpret these nightly messages. Not interpreting a dream, said Sigmund Freud, is like not reading a letter that's been sent to you.

People often suppose that their dreams are just too pointless or silly or fragmentary or scary to bother with. But even if you do want to interpret a dream, sometimes it offers no obvious handle, no way to pick it up and turn it around slowly to scrutinize its meaning. Sometimes a dream seems so long and confused, just a bunch of vague mishmash…so why bother? Maybe dreams are just random residue left over from the daily intake of experiences, some say. Maybe dreams are just garbage in, garbage out.

But as a friend put it recently, "If dreams don't mean anything, then why are they so important?"

Exactly. It's the kind of observation worthy of Gracie Allen or Oscar Wilde or a Zen koan. It goes in a circle yet arrives somewhere new. It is analog, like dreams. Dreams make great sense, yet they are inexplicable to the rational mindset that has been approved for so many years in Western culture. Cartesian logic favors the scientific method of testing for statistically predictable and exactly repeatable results by setting up laboratory conditions such that anywhere in the world, a certain experiment will offer the same results each time that scientists go through those same steps.

Sure. Just try it with dreams! Get a hundred clones and put them all into beds around the world and tell them all to go to sleep simultaneously and dream about the same thing. Good luck.

Dreams just aren't delivered in the statistical linear way favored by Newtonian science. Each dream is unique, just as you yourself are unique, not just a statistic. Just as your lifetime, and even each day of it, each moment, is unique, never to be repeated exactly, no matter how many people will eventually live throughout the whole history of humanity.

Why not write a book? A book showing a month of an ordinary life—like mine, for instance—within the context of its dreams. The eventual result became this record that goes from Friday, November 4, 1988 through Saturday, December 3, 1988.

This book is not abstract theory; instead, it records events and dreams in a day-by-day log. It is a chronicle weaving dreamtime and real time together, so that the symbolic life and the physical life become one. It reads sort of like a novel, I am told, yet it is basically a primer of dream interpretation. And it is all true.

To protect everybody, I have changed names in all cases but that of Flem de Graffinreid, a classmate from high school of thirty years ago—and his name is just too beautiful to change.

So this is how *Dream Mail* began. It started with that wonderful dream of my childhood dog Happy straining at her leash, her plumy red tail waving with excitement and curiosity as she leaned forward into the future. Why not write a book showing dreams from the inside out, I thought drowsily. At that moment, it all seemed possible, and I just needed to begin. With a peaceful heart I went back to sawing logs.

And I dreamed:

CHAPTER 1

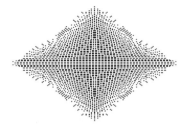

Sawing Logs,
Building Dreams

He and I are traveling together, going beyond the ordinary tourist stops. I see a green, inviting bosky dell down to the lower left and I point to it.

"Horses are in there," says a man. He's suddenly standing there before us, at the gateway to this inviting place. "It's where we teach rope tricks."

We go through the gate, my male companion and I. I'm acting rather casual about all this, yet I'm delighted too.

We find a house. We go inside where there's a single bed for us to sleep in, with a warm fuzzy-looking blanket—puffy wool—tucked around it. This bed has no frame; it rests solidly on the ground. Other single beds are here too, where other people can come in and sleep. Somehow it doesn't bother me. I don't look on it as an invasion of privacy, but rather as comforting and companionable.

We go out the back door, on down to the wonderful seashore. It's an odd mix of grassy patch and water's edge, with ferns rising by the lagoon. The ground is submerged into ocean in spots. So green and inviting. I walk about, describing things as though I'm a guide, but in a slightly exaggerated, amused tone that signals I'm also aware of the humor in doing so.

"And here we see the beautiful seaside lagoon, the shallows by the land. Millions of years ago, and perhaps a hundred feet down, the ocean poured in, covering this interior. Bog and fen, fern, palm and frog, this land slowly emerged from the great interior sea of the past into the solid ground we walk on now. But strolling along the edge of this lagoon, we can still see the most amazing sights."

I point out a little creature submerged in the water, a black and white spotted colt. So there really are horses here? How to rope and use them, though?

"Dobbins," the man says beside me. "That's a sea horse."

"Really?" I am amazed. "But I thought...." And I get a moment's silent image of what I've always called sea horses, those tiny S-curved, decorative but rather useless creatures that are sometimes dried out and pasted into a scrapbook as a memento.

I look at this little black and white colt lying on the wave, resting in its curve within the current, so comfortable and at home there. I know it will grow into a strong and reliable horse. Domesticated to do work. I thrill at the wonder of this. I hadn't known this about sea horses.

"But there are other creatures too—" and he points to a little dragon "—and here are fish."

I see four fish that come skittering up into the shallows. They move onto a concrete step where we can look at them more closely. They are lying there flat as flounders, almost transparent yet brightly colored. And then I see that some of them are frilled with cilia hairs roundabout, rhythmically waving. They look like diagrams of complexes, I realize. Like networks of relationship, or ways of organizing energy. Oh, that's what these fish are doing as they move to and fro, waving their fringes. They are relating.

The man names them now. "That one is Blast" —or maybe he said, "Brag"—I'm not sure which. "And that one's called Jewing Eyetie."

"What?" I'm shocked, certain that I haven't heard him right.

"Jewing Eyetie."

"Really?" I don't like these pejoratives.

"Really. Watch them, you'll see. We name them by how they act with each other." Then I see that they are skirmishing, these flat complexes, and that Jewing Eyetie has just been provoked to fight back against the others and defend itself.

I wake up…to realize that this dream is showing me the way! How to write the dream book! This little sea colt is my transport to start swimming in the unconscious, developing some rope tricks to harness a dream's horsepower. We'll learn to ride this new power. We'll develop techniques. First though, let's just get to know the wild, skittish sea colt and befriend it.

Welcome it. Like any good friend, your dream wants to relate to you. It works in analog fashion, telling you a little story instead of a set of statistics. It gives you an analogy about conditions going on inside your psyche. So rather than dissecting a dream distantly and logically, relate to it. It wants you to become acquainted with it.

Approach the dream first by considering its mood or tone. The mood here—note this spotted sea colt lying goodhumoredly in the curve of the wave—says that this trip will be fun, quirky, and informative. Its setting is verdant, full of mystery. I and my dream companion—is that you?—are traveling beyond ordinary reality into a fertile green domain, a bosky dell nourished by the watery unconscious.

Look, through that gateway are many horses—but the gatekeeper says we'll have to learn some rope tricks first. This chapter will show you how to tame and ride the horsepower of a dream's libido energy.

Now let's move on through the doorway—as one does when settling down for the night into sleep, perchance to dream. Here in the great collective bedroom where everyone meets to sleep, we find a comfortable, secure bed. A single bed, so perhaps this male companion is some part of me. Jungians would call him my animus. (Or female anima if the dreamer were a man.) This inner companion of the opposite sex is my psychic partner, my inner guide. One often unfortunately projects this guide onto a real partner in everyday life, making impossible demands on that poor human. Nobody can be as flexible and helpful as a good dream mate.

Oh! So many beds are in this shared house of dreams. Notice, there's a cozy bed for you, too. I won't consider your presence to be an invasion of my privacy. Even in our separate bodies and beds, we all travel together down to the ocean each night, into the collective cradle of dreamtime that rocks us all.

I will act as a rather casual guide here, using a slightly humorous and exaggerated tone to make my points—after all, it's quixotic to take a word tour through the wordless imagery of dreams. But this is exactly what will be happening throughout this book. How amusing.

And even as I am guiding you, I am learning too. My inner companion (who exists beyond my waking ego boundaries) points out details to me. He even names the black and white colt lying curved in the wave—"Dobbin"—and he tells me it's a sea horse, a notion that thrills me…and does even now, when I'm awake. For I know this sea horse will grow into a strong transport. But here at the beginning, it's only a colt. Hmm, black and white...colors that I associate with yin and yang of the Tao.

My partner also points out a dragon of creative energy. And the little flat fish skittering up onto the step of concrete day so we can study them more closely. They represent complexes, nearly invisible, yet brightly colored by emotions. A dream shows complexes at play and war in the psyche. Just look at their names: Brag. Boast. Jewing Eyetie.

My companion calls one complex "Jewing Eyetie." Yes, I don't like such slurs. But this nasty edge to the dream is making a point. Much of real life is not nice or polite or politically correct. People call each other names and act hostile and make war. One cannot gloss over embarrassments in reporting a dream. I must observe the dream carefully and report what really goes on—not just what my ego would prefer.

A dream can be frightening or overwhelming, like the ocean. It can be soothing or awesome or enchanting—like the ocean. Everchanging yet ever the same, its waves shift over the deeps in the psyche. We can never plumb all of this ocean nor uncover all its riches. We cannot stay in here too long, either, or we become lost in the enchantment of the deep and drown. People in mental institutions are drowning in the oceanic unconscious. Dream readers, though, can learn to swim in it with delight.

This great ocean is a primordial symbol in the forgotten language of dreams. It is our first and deepest home. We humans rose slowly from the ocean, evolved on its edge, climbed into the trees and ran on the savannahs and finally settled into the towns of clustered development. But every night we still fall back into this ocean when we sleep, slipping as disembodied psyche into the flow of a boundless ocean.

Yet when we wake up from a dream and talk about it, we are standing on the land peering into a salty lagoon. We ponder the creatures that have swum up into the shallows of our dreams for inspection. We can only actually interpret them from the solid ground of consciousness.

So how shall we approach this unconscious ocean to utilize its power? First, respect its force as a mighty friend larger than your human ego, a huge power that you can befriend or outrage. Learn to ride your sea horse bareback. Tame a sea serpent. Meet a mermaid. Or be one.

Honor the power of the dream. Acknowledge its stormy face and its sunny sparkle, its crisp breezes and calms and Sargasso Seas of tangled impediment. All aspects of this interior ocean offer messages about your changing inner life. Waves have their hidden rhythms and intent.

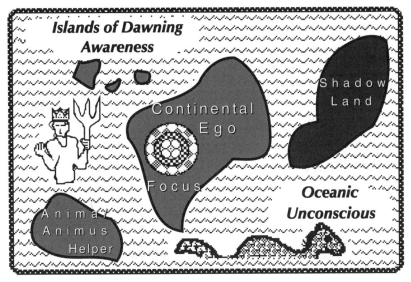

The Known World of the Psyche—A Partial Map

In this ocean, beyond the ego boundaries "there be dragons." Ancient mapmakers printed such warnings on the seas running off the edges of their parchment—and indeed, it is true.

Here's an incomplete map of the oceanic unconscious. It shows a few major continents and an archipelago of emerging awareness. The Continental Ego with its personal focus suggests the solid ground explored by the ego's awareness when awake. It also charts Shadow Land and the Anima/Animus Isle. But beyond the known world there are indeed dragons, along with other larger-than-life archetypes symbolized in mythology, such as King Neptune, Circe and the Flying Dutchman, to name just a few. All these complexes of libido energy have formed around certain triggering nodes.

This ocean is often called *she*, the colossal *she* of our collective mother, full of mysteries that we can sink back into, just as we came out of her at birth. She is both beautiful and threatening, a good mother, then bad, next indifferent, and then enchanting. Everchanging, yet ever the same. Spellbinding. Men sometimes marry the sea instead of a fleshly woman—or sometimes they just seek her proxy in every port. Lonely women in New England climbed to a little railed "widow's walk" up on the peaked roof to gaze across the empty horizon searching for the masts of a husband's ship returning from a long voyage.

Not only the ocean, but any big swallowing collective can stand for this primal sea of the unconscious. It can be any vast body that blindly swallows the individual—take for example, those gray-flannel suit and white-shirt days of the early IBM corporation, the monolithic Ma Bell, the Church, Mother Russia, Red China.

Bureaucracy tends to become a vast, amorphous, swallowing ocean. Sea widows become greenbelt widows—and widowers—who surround a downtown complex as their mates drive in to tend some vast corporate or bureaucratic hive that employs people who often feel like sexless droning workers used as brief disposable partners. If some vast inert body demands your slavish devotion for its mindless maintenance and the continual enlargement of its inertial mass, then you are lost in an oceanic void. It drains your energy instead of renewing your creativity.

If you decide to become heroic and take a trident to the sea and claim your personal power, why then, you become like Neptune. You become a mermaid singing to calm the waves. You become the ruler of your inner ocean by rising above its overwhelming power. You become heir to a realm so rich and deep and wide and full that no foreign power can dominate it all, no complex can poison it all, no human can know it all. It lies just beyond your consciousness, waving and waiting to be explored and lived in. And you share it in common with others.

In 1580, Queen Elizabeth I of England implied as much when she spoke to the Spanish ambassador of our planet's oceans: "The use of the sea and air is common to all; neither can a title to the ocean belong to any people or private persons, forasmuch as neither nature nor public use and custom permit any possessions thereof." So true. It is likewise true with this inner ocean that is somehow shared at the deepest level. We all connect beyond our personal boundaries into the larger ocean.

Remember those dream fish? They are the complexes you glimpse in the great night sea. Everything in your psyche is organized into complexes of energy. For instance, the ego itself is a huge complex that postulates your individual identity. It can be a useful thing too, this ego. It gives your psyche a solid place to stand for viewing the universe.

Smaller islands arise from the deep, too—like the shadow and that inner guide called anima or animus. Many semi-autonomous little complexes skirmish around the boundaries. They act and react to protect themselves. For example, take that flat-fish complex named Jewing Eyetie. It was fighting back against an attack. Sure. Name-calling triggers a defensive reaction. In just this way, each dream reveals its message in wordless mime. So watch your dream closely and honestly to decipher the complexes that it is acting out.

These dreams are the fish that you catch every night in the oceanic unconscious. Do you catch them or just let them swim by? Go angling in your dreams. You can catch, cook, consume, and absorb them daily to power your waking life. How well you nourish your waking life depends on how you handle the catch of your dreams.

Each complex is a cluster of things organized by its feeling tone. It joins apparently disparate items and organizes them around a common emotional tone. Below are a couple of complexes in Joe. One is organized around loyalty, and the other is organized around dogged determination. They happen to relate through the common tie of duck hunting and Hershey bars. That Loyalty complex on the left shows what Joe is loyal to. The complex on the right shows what triggers his dogged determination. The coil at the bottom shows the tie that binds them together. Joe likes to take Hershey bars along with him when he goes duck hunting on the lake, and he has in fact developed a loyalty to this brand of candy while duck hunting. And eating a Hershey bar somehow triggers in him a sense of dogged determination.

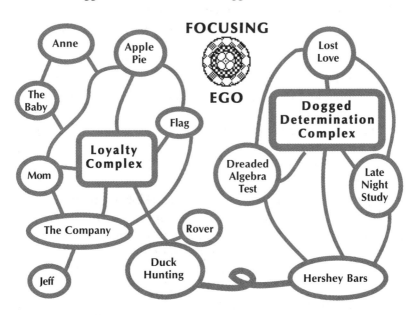

Two Complexes in Relationship in Joe

How come? Well, long ago in college Joe doggedly crammed for an algebra test while brooding over a lost love and eating Hershey's candy bars. Now, eating Hersheys triggers in Joe a certain poignant loss that needs consoling, a resolve to plug on through, and a feeling of being without women as he sits alone in the duck blind eating a Hershey—even though none of this is conscious—certainly he doesn't think specifically about lost love or an algebra equation.

Complexes are neither good nor bad. They just are. Complexes are merely the organizational patterns in the psyche, so the word "complex" is a neutral term. They can help or hinder us, depending on how they're structured, how they hook up together. These networks of energy seek to maintain ecological balance in the life of the psyche. Some complexes are useful—like that inner prod to board the daily train and reach the office by 9:00 a.m. Some are not—that same urge in a workaholic who's on vacation. The urge to smoke? Your ego says, "Hey, it's stupid, unhealthy, smelly, addictive, and expensive." Your complex retorts, "Hey, I like it." Likewise with the addiction to a destructive partner, heavy betting, or shoplifting...you name it.

Complexes don't listen to simple reason. They just aren't motivated by linear chains of logic. Instead they are entrained in analog networks of emotional resonance in the right brain. That's why whatever you learned in childhood is still so powerful later on. These networks of affect hang together in clusters in your psyche, sensitive to emotional tones, sending out feelers that wave around their edges like cilia...fighting and feeding on each other's energy. You tame a complex by bringing its pattern up into the shallows of consciousness for examination. Then retune it into harmonic balance with the whole. Treat it gently—train its analog cycling habits using both your empathy and logic. Then it can evolve.

Complexes do evolve...which affects all the others around it. When an old pattern decays, a new, more evolved one is being born. In chemistry Nobel laureate Ilya Prigogine's phrase, it escapes to a higher order.

Sometimes you develop a nasty monster of a complex that just scares the marrow out of you. A predatory shark or octopus or manta ray of a complex that pursues you in a life-and-death struggle. You can see such monsters of the deep in ancient mythology. The kraken was a giant octopus that dwelt off the coast of Norway. It overwhelmed ships and pulled them down. It appears in the movie *20,000 Leagues Beneath the Sea*, a cautionary fable about a predatory monster of the deep.

Such monstrous complexes can grab your ship of life and pull it down into the fathomless deep, seeking to destroy you. It will do so by setting up a suicide motif that is overwhelming. It will force a life-or-death struggle, shouting: "Being, die! I possess you completely. I've got you forever unless you die! I'll outlast you. The only way you can escape me is death. Better you die than me!" This monster complex doesn't want to die. It consumes the person instead of vice versa. Such an overwhelmed and swallowed person chooses suicide, unable to imagine a life free of this monster complex that is forever chasing and chewing and digesting its poor ego.

That person's finite ego has forgotten how rich and abundant is the oceanic unconscious, how much vaster than the ego's view of the visible horizon, has even forgotten the great mystery that gave us birth can also give us rebirth.

How can dreams do this? They occur in the electrochemical bath of the brain, not in the ordinary hardware of the body. The brain is wetware, a chemical receiver/transmitter that is operating at the level of electrons. Its flowing electric energy lets the brain create analog patterns of holistic connection by forming and reforming networks of references to whatever we do and note daily. It can operate in the holistic realm beyond time limits.

Do you perhaps still think that a dream doesn't matter much? That yours are just too few, too fragmentary, too insignificant to bother with? It's just a picture! Some silly phrase. Makes no sense.

If so, that is simply your conscious ego talking. It uses the linear, cause-and-effect style of left brain analysis that our culture is trained to value highly. But every dream matters. Each image. A word. Each shard is a part of the dream hologram, and it holds the message in miniature.

For instance, when I first woke in the night with that Happy dog dream, it suggested the notion of a dream book. But I needed an intro chapter. So I went to sleep and along came this sea horse dream. It shows how to begin, how to walk down into the bosky dell with your inner guide and rope the sea colt and peer at the fighting fish complexes.

Then later in that night came one of those fragmentary dreams that seems so pointless. Just three words and a feeling:

"Well, old Dobbins...." and also the feeling of dealing with some bureaucratic details.

The next morning, I lay in bed pondering this name Dobbins. Why, it's the name of that sea horse! A plow horse was sometimes called Old

Dobbin. But wait—the dream said Dobbins with the s—that sounds more like a person's name. And S makes a sea horse shape.

Now I remember! In the dream, when my companion called the sea horse Dobbins, I thought, "Hmm. Dobbins. Sounds like an English butler—like Jenkins or Jeeves. Not just Dobbin, a horse's name, but Dobbins, a butler's name." But then I'd forgotten it again.

Until this little dreamlet of three words and a feeling tone reminded me to ask, "Why is this name Dobbins so important?"

Well, look. One name contains the other. The human version holds the horse version, both presented as a faithful servant to the psyche. Dobbin humanized becomes the centaur butler. So these three little words in the dream fragment, "Well now, Dobbins..." were important. Likewise, the feeling tone reminded me to include a list of dream tips in the back of the book, but to emphasize throughout this introduction simply that your dream wants to be domesticated, it wants to become a servant to your soul, not some raging monster that looms from the collective pool in nightmare.

This book reveals a month of the dream mail for my soul, along with the daily events and memories that meshed together in the synchronous becoming of a life. Connecting its apparently pointless, random details into a transcendent pattern offers my life its unique meaning and value.

The bosky dell is the gateway. Its entrance into dreams is yours alone. And mine alone. Each dream you catch in this ocean is uniquely yours. Or mine. It is private territory to explore, to wonder at, fish in, find mermaids in—to poison, or to walk away from. Do with it what you will, but remember, somehow at the deepest source of the collective unconscious, you also join me. In the oceanic unconscious, you deepen and subtly alter the whole pool with the single drop of your being. What you do and are affects the depths of my interior ocean somehow, and what I am and do affects you.

Welcome. Bring along your inner companion and find a bed. I cannot tell you what amazing treasures await. No one else can interpret your dreaming nearly so well as you can, given some practice. Other people may suggest ideas and help things along, but they cannot ordain what your dream means. Only you can befriend and tame and ride it into fulfillment. Your dream is yours. Mine is mine. Let me share a few of mine with you to convince you of their authentic connection and effect in my life, and to help you spy the treasure in your own.

CHAPTER 2

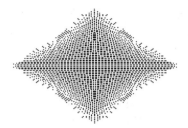

God is Dog
Spelled Backward

Dream Log—Friday, November 4:

Dream: He and I are going together to find the right place to live. With us is my childhood dog, Happy. Happy is on a leash but she's straining forward with excitement and curiosity. So joyous now. I look in delight at her graceful body—Irish Setter—at her long luminous, rusty-plumed tail and feathered legs. So beautiful.

My mate and I go with Happy, who looks radiant, into various places. She's leading us to the right place to live. We reach a landscape that I recognize as familiar territory from long ago. It's a house and view and scenery that seemed wonderfully expansive back then. But now as I stand here and look out, I realize that the view from this window is much smaller and more closed in, more limited than the real landscape stretching around the house outside. The view from this window doesn't show enough. It's too tight, lacking in perspective.

So my mate and I continue looking for the right place to live with Happy leading us.

I lie in the dark, breathing into the pillow to keep my nose out of the cold air. I left a bedroom window cracked too wide last night, I'm realizing now in the real world of thermometers—even as in the dream world I'm still seeing Happy's body tremble with delight. Irish setters are such sensitive dogs. Why is she in my dream?

What was Happy to me anyway, this dog who looks so beautiful here, her coat aglow, stretching forward with her nose sniffing in anticipation and her eyes shining, so alive and realized in this dream?

21

The Happy in my memory is a fluke of my childhood, a grown Irish Setter that my father brought to us children one weekend when we were living with my mother in the tiny town of Rosebud, Texas. This doggy addition to my meager eight-year-old world was a wonder, a mystery of purebred elegance brought into our family only because Dad had promised a friend he would find a rural home for Happy, who had not adapted well to the city of Waco thirty-five miles away where my father worked, traveling back to visit us in the little village of Rosebud on weekends maybe twice a month.

Why so seldom? It wasn't that far away, I say to myself. Commuters do that daily. And why were we living apart from him, in any case? Because they argued all the time, my childhood emotion answers.

But remember, my adult self chides, how hard it was for Mama to find a job teaching school in Waco—only occasional substitute work when we needed more money just to subsist. And remember that it was 1948, when gas was expensive and we were poor and my father was trying to make a go of yet another foundering business.

Remember all that, and how Mama finally got work in the Rosebud public school system and began teaching the only third grade in its only school—with me in her class.

Oh, the peculiar comfortless horror of that! Of being teacher's child in a classroom where Mama daily ignored my hand. She said she could always answer my questions at home. But she didn't.

Ignored in the classroom and yet expected to make good grades as the teacher's child, I sat numb with neglect. No father most of the time, and a busy mother who was there and yet not there for me. And I saw her treating my younger brother with a tender regard that she didn't show for me. So mine was a meager world, emotionally cramped and bereft of much body contact, of animal warmth and spirits.

Then Happy jumped into my life, a panting, drip-tongued, electric quiver-muscled glow that stayed only a few weeks before Dad took her away again. Because of an ultimate, irredeemable crime: she killed a neighbor's chickens.

I cried. I missed Happy with a hope gone sour. And I felt bereft not just of my dog and her elegant fiery beauty, but of some lissome quality of happiness that I cannot even now define.

Lying here, I recall how her beauty flowed out of traits bred into a hunting dog. It was Happy's animal nature to bring us birds, even if she had to kill a neighbor's chickens to do so…as she'd done before in Waco.

So she was killed for it, I think. Because I overheard my parents talking…if Happy couldn't settle in the city and she couldn't settle in the country, why then…. And they grew ominously silent when we kids asked well, where was Happy going? To a better place, they said. We cried and cried, my brother and I, but he was younger and I guess he forgot about Happy eventually. Well, I finally forgot, too. Except now in dreamtime.

Happy was out of place in my childhood. Our thudding family rhythm was the vaguely lapsed-Protestant ethic of my father struggling to establish a small business in a town off from the rest of us, of my mother teaching in a village where I felt invisible by day and somehow also by night. I was miserable in the odd-child-out triangle of me, my mother and brother. Around them I felt stifled into silence by inattention. I was the good ghost.

But of course, this is only how my child's eye saw it back then—not how it "really" was. Parents usually have very different perspectives, and even the other siblings do, too. None of these perspectives is "the way it really was." Each is only a partial view of a greater reality that we've all traveled through together.

Back in those days I viewed my mother harshly. She was easy to blame because she was so close, and because her flaws meshed like gear teeth into my own. It's easy to forget all those carefully-sewn dresses, the spelling lists she coached me in weekly, the lunch money she handed out daily. It's easy to remember the frown that made them seem like duties completed, the cold arguments that chilled my father, the favoritism to my brother that turned him into an apron-string child. Now I realize she was caught up in that archetypal mother's jealousy of a girl child—which I played to so effectively by championing my dad's views whenever possible.

So I was caught in the complex too. Why, at three, I already knew how I infuriated her whenever I coaxed my father into taking me along on a car ride to the drugstore, although I didn't know why. Mama forbade any more car rides, declaring bitterly that I was a spoiled daddy's girl. Her tone said that preferring Dad so adamantly was a vile betrayal. But it was also my power against her.

Archetypes are impersonal. They form huge complexes of energy in the collective psyche. They develop dramas bigger than individuals and possess us with a cold manipulative fury. They pull our strings to watch us dance. They stand above us and oversee our actions so that they can live through us, take shape and manifest their latent patterns through us. We provide the specific contents, they the general form—of jealousy, denial, whatever. We puppets compliantly bend our bodies to their melo-dramatic plots and parrot some old stale script, even as we think dazedly, "How could I say that? Why did I do that? What came over me? What a stupid exaggeration! What possessed me? Oh no!"

But in those days I took Mama's fits of fury as aimed straight at me. I didn't see my own three- and four- and five-year-old role in our family drama…that of the aggravatingly cute ingenue. Gee, why blame a child? So sweet too! For of course, I was the protagonist of my own life.

So despite all the dresses and hot meals and dental appointments that my mother made for me, I still chilled to blasts of cold disaffection rolling off her body and tongue. Though she occasionally said, "I love you" and she did the right thing by making me a birthday cake or cutting my hair, at some level I felt radiating from her a wordless rage, busy in a contest I couldn't understand, much less compete in equally, much less win.

Of course she did love me. But whenever that class-action jealousy took over, it placed her in a terrifying role. In the typecasting of the archetypes, she became the wicked queen, the controlling witch, the bad bitch, and my father became the kindly but ineffectual king-hero-father balked by her jealousy and temper fits. I was poor little Rapun-zel locked away in a silent tower of stony isolation, lonely and guarded by the witch's possessive jealousy.

So how did this happen? I can only report that this complex is bigger than consciousness. It appears in my earliest dreams and in my astrology chart, although planets and positions do not create a karmic contract—they just record it. My job has been to live it and grow my soul by it.

During those two years in Rosebud, we lived my mother's lifestyle, not my father's. My brother was not my friend, not even at that young age. He somehow became my mother's ally and hostage against the loss of her husband's presence.

And where was I? Untouched. Uncherished. Unseen. I had a meager, frantic feeling that I can only call skin hunger. I needed to be held in a tender regard that actually noticed me. And I needed to return it as reciprocal love. But I was invisible, no matter what I did, good or bad.

Lying here in the dark, at last comfortable in myself, I am finally able to muse over this rough-hewn past. All its pain has eventually brought me somewhere good. I can see from this vantage point that my mother's complex was culture-deep. It caught her, it caught me.

Our very culture fears, distrusts, subdues, ignores, punishes women. For being women.

But I long resented her treatment. Took it personally. Pained, outraged, angry at the injustice of it, I hated Mama—because the poor pitiful pearl of an innocent little me, I wasn't at fault! That archetype pulling my strings made me fear, distrust, punish the closest woman. My mother.

Oh, our collective mother image needs rehabilitation, just like our Mother Earth needs it. Mother Nature has cancer, and the mother image has gone bad and runs like a spider along the curving, sly web of our culture.

Well. For a long time I too worshipped at the linear logical shrine of the father, the male domain, the patriarchy that brought us logos and science and the bright ray of reason. I was too afraid of the dark.

These days I'm glad to say that I go weekly, even daily into the dark. Constant little ego deaths. But each brief descent of my ego into the darkness becomes rich beyond measure. Each little going down into the dark brings the sunrise of a new vision with a broader sweep. To go into this and survive it and return daily with treasure is a feat. And I can do it now. Because of what my mother taught me.

So I willingly recall lying in the dark in that tiny town of Rosebud, lonely on the bottom bunk of an old green army double-decker. I gazed up into the rickrack wire against the thin mattress overhead, feeling alien to all around me, shut away for the night in a temporary roost until my mother could find a better job elsewhere. Maybe that was why my skin thrilled so much to Happy.

There was no room in our landscape for what was bred into Happy. Her very name, her tremored excitement and quick leaps, her exuber-ance on long bounds across open countryside—they didn't suit the narrow ways of my family. Our house was in a village, but you'd think it was a tiny New York closet apartment, for all the constriction in our daily lives. A cotton field lay at the end of the street, but we had no romping room for boisterous animal spirits. Not for Happy, our failed-family totem, nor for ourselves. Neither inside nor out.

I thought I had my mother's number back then. I'd toted up all my grievances and the sum came to—Her Fault! I'd noted everything—her petty arguments, her jealousies, the cold furies like the time she threw a mixing bowl of water into my face to drown my tears.

So she always took the rap in my inner courtroom. How strange it is to remember all this now. After I've let it rest it for years, have even dismissed the material as sifted through enough, talked over enough and rearranged in its import, and reconciled.

But wasn't it just yesterday that I thought about my mother? Wished I could express my love to her better. Now that I know it exists. To let go of those old grievances hidden within our new ease together. Hey—just where is this Happy leading me?

Remember, the dream said I would recognize familiar territory from long ago. A house, a view, some scenery that had seemed wonderfully expansive back then. But now as I stand at the window of my past and look out, I realize that my view was much smaller and more limited than the actual landscape stretching outside. The vantage point from that old window didn't show enough. Too tight, lacking in perspective.

True. Even at three and five and eight, I supposed that I saw it all. By nine, I more or less measured the whys and wherefores, already full of speculation from books read alone and undiscussed, and from long thoughts stretching taut from not being spoken.

Often I felt sad. Happy, I thought, when my dog was banned for chicken-slaughter. What an ironic name. Happy had to go because obviously happiness was not a welcome state in our home.

Yet Happy was no more out of place than the other totem dog of my childhood, Tiger. Tiger came two years later, after we'd moved into Waco when my mother finally found a full-time job in its school system. We moved into three rooms and a bath over my dad's dry cleaning business. Apparently they were getting along better now, my parents, digging in to make a go of this marriage despite its limitations. It was a setting-the-shoulder-to-the-wheel and tongue-to-the-grindstone time. My father didn't bring home buddies to the apartment anymore, the way he had before our Rosebud sojourn, and probably that helped.

Then Tiger came one day, and like the previous dog, he was an adult afterthought. A friend of my father's didn't want him anymore, so Dad responded in his spontaneous way: "Oh, I'll take him home." Tiger was a medium-sized mongrel with a short-haired brindle coat, all orangey brown whorling spots, like Australian dingo dogs I've since seen in zoos. My brother and I sensed that he was primeval, so we named him Tiger, the closest we could come to naming the force that was in this bunch-muscled, multicolored, wiry, adaptable body. So different from that elegant and fiery Happy…so maybe this little toughy could stay.

26

We kept Tiger too, for several months, even after he got the mange. My father doctored it with home concoctions of bacon grease and sulfur—we couldn't afford a vet—before my mother finally said one day, "We have to get rid of that dog."

It was summer time, no school, so we kids had lots of time to argue, "No, no, we'll take care of him!" A reluctant decision was made to wait a little longer and see if Tiger's mange improved. Because he certainly couldn't come into the apartment with that gloppy mess on his coat. And he couldn't stay outside without one of us children watching him, because we had no fenced-in yard. So my brother and I spent lots of time trotting Tiger around the neighborhood, taking turns to run upstairs and get drinks of water and go to the bathroom. Sometimes we put him on a slip leash on the apartment building's back clothesline and let him run there.

Pragmatism won. Tiger was too messy and too much trouble. Dogs are too much trouble. No more dogs.

I resolved that I would have a dog when I grew up.

Now I think back, rather sad and ashamed, to those woeful adult years between the dawn of my say-so about dogs and the dawn of my realizing that I didn't really know how to treat dogs. I didn't know how to care for a dog properly, just as I didn't really know how to care for my children well, or for myself.

It was a notion from childhood, this assumption that going through the gestures of lengthening into adulthood makes it official. I made the right moves. Babies, food, diapers. Ballet lessons, little league. And they turned out to be hollow gestures of a child who still had skin hunger.

Several times we kept a dog a few years before it got run over by a car or poisoned by a neighbor—one who (so went the neighborhood whisper) left out poison in globs of hamburger meat because he didn't like dogs running loose in the alley and knocking over his garbage cans. Cheerio, a bouncing black bundle of Cockapoo curls, did several times manage to wangle his way beyond our fence. Cheerio died in my son's arms from strychnine, a black mop of stiffening silence.

But Jeannie came later and had a different fate. She was a Shetland Sheepdog, a lovely miniature of long-haired Collie loyalty, very gentle and sensitive—too sensitive for my splaying-apart family as it turned out, an unheeded barometer of what was happening inside the house. Jeannie developed a skin disease, an eczema all over her body. It was ugly and painful and wouldn't go away.

I recall suddenly—heavens, I too had rashes! Mother said I had a horrible, persistent eczema as a baby. For months and months it spread over my face and body. She finally took me to a doctor, who said it must be a food allergy. Said to cut back on my food variety. She switched me to orange juice and cod-liver oil and Post Toasties. For two years I ate Post Toasties and orange juice tainted with cod-liver oil. I still hate Post Toasties. And cod-liver oil. Orange juice has recently become okay.

So here I am now, just as my dream predicted, traveling with Happy back into my memories, far into the past, reaching an inscape that I recognize from long ago, until here I stand at an old cramped window assessing the territory.

Nowadays my view has opened up considerably. Long years later, after studying psychosomatic illnesses, I discover that eczema is a sign of allergic sensitivity, true, but also of overstrained nerves, of something that is emotionally wrong in the environment which the subject can't adapt to. It warns that some terrible stress is overtaking the organism. So the body protests nonverbally with eruptions over the skin, with falling-out patches of hair. According to the Greek root, eczema means boiling from within.

Skin and hair together, archetypally speaking, symbolize the soul. Skin and hair enact in mute matter what the ego cannot say in an intellectual, verbalized way about the state of the soul. Your skin is your container of finite being. This seamless whole intact net has the potential to shine as an unblemished, radiant container for your identity. And your hair? It pours out of your skin—literally—sieved fine and waving in filaments that are thin tendrils stretching beyond the body's material limits.

We cut our soul-tendrils short in military years and grow them long and luxuriant to make music—*Hair!*—in consciousness-expanding years. In the name of style, we dye this soul symbol in punk artificial colors and crimp it and de-kink it and shave out tonsures and comb it over bald spots and Psyche-knot it and tease it into Fros and transplant it in little chunks—all to hide and disguise and denature and advertise and inflate and decry the state of our souls. It's a code writ in hair.

I lie here thinking that fortunately for me, you can't kill a baby for having an unmanageable eczema the way you can dispose of a dog with a stinking "untreatable skin condition." Because that's how Jeannie went finally, under the syringe of a vet, with all her little stresses and tensions etched deep into her flesh, written into mute trembling matter. My daughter cried and seemed in shock for several days. As I had done with Happy.

Shades of *deja vu!* I'm suddenly remembering my mother's long-ago tale of losing her own childhood dog, a beloved Collie. It occurs to me that we are carrying on an infamous doggy tradition, with slight variations. Shades of patterned chaos! Of self-similar pattern repeating across the family years.

Why didn't I catch on sooner? For example, before tiny Jeannie got put down? Well, I'd learned how to ignore my own psyche's stress. It was easy to ignore a dog's. No wonder I couldn't read the message pantomiming in our family dog's body as eczema, spelling out in skin and hair the imbalance in our atmosphere that I couldn't afford to admit or allay. Outgrowing my own eczema had meant learning to hide in the rosebush, or behind the four-clawed bathtub, or in a book, or crying in the dark triangle behind the dining room door, away from my mother's raging face and bitter tongue and my father's baffled, injured blue eyes. My quiet father. So blue-eyed, as the Germans say of a very sensitive person.

Very soon I learned to hide my head and psyche in books in order to jump into mental rhythms foreign to my own and thereby gain a bit of ease from that insistent whine of my own interior tension. When we finally arrived into the middle class and I got my own room at twelve, why then, I could really hide in layer after layer of apartness. Feeding my intellect with knowledge while my soul continued to starve. Linear chips of dry data made a long trail to nowhere. No exit.

It took me a long while to learn how to feed my soul, and to find out that is the true relief for skin hunger. The skin is the organ symbolizing the soul, the biggest organ in the body. It wraps up the whole package. It extrudes hair reaching out beyond the skin's boundaries to seek soul growth…and it gets shorn occasionally. Now that I know how to nourish my soul, I can look back on those first thirty years with bemused shock—how could I have lived so miserably stunted in soul and still possess all the appurtenances of a normal American life? By contrast, these days I am also shocked—how can I live so richly in my interior and still possess the normal trappings of an ordinary life?

From hindsight, I know that Jeannie's eczema—the scaling skin and loosening tufts of hair—said that something was dreadfully wrong in our household. Soul was getting short shrift in all those rounds of rushing car pools to ballet class and guitar lessons for my daughter and little league and boy scouts for my son and working and makeshift meals around a newly-husbandless/fatherless table, where the mother was both there and not there for her children. And for herself. Does that sound like *deja vu*?

It was *deja vu* squared. In trying to become *not* like my mother, I acted even worse. Maybe my constitution was more vulnerable to stress— being more blue-eyed—or maybe I just had more options, so I went to more extremes. In my twenties I was half in love with death. Then in my thirties, with sex. But Freud was wrong, because both sex and death palled, and then became waystations to something more interesting. The god that I had scorned as unrealistic and kitsch became not just an idea but an experience. God sneaked up on me out of the shadow. Had been there all the time…waiting beyond the dark borders of my ego.

Meanwhile my mother did the trickiest thing she could have done— she grew less possessive, critical, frantic. More easygoing and lovable. Which left me in the lurch. Where could I pin the blame now? I didn't have a negative mother to deal with anymore so much as a negative mother complex. It stayed with me more years. The mother I lived with in my imagination was an ogre, unrecognizable to the normal world. And the father I lived with in my imagination was still not there. An absent father. The disposable and disposed-of man.

Or at least that seemed his fate in my childhood. He retreated into work, where so many men do disappear. I seldom saw him. At home, he was more or less invading my mother's territory.

But these old resentful memories from childhood don't hold up anymore. Why? My parents evolved. So why blame people who no longer act that way? Who should I blame? Myself? Life? How do you clear away the debris of old grievances that have outlived their point?

People say that you can't change the past, but you can. I am doing it right now. My life is actually a hologram. As I walk around it in my memory, some event from the past will pop out and throw things into a new perspective. As I stroll down Memory Lane with Happy, my viewpoint continually shifts on the old details. Sometimes I even come upon new details, perhaps in a Bible frontispiece or a photo album. Sometimes I discover a panorama that I had missed in the forest of trivia. As my perspective changes, so does the meaning of my past.

My poor mother, jerked by the archetypal melodrama into that witch role despite her best intentions to be loving. Poor me, playing against her as the kid ingenue until I outgrew that part…and took up the witch role myself as an adult for awhile.

Here I stand at the dream window and take stock. Knowing that I've jerked my daughter around in this archetypal play. And the beat goes on, generation after generation. All we can do is get more perspective on the trite plotting and then start to rewrite the tired lines.

I must admit that my long-ago perspective, so crystal clear back then, seems woefully limited and two-dimensional now. Back in adolescence I was—oh, wow!—so much more with it than my parents, so much more savvy. I saw absolutely every fault of theirs perfectly.

But as I stand at the window with Happy and gaze into the tight landscape of the past, I know that the view from this old window is more limited than the larger landscape stretching around it. It's too tight, too incomplete, too uncomprehending.

It took me a long time to quit blaming various people and discover the puppet-string scenarios where we go unconscious and get jerked along in the tawdry old scripts written by the archetypes. But we're meant to evolve those archetypes, not let them jerk us around. We're here to become differentiated individuals, not just remain the knee-jerk masses. Each of us is here to explore a tiny unique drop of being in the great genetic pool. Each of us has a reason and a way to evolve this dream onward and not get caught in the stale past.

It's taken me a long time to start writing my own script—to the extent I do. A long time to start moving my own body about instead of having it pulled around in twitchy, melodramatic passions that I can't fathom or justify or wish to claim. "What!—did *that* come out of my mouth? I didn't really mean it. Something just came over me."

Yes, a puppet master looms in the collective unconscious. A possessive archetype can take control of a person so that one's unique identity is lost, submerged, drowned in the simplistic roles of a bad, stale script.

I guess that's why soap operas are both lousy and enthralling. They are trite with the old gestures bigger than individual life. They do not show one unique spark at the forming edge of an individual awareness. Instead they parrot and pantomime all the canned collective archetypes. And we think, "I know him! Her! That plot!" So what's new?

Taking charge of my script allows me to follow happiness in the midst of pain…the pain of others and my own. To acknowledge it and yet be led by happiness tugging at the leash is my life now.

Who can guide me on this path? I look at this dog of my dream, this Irish setter leading me. She conveys me into the underground of my own being, where my hidden panorama lies revealed. And here I stand musing upon my own interior landscape opened up and spread out beyond the dream window. And then I go on.

Where are we heading, this male companion and I with Happy? Do we ever find it? Or is the journey itself the point? Happy is leading us, straining forward with excitement and curiosity. So joyous now. I see her long luminous red plume of a tail and feathered legs, her graceful body—so beautiful. But look, she's not just luminous. She's numinous—touched with god. See that feathering fire that runs around her body…flaming filaments of soul-plume stretching out beyond the limits of her being.

Maybe I'm almost ready to afford a dog again. It costs a lot. Because I will not have a dog in the old way. I won't build a new dog house and set it into the old landscape. Instead, I've been developing a new territory around me, one with a more comprehensive view and easier lifestyle.

But the cost is quite high in this culture where there's so little room for animal shit and everything is paved over and squared off and sterilized, barricaded against animal spirits, with every hour is tiled on a schedule that becomes glazed over with obligations and commitments and maybe a few drinks or pills or snorts to hide that interior wasteland.

It is still a culture where oh, no, there goes another neurotic, frustrated, yapping, lunging, lonely, compartmentalized dog, eroding its barren track in the backyard patrol against a fence or howling for-lornly and scratching the paint off the bathroom door for something to do. This lonely dog guides us to the inscape of our own modern life. In here we find little time or space for connective ease and indolence, for the sheer joy of movement or stillness, for being in oneself and lounging about in one's own soul. Abraham Lincoln joked about getting comfortable in this way: "I think I'll just take off my skin and lie around in my bones." Me too.

This dog that I'm contemplating costs too much for me to afford it and keep up with the modern pace too. Or maybe a modern pace costs too much for me to keep up with and afford the dog. So I want to do this slow and right. If the outcome is too expensive, I'll pay for it in money and time and irritable inconvenience, but the dog, as my soul's barometer, will pay in skin and hair and the whining tics of dis-ease. So to that I say, "No more!"

It sounds like a daunting challenge to find the proper space for a dog in my life. Yet I will pursue it. For it is this humble dream dog that is leading me into connection with my inner meaning. To my unique reason for living.

Long ago I read a witty, depressed book called *Dog is God Spelled Backward*. It was a minor masterpiece of dark sardonicism. Its tone demeaned the god-dog paradox spotlighted in its title as no more than a cosmic pun. Although I couldn't find god either back then, still I sensed that the notion of god might be more than a cosmic joke.

But what? God-dog it, I didn't know. But I was searching.

Now maybe twenty-five years later, I recall that book as I stand here looking out the dream window at a landscape that is bigger than I once knew. I see dear old Happy who was doomed to die for what she was bred for—even as I walk on with my inner companion and this inner Happy that is still alive in me, joyous and straining at the leash and eager to guide me toward the right place using that intuitive nose.

That old house and view became just too limited. Too closed-in and closed-down and closed-minded. From this new perspective enlarged by the years, I can see the god-dog paradox better. It's not that god is negligible and trivialized into a dog. It's really that a humble doggy companion is majesty going incognito.

Uniting the poles of paradox is a simple human way of describing the immensity of god. In the old mythologies, a dog-god guided us into the spirit world. And the lowly beggar at the table turned into Christ. And in eden the lion lies down with the lamb. Offhand paradoxes like this encapsulate the divine union of opposites. Here all paradox is united, since god is comprehensive beyond comprehension.

So who is on this leash? Me or the dog? Or is it god?

Just such tiny paradoxes fleck my days with diamonds and my nights with dreams. Incongruous glimpses of god rise up from the nightly dreams and daily peripheral vision in plumey fire at the borders of my sight. God hides in all of life, cloaking such awful fiery majesty because I am finite in this individual container and cannot bear the full brunt. God gives me only a whisper. A dream. A feeling, A glimpse.

But each time, it is uniquely my own. It can never codify into a religion or rigidify into a statue or sanctify into a dogma. After all, who would build a cathedral to an Irish setter? Too dumb for words.

To think that something so simple, common, and humble as a dream dog is leading me into this book. Let's go together toward the place where dreams have meaning and guide us aright, if we let them.

CHAPTER 3

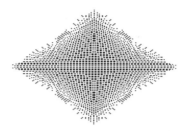

Three Witches
of Entropy

Dream Log—Sunday, November 6:

Dream: Three women are going up in a long spaceship. I am one of them. Then we are doing tedious but necessary tasks, getting things ready. The voyage will take a long time.

I lie here in the dark feeling annoyed with this dream. I don't want to turn on the light and write it down. It's not that important.

But then I say, Hey, remember? You made this commitment to write down each dream, no matter how dumb it seems.

And you can't tell all that much when you're just waking up, and your ego is pooh-poohing it all. That is the ego's most primitive moment…when it's just rousing to grab possession of the mind's reins.

In the dark I hear the train go by. Nearly morning already. I'll write it down when daylight comes.

I do. Not much to grab hold of.

Mostly it leaves me with a feeling. And I'm annoyed with that feeling. I don't want it. Ugh! All that tedious work of necessary tasks, absorbed in *women's* work, while the ship moves on.

Silver ship. Spaceship, long and pointed upward at first, then it arcs out into a long voyage. Where to?

Not a trip into the past, not into the watery unconscious with those ego islands rising from the deeps….

No, this is a spaceship. What does a spaceship mean to me? I associate this with the future, not the past. And it goes—where?

To another world. A spaceship goes to a new world. So I'm going to a new and different world? Traveling with these two women whose faces I cannot even see.

I shift on the pillow—ah!—slightly more interested now in this dream. But still. I don't really want to own all those tedious *feminine* tasks on the dream ship. Why? Because my ego is really rebelling. Why must it be *women* who do this tiresome work?

But dreams see beyond the ego boundary. The landscape of dreamtime is bigger. So the question becomes, did I feel annoyed or bored or tired *while I was in the dream itself?* Because what I feel on my waking observation of a dream is not necessarily the same thing as the feeling tone *in* the dream. After all, I created that spaceship dream, so I'm really *everything* in it: the women, the spaceship, the tasks of necessary tedium. I created it all in the theater of my dreamtime being.

Hey, that's right! The *me* in that dream wasn't bored. Just busy living, contentedly absorbed in tasks, doing necessary work.

Well okay then, I'll accept those tasks.

Hmm. Yesterday's dream looked back at the past. But today's dream points to the future. To a long tedious trip filled with continual effort to reach a new world. These women are on the move. My unconscious says so.

Why is it *three* women? I don't even know them.

Well, this 3 is the number of transformation. A third is born out of two. Man and woman create child. But these are three *women,* not man- woman-child. And all three women are doing necessary work. Is it work that the feminine must do?

What work must three women do together? Hey. During our last walk along the creek, my friend Ward and I were talking about the transformative power of the 3 and the triangle that is inherent in its three points—and he said suddenly in his British accent, "Witches come in threes."

And I said, "The Three Witches of Endor."

Then I walked along silently for a bit, thinking of how witches have gotten such a hard rap historically. Burning, drowning, hanging. The Middle Ages. Cotton Mather, Jonathan Edwards. Witch trials in Salem…Salem short for Jerusalem. Jerusalem, focal point for the rise of three great Western religions—Judaism, Christianity, Islam. All of them male-dominant…while women's power sank into obscurity. Went west into the dark and witchy underground of consciousness.

35

What did they know—those old witches? What was their magic? Basically, it was just how to concoct herbs into medicines, how to watch the moon to mark their periods, how to perceive psychic force in a dark territory that most men shied away from as out of bounds to logic.

True enough, sometimes women used hexes and curses to gain a power they could not wield by brute strength or role in the male hegemony. Sometimes, instead of being wise old women, they flaunted their knowing as perverse spells. They made men fearful of their herbal knowledge, quick to scorn it…so that a capsule from a pharmacy bottle is currently considered more reputable than a cup of herbal brew. Our male-heavy establishment has ordained it…even though aspirin comes from birch bark and reserpine from Indian snakeroot.

We three women on this spaceship…are we witches, then? We don't feel evil to me, though, just normal women busy at humdrum tasks. Riding this rocket? Like a broom once carried us?

Hmm, I don't believe in witches. A witch can't hex and possess you—not one, or even three. But a complex can possess you; it can hex you three times roundabout and put a demon in you. It can obsess you. As though you've swallowed a love potion. A hate potion. A paralyzing potion. It can debilitate your potency into fear and loathing. It can turn a grown woman into desperate Rapunzel still locked in the stone tower by a witchy mom. Turn a grown man into putty. Bewitched.

But witches claim power without relationship. Witches live alone in a gingerbread house in the middle of the deep, dark psychological forest where the inner child loses his way till he can't think straight: "Dammit, now I'm lost and going in circles. Somebody's bewitched me!"

Witches know their way in and out of the dark, tangled forest of complexes. They fly over it on brooms taking the shortcut home as the witch flies, right over the lunatic moon and society's linear logic that goes stumbling this way—no, that way—no, go back around—in turns and twists.

And don't they say that witchy women have loathsome, fascinating appetites? They possess enormous, perverse hungers. They can eat you up whole. A witch fattened up Hansel and Gretel for eating. A witchy woman nearly gobbled up Michael Douglas in the very popular movie *Fatal Attraction.*

Wow—if you *were* a witch, living out this archetype with such great gusto and grue, how could you ever give up such awful power? Such satisfying, far-out, scary power that no one quite comprehends?

But you better be careful, you dark witches out there flaunting your enchanting power. Spells have a notorious way of dissolving at the most unexpected, inopportune moment. Magic is only an unexplained phenomena—for example, electricity is magic if you don't understand the concept of electron flow in a conductor such as a copper wire. My old hippy Peace Corps friend used to do magic every night in Ghana, he said, just by turning on the light.

A witch's magical power with hexes and voodoo dolls is really just a sleight of mind. Primitive cultures often use such techniques to mold and manipulate the psyche. They tinker with the power of suggestion, they command it sometimes without knowing why.

A client once told me that as a child she had been tormented by a recurring dream of a lion that was always starting to eat her. Finally her mother told her to draw the lion on a piece of paper. Then they burned the paper together. And the lion disappeared from her dreams. Wonderful magic, you say?

But the disturbance behind that ravenous lion did not disappear. Banned from the psyche, it next began to manifest in the body, as anorexia and suppressed menstruation. Although her mother didn't foresee this, instead of destroying the lion, it would have been better to work with this recurring dream and find out what the lion was trying to communicate through its ravenous hunger to consume the girl.

A dream is not going to recur again and again unless the psyche is whapping the dreamer's ego with a big stick to get its attention. Such dreams are a signal that something has gone wrong rather than right. A dream reiterates a recurring message only when it has moved out of the paradoxical health of "random chaos" into the narrow confines of a frozen, repeating alarm. Only a frantically traumatized psyche keeps screaming the same message. It knows whether you're paying attention or not. If you keep ignoring the message, it gets more strident and nightmarish. Until it then somatizes into body symptoms.

As for that lion, during analysis this client moved eventually into embracing her femininity, and that ravenous lion one day turned into a fantasy of seeing me as a friendly female lion curled up in the chair across the room from her, offering her courage and companionship by example. I was serving as a non-devouring, yet powerful mother figure whereby she could start to trust the feminine force in everyday life. After all, a lion mother can eat you up…or it can protect you with a brave heart.

Tame the monsters and dragons and lions by your loving attention. Even a child can do this. Some years ago my friend Janice mentioned that her young son Tom was having repeated nightmares about a monster. I remembered seeing some transformer toys in their living room, those jointed toys that flip from, say, a dragon into an airplane into an open-top jeep, depending on how you flex the parts.

So I said, "Tell Tom that monster is like a transformer toy. It won't hurt him if he makes friends with it. He can walk up to it and turn it into something better…like it's a transformer toy. Tell him that next time he sees the monster in his dream, to ask it what it can turn into that will help him instead, like an airplane or a jeep. And then he can ride it to a good place."

We also talked about a situation that was evoking in him a monstrous rage and envy of his older brother Joe. So what particular talent did young Tom have, I asked? Janice said that he was very coordinated and limber. I advised her to find a way to emphasize and praise this trait.

A week later on our walk she said, "I told Tom about the transformer toy. Thursday morning he came running downstairs yelling, "Mom, Mom, the monster came last night and I talked to it and it turned into a horse and I rode it!" Then a few weeks later: "Tom is taking gymnastics now and his teacher says that he's a natural. So now he's got his own area of expertise." He'd ridden his horsepower to a good place.

This little boy of seven didn't need extensive theory or therapy. He just needed to befriend his dream and go to a good place in it. The key is to tame your dream monster and transform it rather than kill it. *By changing your approach,* you can harness your nightmare's wild energy into a sturdy, friendly beast of burden that will carry you swiftly and joyfully through the nightly underworld into the day's adventures.

Killing an enemy instead of transforming it is dangerous. Just as cursing an enemy really puts a spell on you. Voodoo is full of these shortsighted power plays. Wade Davis' amazing book *Serpent and the Rainbow* tells how Haitian voodoo taps into a startling wealth of psychic power. From Africa came the heritage of right-brain wisdom, where all is seen in a holistic web of meaning. Voodoo recognizes the power of the personal unconscious, which it calls the *ti bon ange;* the collective unconscious, or *gros bon ange;* and even the archetypes, or *loa.*

Voodoo's great psychological insight is at present, however, largely unavailable to the culture as a vehicle for conscious improvements. Voodoo is still stuck in poisons and curses and power plays, unable to use its psychic wealth in a way that will serve the larger society instead of just a canny, conniving individual hungry for personal power.

Power-mad witches and warlocks just wind up cursing themselves. They stunt their souls into ever more wizened shapes. In the mythology, they don't have spouses and children and pets. They live alone with bestial familiars. A witch's natural companion is an aloof black cat. Remember Rudyard Kipling's *Cat That Walked by Himself*: "I am the Cat who walks by himself, and all places are alike to me." This slinking self-sufficient creature can calmly play with a half-skinned mouse, releasing it to watch the mouse hide before catching it yet again. A caricature cat humps its back in indolent disdain on a broomstick that the witch rides over the full moon. Such nasty traditional images of a witch symbolize a solitary feminine energy gone edgy and lunatic.

I've been a witch too—for oh, so many years after my first and then my second child were born. All the ingredients were there. The facade of an attractive gingerbread house, a vast power over my little isolated lonely suburban domain that was called home, those weird unsatisfied appetites that I felt, my lack of relationship with the larger world.

I got so tired of changing diapers and hauling sacks of groceries and carloads of kids in the dim world where Mommy is Queen all day, so tired of seeing my domain of tiny faces starting to frown, complain, or maybe just fall into silence at whatever decision or command Mommy spoke (with such vast power over everything I surveyed in the little isolated suburban queendom that my husband seldom entered).

I wanted more sex and more free time for myself (these were the weird unacceptable appetites, according to my then-husband). I secretly imagined chucking it all and going away to find myself—even leaving my husband and children, like Meryl Streep did in *Kramer vs. Kramer*. Maybe I too would even turn out to be nice, like Meryl Streep, instead of lacking any felt connection to what was going on around me.

Yep, I felt just like a witch—isolated, ugly, and perverse. Although I didn't put it that way. And I hated it. I had more power over those children than I knew what to do with, but less over my remote husband than I wanted. Perhaps the worst horror was that I even knew how my husband felt about it all. Under a sex-instigated spell that he couldn't escape now. Add babies. Add bills. He was caught, for sure.

Witches know. They can go into another's skin, into a tree, into a rock or a cat. They have no ego boundaries so they can go anywhere. Full of empathy. Not sympathy. Empathy gone wrong and diffuse and out of control. Some women get so diffuse that they lose themselves in others and never come back. Oh yes, I recall the witchy feeling that went along with my being a suburban mommy with pseudopower and devalued sexuality and no room for free time or adult interests. Some mommies do manage it all, but I couldn't.

My children are grown now. Actually, through it all I was trying to be a good mother. My definition of it just kept changing, though. Now I don't reside in a little hidden domain of power and harbor weird unsatisfied appetites, locked in my isolation. I've left the enchanted greenbelt for good.

So we three women are riding inside this spaceship instead of on a malign broom stick. Is this penis-shaped rocket our hidden yang power? Is our newly befriended-animus power taking us into a new world? We're doing the necessary, tedious tasks to arrive. But I sense that my mother has been on this spaceship before me, and her mother, and hers, going back through the centuries. And my daughter is on it, now. We're an ever-extending threesome of women riding this rocket.

I'm glad now that we're on this voyage, we three women. We are *not* witches, just women. Each of us has a personal power and can express it through normal, healthy appetites. That old witchy way of possessing the rocket—that classic penis symbol—by enchanting and enslaving it is changing now. Such sly old-style witchery is dying an entropy death out there beyond the silvery rocket skin in the chill reaches between one world and another.

So at daybreak I get up, pick out some clothes from the shelves, and go into the bathroom. In the shower, I suddenly begin smiling as I realize what I've laid out to wear today. It's a space-crew suit! I chose dark blue knit pants, a red knit turtleneck, a royal blue knit top—even with an emblemed zipper pocket over the left breast. In a pinch I could serve as background crew on *Star Trek*. My unconscious has gathered this outfit from the closet for my body to wear today, and now it's even good-humored enough to let me in–belatedly–on the joke.

CHAPTER 4

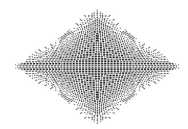

Uncle Sam
Meets His Other Half

Dream Log—Monday, November 7:

Dream: He and I go under a large, multi-pointed canopy made of rigid material into a tent-like interior. Here is a convention called by the government. It has discovered that information floats in the air, tiny as the synapses in nerve endings. This information changes things. It is frightening to the National Defense.

But not to me. I knew it. What surprises me is that they realize it.

I stroll around while my male companion is setting up folding chairs. I walk here and there, exploring. I wait in line to get a drink, standing ahead of a man who is large, mature, well-dressed in a tweedy, leather-patched way, good-looking. An academic. We chat a bit, and then I realize that he is following me back to the chairs.

I introduce him to my mate, not knowing just how to phrase it, because my mate is almost my husband but not exactly. I say to the man, "You're welcome to sit with us. There are plenty of chairs here." My mate says, "Yes, there's plenty of room."

The academic is dumbfounded, although he's politely shaking hands. Obviously he hadn't expected my mate. He'd thought I was alone. He starts to walk away. I sense that what he really wanted was just a woman to take up with during this convention. A brief fling.

Over his shoulder, the academic names an obscure book. He asks me to remind him of the author. I say I don't know, aware that his subliminal message is that I am not knowledgeable enough for him. I smile to myself, not at all bothered.

DREAM MAIL

My mate and I sit down to listen as the talk begins. The area is full of people of all kinds. A military scientist gets up to speak. He is in charge of this meeting. He is nervous, I see, tall and very lanky, but his bony frame is covered by a good suit. His faded reddish hair has a strange, brutally chopped cut to it in the back, and he has a beard that I abruptly realize is meant to hide his youth. This guy is a kid masquerading as an old man.

He talks about data that shows a deeper, subtler level of universal organization than they'd expected. But the sound system is bad, though. People are complaining all over the auditorium.

A silver-haired man on the lower left near the front—he has beautiful silver hair—mutters a complaint, but he won't speak up. I say loudly from the rear center, "My hearing is good and I can't hear you." A black-haired woman on the right nods agreement.

The bearded kid just keeps on going, annoyed, refusing to change his approach or adjust the sound system. Every few sentences, someone else complains or contradicts him or asks him to clarify. Finally he is so frustrated that he stops, saying, "If you don't hear me, then I don't know what to do. What'll I do?"

Is he telling us to read his lips, I think? Will that work? Will we get the message? Who even cares anymore?

But still, I want to hear him. I'm curious. What's he got to say about this new information? People start getting up. The whole area is full of babble. People are leaving.

I go up to the front, and as he's starting to walk off bewildered, I say to him, "This convention center wasn't well-chosen. It's too near the traffic noise on the road, and this cheap building material doesn't muffle it. The space in here has bad acoustics. The sound echoes around and gets lost out the various exits."

I look around. "Let's take our chairs," I say, "and move over to a place where we can hear each other and talk better. I am interested, many of us are interested in this topic."

Some aides are scouting for a new location in the center. The thin, tall man and I look around at people rising, folding their chairs. I see the old concrete floor under their chairs is bare now. I don't know if they are all leaving, or if at least some of them will be moving into this new location. I hope that we're moving to meet.

Puzzle, puzzle. The first part of this dream, about the academic on the make, I can understand that in a flash as I wake up with my head rammed against the headboard by the force of this dream. But the other part, this stuff about the collective meeting? I don't get it at all.

Okay, so take the dream a bit at a time.

This inner male companion, my animus, and I—we always do things together. He goes everywhere with me nowadays. Used to be, when I didn't know that he was inside my psyche, I looked for him in the outer world. As a teenager I saw him in each new heartthrob. I searched and thought I'd found him in every new lover, each new husband—but it turned out he wasn't there, not in the outer world. I'd only found some mesmerizing projection of him in the shape of whatever man would hold still long enough to reflect that gleam in my eye and shimmer enough to become my screen idol, to accept my projection of dauntless courage and loyalty etcetera. For awhile.

The guy would play the role of my perfect complement who'd never leave me and always love me and help me and never betray me and etcetera. What guy wouldn't want to be the perfect hero, at least for awhile? Until the leaves dwindled down and the crunch came and push shoved and the idol turned human despite himself. That moment came along when he finally had to be his own person, not mine. To stay himself, not a symbiotic part of me. I'd say, "What? You mean that you're not my perfect complement here to complete me, but another separate person?"

Heartbreak hell! What a disillusionment!

So man after man in one way or another pushed me—slowly—into finding within myself the courage and loyalty etcetera that I'd projected onto them. I realized that my female body carries male chromosomes too, and my psyche holds a male factor to complement my basic feminine identity. Likewise, in reverse, for men

I meet him often now, this soul mate, in dreamtime. Not in fantasy—I seldom bother with that anymore. At first in my dreams he was so young—sometimes wounded—sometimes only a baby or a toddler. He was mirroring the pitifully undeveloped masculine side of my own psyche that wanted to mature and support me in psychic wholeness.

Before I knew this, though, he tried to manifest in projections on the men around me. I didn't see a real guy, but whatever I needed to complete myself. So men become meat markets of transposable parts and I'd get out my shopping basket and my current menu of needs.

Whatever my psyche required must be waiting out there somewhere—wasn't it?

Nope. Take my word for it, you cobble something together like that and it turns out to be Frankenstein. It was only when I gave up beating the bushes for the right man that I found the masculine power was already inside me, but pitifully undeveloped…needing nurture.

Oh lord, the dreams that came then—of the skinny little five-year-old kid in cowboy boots who rode in a plane with me but dragged his heels on the ground to keep from going too fast. Then of the hulking teenager whose right arm was completely crippled and puckered white, drawn up and tucked up behind his back into an atrophied chicken wing by means of a harness that he'd kept hidden under his shirt.

That one really shook me up. It showed the limitation I had put on my masculine side, crippling its good right arm of logic. In that dream the teenager had taken a dare to work only with his left side—in other words, his more feminine, receptive, holistic side—but his face was drawn into a continual bitter, secret smile that was aware of what he'd given up. A proud perverted smile at the agonizing pain of that strapped-back right arm withering under his shirt, but still he was smug about managing to get along using only that left arm and shoulder that was so overdeveloped and out of balance from swinging his ax to chop the wood left-handed. All because he'd taken that dare so long ago from the boss, that old man standing by the woodpile. You know him—the big boss guy who believes women can't think logically.

Oh! I recall that woman who stood at the kitchen door watching, horrified, as the youth stopped chopping to take off his shirt because it was so hot. It revealed his strapped-back right arm. She hadn't known before. She'd never realized that this teenager had stunted himself so badly just because the old man dared him to do it, and by it, had shriveled his good right arm. What power was laid to waste, made so twisted and tiny…much like the bound feet of a Mandarin Chinese woman.

That watching woman in me mourned. She'd never known; she'd just thought that the righthand logic in me was naturally handicapped.

Yep. That was me. I discounted my logic and hid my "masculine" gift for math, simply because my culture ordered me to bind up that side of myself and manage without it. What pain came, though, from trussing up that side of myself! Crippling myself! But for a long time I accepted it with a secret proud smile—so I just tried to get some man to become my good right arm instead.

Years ago, when that dream came, I told it to a casual acquaintance, and he laughingly tossed off the remark, "You'd better give that crippled kid some rehabilitation."

How succinctly true. My good right arm of linear logic needed some rehabilitation. So I set up an exercise program. Doing it, I recalled the old days of hanging back from logical syllogisms and physics and chess and things that "men do." I recalled Mama saying that I couldn't think as well as my brother could, that she was afraid of math, that I should stick to the humanities in school. So I'd space out whenever I didn't understand a math problem instead of seeking an explanation. Forget it—I could get along without that stuff. Society told me so.

After all, wasn't logic what men did, and better? A girl who tried that stuff was too competitive. So don't compete at all—that was the dictum of my generation of women and a lot before me. Men were getting the same thing in reverse. Men don't cry, cook, care, etcetera.

What a shock it was hear my ten-year-old daughter say in the kitchen one night: "Mom, don't laugh. You know that man Kissinger? I'd like to have that job when I grow up." I didn't laugh. I admired her. Secretary of State! But didn't she realize, I thought? You can be born a foreigner for that job, but not a woman. Society said so.

Not in so many words. It just floated in the air, in the culture. It whispered in the collective values. When I was her age, I put a pillow over my head at night trying to drown out all the whispering strictures I wasn't measuring up to. I'd lie in the dark cringing as that condemning voice replayed my day's deficiencies. That voice spoke in a collective dogmatic intonation that parodies male authority—or conscience, my mother told me. It would decide that I still wasn't good enough, careful enough, pretty enough, kind enough, you-name-it enough.

But I grew up anyway, and much later, I even got wise to this inner patriarchal carper. He was my alienated, bossy, and negative animus. Eventually I got up enough courage to speak to him firmly: "Look, animus, I'm in charge here. I own this body and it's female. That's just how it is. But hey, you've got a big investment in me too, in the psyche. And I love you. So don't pick me apart. If I can't count on your help inside, I'll pretend to find it outside. I'll project you onto some man and let him fail me instead. So please, please, please be my own true inner guide and helper. Dammit, grow up and be supportive and help me get whole inside, so that maybe eventually I can even live with a whole man outside."

Gradually he grew up and we became great and good friends, and I depend on him when I need masculine steel and logical thrust and evenhanded decision-making. He is assertive, not bossy now. We go everywhere together. And of course my real husband comes too, who could not love me half so much, loved I not my animus more. It's the only way I can be true to my husband, by being true to myself first. Because of it, I don't flit off with stray guys like this academic in the tweedy leather patches who was cruising for a brief fling.

Okay, so that part of the dream I understood in a flash. I recognized my animus going with me into the tent, saw him unfolding chairs, doing my psyche's piddling maintenance chores while I had fun. I trust him to do this; he handles it comfortably—all this I can count on.

Meanwhile I explore and get a drink. Hmm, this good-looking guy behind me?—well, he chats and then follows me back to our chairs.

Fine. Even sort of a compliment, right? There he was, standing in line alone, so he mistook me for being alone too. No, he mistook me for being lonely. But I have my partner. So when I introduce my other half, the masculine yang energy, this guy is shocked. He doesn't know how to deal with this sort of woman. He doesn't want to know me anymore. He even puts me down. He just wants a hungry frail he can put the casual academic make on. A brief fling.

Maybe this academic guy is wary of long-term commitment. Afraid of my competence. Cynical about all those shattered women lying behind him along the trail. Those incomplete, susceptible women who can't hold him longer than a few nights because otherwise it would all matter too much.

So what's he doing in this big meeting tent? I guess he's a member of the collective. Remember how he delivered that subtle putdown as he walked off? That little throwaway line showing I wasn't knowledgeable enough for him anyway. That I didn't know the right stuff.

Well, he was on target—I didn't know that book. But I don't care. He was accurate but petty; he'd picked just the exact book for me not to know. He was that voice from under my pillow in childhood that picked flaws in me...on target every time with the technicalities. A logic-chopping hairsplitter. Great on right-armed axing. But way off the truth. Busy at his malicious task of sundering my body from soul.

Hey, I'm still not perfect, but I'm enough. And I don't feel lonely or left out. So maybe this guy was peeved that I didn't fawn over him and stumble embarrassed at introducing him to my main man or secretly yearn for him instead and arrange to meet him on the sly later and have a quick fling on the couch of inner conflicts. Just to keep my inner male side betrayed and my complexes in fighting fettle.

Well, tough. That's the great thing about having a capable inner man around. Root Man, a friend calls him. He keeps being recast in updated versions nightly, sporting new hair colors and demeanors and professions as my psyche's need arises. He's stable yet forever renewing. It's far too much wear and tear on a real man, though, who deserves to remain himself and not become a play toy of my shifting needs.

Oh yes, I do love real men. Walking, talking, giving, taking, loving whole men. They are so gloriously themselves. You see, yin energy I can understand instinctively—the holding, the ocean, the soil, the receptive embrace. But at this active male force, I thrill and wonder and offer myself. To him. For he is the symbol of the infinite other.

Maybe that academic felt lonely. But I didn't, because I already found my mature inner male side.

So what is this collective tent gathering about? I look around.

A military scientist is getting up to speak to the group about a big discovery: things are a lot more connected than they thought. Information floats in the air, so tiny that it goes right to the nerve-endings.

Well, I knew that already. But I didn't know that they knew. Not officially. Don't we all know this secretly, though, in our deepest selves? I've known it all my life, been aware of subliminal information tingling at the tips of my nerve ends—yin connectivity. I sense the future as it shapes clear for a moment in the fog. It's the precognition that women are accused of using instead of brains.

It has its power, this yin receptivity. It's the information network that lets me pick up the phone to call my friend Susan and find her already on the line. "Susan? But it didn't even ring! I was just calling you! So you were thinking of me too?"

Pondering this dream, I watch that tall, skinny guy in front of the crowd, the military scientist with a good suit over his bony frame. Hair chopped brutally short, that scraggly beard to hide his adolescent face.

Hey! I know him! That's Uncle Sam! He's out of his wartime top hat now and the red, white and blue garb and into a well-cut pinstripe suit of the techno-military-industrial complex. That's a fake beard! He's trying to hide the fact that he's really still just a gawky kid underneath.

He talks about this new data that worries the Defense Department, this deeper, subtler level of information that no one has suspected.

He's trying to lead this meeting, but he can't be heard. We can't read his lips. People keep complaining. But he still doesn't change his ways. From the left and the right, people complain and contradict and ask for clarification. Discouraged, he stops and wonders what to do.

But I want to hear this talk. So I try to help this guy out. Okay, it's true, I do love my country. So I'll give him a little advice. Get away from the shoddy material, Uncle Sam. Find a new location in the center. Adjust the sound system.

Sound system. Yep, there's a dreamy pun. Dreams are pretty darn punny. Like that advice for him to find a new location in the center. It's not just the center of this flimsy tent-like place—it's the center of the culture. That's what American government is all about, serving the majority by staying centered in it.

I'm irritated at this political hoopla and flimflam going on right now in the Bush-Dukakis campaign. It's the day before the election, and I feel jaded. But in this dream, the government is realizing that something new is going on, the climate is changing. Politics needs to center itself and become heard by people on both sides. Because many of us do care. After all, we came in here and sat down to listen.

Odd that I, an unknown woman from the central rear of the audience, I am giving advice to Uncle Sam. He even looks like he's considering it too. It's advice that this government needs to hear. Sure, a lot of us are folding up our chairs and walking off. But maybe we can meet in a more central location.

Yes, my unconscious says that young Uncle Sam needs to do some growing up. He needs to realize that we're all connected at the floating information level, that his persona of old man's authority isn't going to work anymore. Hey, I'm glad that Uncle Sam is finally discovering this, even if his defense system feels threatened by it right now.

This deep network can actually work for us, not against us. It can consolidate and center the people, make a basically sound system better. I'm willing to help, talk, listen.

Hmm. I never thought of something before. Do you suppose that Uncle Sam has a girlfriend? An anima figure? What would she look like? Olive Oyl?

Smiling, I get up, take a shower, sit down at the breakfast table, all dressed now except for the soft knitted slippers that I'm about to pull over my feet as I glance down at the folded newspaper lying on the table. My husband has brought in the *International Herald Tribune*.

A headline stares up at me: **"Vote? More Americans Just Say No."** Skimming it, I blindly pull a slipper on over each foot. "Voter turnout is in a downward spiral—experts predict a new low—dip below 50%—cynicism and apathy."

Yes, Americans are walking out of the tent now. I read on: "Americans laugh at the scripted roles during debates—wimp image—grooming by media advisers—lies and distortions of big-money TV ads—NBC political mini-series *Favorite Son,* where the central character is an empty-headed and successful Washington politician."

Then I read Johnny Carson's joke: on Halloween a kid came to his door dressed as President Quayle…it really scared the hell out of him. If he thinks that's scary, what would he make of this dream where Uncle Sam is just a gawky teenager dressed up as a wise old man? Maybe the notion of *President* Quayle scares him because it presents Uncle Sam without the age mask. Callow behind that stiff forefinger and macho bluster.

I read on: "Experts on voting say that it is no longer a default of civic responsibility for an American not to vote. In this emerging school of thought, voters are victims and the culprit is politics."

Well, it's because we haven't learned to cope with political shadow yet. Public figures must be perfect—and they can't. When that wise old man/good old boy facade slips and shows that Uncle Sam's beard is held in place with a rubber band, the platoons of reporters scream, "Fake! Phoney! You slipped! Get perfect!" instead of "Hey, kid, take off that false image and grow up. Get real."

But getting real, Uncle Sam, means admitting that you've got a shadow and even working on it. Uncle Sam, face your own shadow.

It faces me as I unfold the newspaper. It's hiding in the Arpanet: **"Virus Revives Doubts About Military Computers."** Yeah, they do it every time, those dreams. They show the day's docket. Today it is shadow riding the infoweb. I read: "…release of a virus into a military computer system throughout the United States—Pentagon gives flat assurances of safety—no evil genius could sneak into critical military and intelligence networks—but skeptics reject blanket statements."

I read on: "…virus written by twenty-three year old—intended to live innocently and undetected in Arpanet, the Department of Defense computer network—design error caused it instead to replicate madly out of control, ultimately jamming more than 6,000 computers—no damage was done.… But suppose it had been the KGB? …And suppose the last instruction in the virus program was to delete itself? You might never know what happened." No wonder the Uncle Sam is scared about hidden information floating around in this supposedly secure network—that's damn scary indeed.

Okay. I have an idea, young Uncle Sam. Get over your fascination with adolescent rocket erections and rethink the way you flaunt those macho missiles. They spew death, not life. It's oversexed overkill. Like semen, it doesn't take much to do the job, but you've erected enough "big boys" pointing skyward in their "constant state of readiness" to depopulate the whole earth thirty-five times over. Talk about sex and death wrapped up in one big blow job. It's like a kid stuffing his crotch with balled socks. Big show. Big deal. Give me a real man.

Grow up, Uncle Sam. Learn that your shadow foils the boast that you can handle anything. Your ego may claim that it's got everything under control. But shadow's gonna get you if you don't watch out. Any time an ego—whether it's in the body politic or the body personal—grandstands on how thoroughly it is in control, then the split-off shadow will inevitably pop up to spoil the effect. Watergate found Nixon. And Hitler?—he took a whole country down with him.

So this program ran madly out of control, ultimately jamming more than 6,000 computers—just shadow getting its own back, Uncle Sam.

Maybe it's time to listen to what the vastly larger human network is whispering, Uncle Sam: even if you assure us that you've got everything under control, that still doesn't suffice to safeguard the people you represent. Conscious intellect is not enough to insure against death-dealing error and snooping and whispering and analog resonance in the huge invisible collective network of shared information. The global body politic is too big now, Uncle Sam, with too many links that can go public or go haywire. And they do. Hide your industrial warts and nuclear waste—they don't stay hidden anymore. Hide your marital peccadillos and attempt to avoid military service and pot smoking and homosexuality and coke weekends and Watergate and embarrassed visits to a psychiatrist and nodding asleep during cabinet meetings and whatnot—it just doesn't stay hidden. Not anymore.

See how this vast global info network connects us all, Uncle Sam? It makes the Arpanet look small. That's starting to make you sweat. Shocking, isn't it, Uncle Sam, to realize the extent of our connectivity?

There you stand up in front, strutting around as a techno-scientist with the right stuff. Looking good in photo opportunities. But it'll keep popping out, Uncle Sam, this shadow polarizing into the wrong stuff. The press will have a field day pulling down your false beard to let your oozy five o'clock shadow leak forth. How can you possibly hide that your beard of venerable wisdom is fake, Uncle Sam? Truth keeps pulling it off.

Surprise! Welcome to the truth revolution. And this info network, Uncle Sam?—it's just nasty bits of unadmitted truth surfacing and sparkling and dancing in the air. More angles keep faceting forth, noted and relayed by so many observant eyes. Reporters can spot the pinpoint lesions on tapes, candid cameras give the lie to official versions.

After awhile, it may get so hard to tell a plausible lie that we even switch over to telling the truth. That's even harder to tell than a lie. But it's a lot more exciting and useful. And freeing. When governments finally can't keep their secrets anymore, we won't need secrecy. As the big stick of the big lie becomes obsolete, we can seek the truth, fleet-footed quarry though it be. Chasing the truth is a real trip.

So Uncle Sam, be a man and work with your shadow, not around it. Quit trying to look so wise and get wise. Develop some depth and substance beyond your image. Shock us all with your new maturity and wisdom. Face your mistakes and correct them *before* the press pounces on them gleefully. Shock other nations, too, by starting to work with them, not for them or over them. Pass the buck back to the public and ask for our help on *our* problems. Help us become again the real source of government as being such radical conservatives that we can honor the ever-new, everchanging, and shocking face of truth. Turn us on and to and with and about the truth. Give us no prelapsarian Eden. Just take us beyond the primeval fall into wholeness.

Uncle Sam, stop rutting and strutting around Olive Oyl. Put down those big guns. Quit bragging that you've got it all under control. You'll never have it all under control, Uncle Sam, least of all when you kid yourself that you do.

Grow up, Uncle Sam, and maybe you'll find that Olive Oyl does too. Underneath that stovepipe-thin costume, she may even turn out to be Sophia—goddess of wisdom, not a silver screen. Or of Justice, not nitpicking adversarial legalisms. Or of Liberty, not just libertine dumping. Now those gals are what I call *women.*

CHAPTER 5

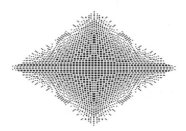

Our Scheduled Night Flight is Delayed; Please Relax in the Lounge

Dream Log—Tuesday, November 8: No remembered dream.

Dream Log— Wednesday, November 9:

Dream: I am working. Then the four of us workers are sitting on the floor talking. A patient is lying on the floor beside us. He's a young man, fully grown, healthy-looking, lying there asleep. He wears blue jeans—bell bottoms with gold medallions and hieroglyphics printed along the seams and down the front. Along the hem. It is all symmetrical, some sort of folk design. His face looks oriental— Chinese, I think, lighter and different from Japanese features. He wears a flattish hat with a little bill. He doesn't seem in pain. I wonder what's wrong with him.

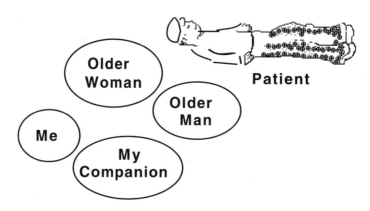

The older woman is talking. She is large, bulky, mannish-looking. She sits on my upper right, talking to the older man. I watch her wide, heavy lips moving as she says, "We should stop work when the money runs out. We should work only as long as the money they've brought in lasts, and then stop."

I look around and wonder where we are. Maybe some war zone, some Oriental theater of war.

"Yes," says the older, gray-haired man. He has a crew cut with silver bristles of hair. I see his scalp showing through. He has a large gut bulging over his wide brown belt of crude, thick leather. He looks heavy, sluggish, pragmatic, a soldier grown old.

I finally realize what they're saying. Interested, I come out of my preoccupation with their appearance. The younger man, my companion, is protesting, saying, "But we can't do that, not in the middle of operations, or they'll die."

I say, "No, maybe they're right. That's what people do nowadays. You don't work more than you get paid for. It's not right, they say."

"But how will these patients live? How will they last while somebody goes back to their home base to get more money?"

The large, fleshy woman says, "Maybe they'll start bringing extra money with them in the first place."

Then the older pair start talking about what they're going to do to the Chinese man's left leg. I look at his bell-bottom jeans with their symmetrical gold design—it's a band of medallions and strange marks put together. It feels holy or something.

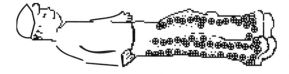

The woman says, "I'll show you how we'll do it." She takes a tool like pruning clippers and starts cutting open the front of his left pants leg. "We'll cut the bone out along here...." She gestures down the leg. It disturbs me. Are they going to make his left leg shorter? I look at the firm pale flesh and I don't understand why he needs this operation. Now she's making a second cut on the pants leg, apparently to lay the fabric back like a flap and show the whole leg. Then she says, taking up the shears again, "I'll cut off this gold border on the flap. It'll just drag and get in the way."

I am furious. I know these pants are valuable and beautiful, that he is poor and needs them. Why is she cutting up his pants when she doesn't need to, just to reveal where they'll operate eventually? Why not just take the pants off?

I take the shears away from her and say, "No, don't cut that hem off. He can sew the seams back up and use the pants again. They'll be symmetrical again. But not if you cut off the bottom and throw it away." I stop her.

Then we're in the operating room. I see that a little baby is being operated on, in the abdomen. I am worried about it. Somehow it seems to me like another version of the Chinese man.

Then, abruptly, Westerners are coming in for the Olympics. A helicopter arrives and a group of men get out, joking. One looks like MacLean Stevenson from MASH, and I wonder if this is Korea. He is holding up a severed eyebrow—it reminds me of an angry oriental eyebrow off a Samurai warrior. He puts it up over his own eye like a raised Groucho Marx eyebrow to give a quizzical look at the remark he's making. They head over to a football field with a stadium. These people act like it is an Olympics—but it's a war zone! I'm puzzled.

Then suddenly, I'm back with the baby. Somehow I know it's the young Chinese man, but turned into this baby. The operation is over now. He stretches and I see his stomach extending out of his diaper. The stitched cut in his belly ruptures. The clipped tubes of his severed intestines poke out. Odd, they look like the stiff white tubes in a chicken's neck in a bag of chicken parts.

I am pushing it back in and holding it all together with my hand, shouting for someone to come help me save this baby. But the older couple are sitting down on the grass eating lunch. They won't come because they haven't been paid for it.

I know that this baby is dying. I feel heartsick. All the babies around here dying for lack of care! I am in despair.

I awake in the night—my god, shivering! What's all this about? Gruesome! Maybe I'll go back to sleep and just forget it.

But no, I turn on the light and write the dream down. Because I've promised, because there must be *something* useful to this complicated mess. And I'll forget it completely if I don't bother now.

So beneath the little night light I dazedly scribble words, not waking up my husband John. Maybe in the morning it will clarify itself. I go back to sleep, groggily sending up an interior SOS for help on this complicated dream. And I dream...

Dream: Events are going on. A short modern tool is being used. Someone is holding it to do work in front of me. I contrast it with a tool that's hanging on the wall. "That's the old tool up there," I say.

The busy person turns around and looks at the wall. "What, that?" The tool hanging up there is verdigreed metal, partly dull green and partly polished copper. It is shining a soft rose. It is curved and ridged like a ram's horn, and I think of that trumpet blown by a Jewish rabbi or official in *Last Temptation of Christ.*

"That greeny-rose thing?" the worker says. "That looks like wood."

"No, it's metal," I say. "It is metal that looks like wood."

We look back to the modern shiny tool in the worker's hands. I suddenly realize that this modern tool is wood veneered over with shiny metal—it is wood that looks like metal.

Abruptly I wake again, awed at the wondrous beauty of the old tool on the wall. It is made of metal that looks like wood. I smile.

This dream I understand immediately. I even know that I'll still recall it in the morning too, without writing it down. Because of the punny humor. Wood-would. Metal-mettle-medal.

The old holy way was to work with metal-mettle-medal that on the outside looked like mere wood. Organic. Soft and curving and natural. With a gentle "I wood-would do it." Curved with intent like a holy trumpet. But the modern way is to put a lot of polish and glitz on the surface so that it looks like metal-mettle-medal outside, but underneath, it isn't hard with resolve. Underneath, it is just soft wood—"I would if I could, but I can't." Inside, there's no real metal-mettle-medal.

That old tool hung up on the wall. So beautiful. I groggily resolve to take it down and use it. And immediately I fall back to sleep.

Dream: I'm taking my Macintosh computer somewhere to get it upgraded. Then I carry it back home, wondering how it'll work now. Gus is coming to visit me and I'm amazed. Because Gus won't fly in an airplane. He's afraid. Has he conquered his fear of flying? I want to get this computer going that so I can show it to him when he comes.

I hear the doorbell ring, voices in the living room as someone answers the door, greeting Gus. I hurry to get everything ready, hurry to arrange all these trays of information disks in order.

But I'm doing it in the dark, in this study that is—now I'm a little surprised to realize it—is built into a huge closet on the left as you come down the hall toward the bedroom.

Odd, a two-stage frame sits over the computer to hold things.

And what are these two items beside the frame on the left? They look like flat, transparent sun visors taken off a car. They are paper-clipped together.

I plug in the computer. A bright surge—wow, I see it's really more powerful now. I hope this upgrade will work out. A picture comes on the screen and I take it through several procedures. Looks like it works fine. Then I glance down beside me. A picture is appearing on the transparent sun visor beside my left elbow. It's just like the one on the screen. And here's another one behind it on the second visor, but they're folded and wrinkled together by the paper clip.

Wow, these visors are portable screens! How funny! You can take them to other places and see what's going on at the computer. But hmm—maybe I'll have to turn off the computer to remove this paper clip where it's bending the picture.

Amazing. Gus will be amazed. And pleased. I giggle.

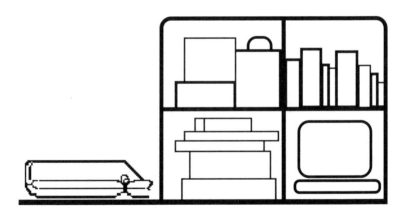

I lie in bed smiling. What a comical dream! It had a thrill of new technology, that kick of a new gadget. It was like a little miracle to the child in me.

The child in me. It recalls that child dying on the operating table. All those little babies dying. Oh my god.

Oh! Suddenly I know what the dreams mean. I'd gone to bed tired. On Monday, I was exhausted—because writing Chapter 4 down took so much time and my feelings went so deep. So it was a relief on Tuesday to wake with no dream recall. Gladly I took the day off. But even then, I felt drained and almost grudging as I got into bed last night. I was thinking, "I'm going to dream tonight, and then I'll have to wake up and write it down, and then tomorrow I'll have to write out a chapter on what it means. Because I made this damn inner commitment to do this book on dreams as a month-long log. Dammit."

"But maybe I won't dream again tonight," I thought. Wondered, "Have I bitten off more than I can chew?" After all, I've got other responsibilities, too. I want to do more than just sit at a computer in my spare time and analyze dreams. It's even narcissistic, don't you think, this sitting pouring over it so hard? What have I gotten myself into? As I turned out the light last night, I was dwelling on the sheer inconvenience of it all.

For one thing, it just takes longer to write this stuff down, spell it out, than I'd guessed. These associations pass through my head lickety-split. A thought comes, and then another, and like tinkertoys they slowly start fitting together and I begin to see the structure. But to write it all down!…it takes hours.

"Maybe I'd better cut back," I thought, "abbreviate what occurs to me about these dreams." I had supposed it would fill just one or two single-spaced pages for each day. A thin little book. After all, it leaps through my head in quick flashes.

Take today. Flashes this morning as I got up and stumbled into the bathroom, started to undress for a shower, suddenly realized as my hand was crossing my left ear that I'd lost one of my gold hoop earrings.

Odd. They almost never come off. I wear them day and night. Gold hoops embossed with flattened sheaves of wheat, symmetrically stylized.

Oh dear, I hope that earring is in the bed. I don't want to lose it.

I go back to the bed and uncover the bottom sheet. No earring. I pull the sheet loose, lift the edge of the waterbed mattress. We have a waterbed for two reasons. One, to ease my husband's back pain from a deteriorating disk. Two, it tickles my fancy to sleep on a slab of water, to float off to dreamland on the premier symbol of the unconscious.

But we don't use an electric heating coil in it, because under the carpet, this Swiss floor is naturally warm from hot water flowing through the concrete in hidden conduits. This whole apartment is evenly warm.

Pulling back the bulging edge of the waterbed mattress, I see a small bright coin. A Swiss five-rappen piece, worth perhaps a penny on a good day. Beside it, there's a black stone from my I Ching set. I didn't even know it was lost. How did this get under here? But no earring.

Then on the carpet beside the bed, I spot my earring! Relieved, I put it back on. Return to the shower. Review the dream as water flows over me. Some of my best ahas! come under this sluicing bath of the unconscious. More insights as I sit at the breakfast table....insights that take hours, however, to write down. All these nuances shift and twist in their avenues of thought and open onto some broad image connecting at the hub—an intersection like the Place de Concorde.

The hub. Oh yes, the hub. That's what suddenly ordered it all for me, put this dream into context. The hub is this child.

I know this child dying on the operating table. It is a child of my mind, this dream book that is still so young. I recognize it because when Katrine and I were walking by the creek yesterday, she said suddenly, "What's going on with you and your children?"

I looked at her, puzzled. She's never even met my children, and they are grown up now, and far away. At my look, she said, "Oh, I don't mean your real children. I mean the children of your mind. What are you working on lately? How is it going?"

But I didn't want to tell her about the dream book yet. I'm feeling too protective about it, worried at being so tired already, wondering if I can manage the month of work upcoming, if it will mature and turn out well...or not. Can I cope with it all. Just like a new baby, I thought, as we walked along. Night feedings. This dream book is a child of my mind, and it demands night feedings. I can't cut them out.

Hey!—the guts got cut out of my dream child. And it died on the operating table. Remember?...my male companion warned us. But the operation went on anyway, and the baby died on the table, its little chicken guts severed and sticking out as it bled to death.

Chicken guts. My ego is chickening out on the dream book, but my animus warns it will die under the cuts, this child of my psyche.

So the dream was set in my own interior theater of war. A big conflict is going on along my Eastern front, my holistic side. This Chinese youth who's lying on the upper right reminds me to say that dreams give oddly pertinent stage directions. Movement at the upper right of a dream usually looks toward the future. "Upward and onward!"—that kind of thing. And this diamond formation with the four of us workers sitting—we're ostensibly balancing each other, but notice how the older female sits higher than me and the older male sits higher than my companion. So this older pair has got the power edge over me and my inner man. They literally sit higher up in the structure. They expect the last say on what to do with this sleeping patient.

They prepare to operate on the patient…no wonder he sleeps while I am warring internally over the decision. Look at his bell-bottomed jeans …out of date now. Bell bottoms—his jeans have bells on their bottoms. Temple bells? The fabric is folk-printed with symmetrical gold medallions and hieroglyphs. Somehow it all feels holy. Beautiful designs along the jeans…valuable…something the poor people need.

Well, that's what dreams are—beautiful golden designs, valuable, something we poor people need. Dreams come out of the blue. They're in the gene (pun) fabric of the folk. They make a harmonious design, if you just string their mandalas into chains of symbols that the waking mind can sort out and deal with. His legs are garbed in balanced harmony. Pants—that's how your cover your creativity, isn't it, your genitalia—so maybe dream pants are how you garb your creative ideas. And legs? That's what you rise up and walk around on. Legs give the stance you take on an issue. This Chinese guy is taking it lying down, this cutting. But he looks healthy enough. Why are they going to cut him? Who are these people, anyway, this thickset older couple who want to operate and shorten his left leg?

The woman is large, bulky, mannish-looking. Her thick, wide lips move in a commonsense voice advising me not to do more work than I've been paid for. "When you run out of money, stop," she says. Sounds practical, huh?

Suddenly I see my old high-school chemistry teacher, Miss DuMonde, coming out of left field. She zooms up like Buzz Sawyer's big bruiser of a kid sister, who wore a football helmet and played tackle: Baby Sister Sawyer. Hey, maybe that's the sawyer ready to cut the bone of that left leg. That dream dame looks a whole lot like Miss DuMonde.

Back when I was in high school, Miss DuMonde was maybe forty-five, what my parents called an old maid school teacher. She had a large frame and a huge bosom under a man's gabardine shirt. It was always one solid color and buttoned right up to that little corner loop sticking up to catch the final tiny button hidden under the collar. Straight nondescript no-color skirts. Men's oxfords with heavy lisle stockings. Women teachers couldn't wear trousers back then. Mannish cut hair, wavy iron-gray. I didn't know it then, but she looked like Gertrude Stein. And came on like the comic strip Baby Sister Sawyer.

What do I remember of the chemistry that Miss DuMonde taught me? Quite a bit. But most of all, I remember her practical advice, her dictums thrown out to the class in this hearty, no-nonsense boom with a little screwball twist on it. Not taking you into logic but to some other place strange and rewarding. Her feminine side outing itself despite her dressing in male drag.

Boom: "Never cut citrus fruit with anything except a knife reserved just for that fruit." Puzzled looks in the classroom.

A hand goes up. "Why, Miss DuMonde?"

"Chemical reaction—citric acid eats up the blade, turns it dark."

Someone else raises a hand. "You could use stainless steel. It wouldn't turn dark." Another hand: "You could wash it." The class snickers.

Boom: "You can *never* wash all the acid off! Never." Deliberate pause. "And *never* use anything but a carbon steel knife in the kitchen. A stainless steel knife looks pretty and shiny at first—it cuts good, at first—but it won't hold an edge. The first time you try to sharpen it, you'll find out you were had for a fool. Can't sharpen a stainless steel knife worth a damn."

Wow! Cursing in class! Miss DuMonde was the only teacher I knew who got away with cursing in the classroom of this Baptist town. The boys figured that Miss DuMonde peed standing up. She also broke local precedent by teaching a "man's subject"—science—better than any other science teacher in my large high school, all of them male. With Miss DuMonde, you learned chemistry from the inside out. Building it up from the kernel elements. Like growing a baby. So I loved Miss DuMonde for her fine mind hidden in her wolf's clothing.

Another DuMonde dictum: "Save those cans from your kitchen. Don't throw them in the round file." (Trash can, in her lingo). "This new generation wastes too much. We grew up hungry as hell in the depression. People throw away too damn much nowadays."

Students glanced at each other bewildered. Save cans? What for? This, you know, was back before metal and glass collection became a normal part of the community ecology. Finally Flem de Graffenried (and I must use your true name here, Flem, just because it is so wonderful)—Flem raised his hand. "Well, Miss DuMonde, what do you save them for? The cans?" It was a puzzle that she'd propounded and he'd finally given up on.

"Anything. These days, I pound 'em flat and put 'em in the cracks in the yard. What with the drought this year, those damn cracks open up wide and fast. And with all my dogs—I've got lots of dogs and dog food cans—so I'm filling up my cracks this year with pounded cans."

That one absorbed me for the rest of the chemistry hour. Round and round the ground file it went. While she wrote chemistry symbols on the blackboard, I sat with images of Miss DuMonde heartily pounding cans flat and putting them into cracks in the soil while dogs bounded all around her. Pounded cans. Filling her cracks with cans. Not with cannots. I wondered where she lived, anyway, that she had so many dogs and so many cracks and so much leeway to fill them up without the neighbors complaining at her weirdness using so many defiantly pounded cans? No cracks in the yard at our house, and I lived in the same clime as she did. Didn't I?

Miss DuMonde was a conundrum. I followed her twisty dictums into their shunts beyond logic's dead ends. I wasn't sure where she lived in her deepest self, under that hearty bluff manner that turned away personal questions as impertinence.

Then one Saturday in Sherwin-Williams Paint Store on Columbus Avenue, I saw Miss DuMonde's other life. First I heard the boom, boom, boom coming along the next aisle of paint cans. I peeked over the top of the gallon cans on my side. There was Miss DuMonde all right, wearing slacks now under her men's gabardine shirt since she was out of school. And beside her walked a miniature version of her. A sister? But right away I decided, no, it wasn't a sister. A lover. Also in shirt and pants, but to different effect—she was tiny, petite, with slightly longer, curlier gray hair. She had a gentle smile and a soft voice that trilled up and down the register while Miss DuMonde sustained the steady solid base note—boom, boom, boom. There they were, base cleft and treble cleft making their own kind of music. And they sounded good at it among all the cans.

Yes, she was just a whole lot like Gertrude Stein. She delivered those hearty opinions that leave you blinking. Uttered those weird dictums beyond logic that somehow wind up making sense as you turn it this way and that, looking for the point. "A rose is a rose is a rose." "There isn't any there there." "Stop working when the money runs out." Logic hides in there somewhere. Doesn't it?

Unless your logic starts to chopping. Chop that holy-medallioned left leg off. Leave that dream baby dying on a table with its chicken entrails trailing. So what if the patient's heart stops when you do? Death? So what? Shrug. Throw it in the ground round file.

She wants to shorten that left leg. Cut off that hem-hymn-him. Turn the dream book into a cripple. Damn the creative impulse anyway, for taking so much energy. Throw it into the round file, where it goes round and round. A rose is a rose is a rose. How do you do when you don't do? Howdy Doody deep doo-doo.

Money is dream-shorthand for energy—it is condensed, unitized, tradeable energy. When I run out of energy, just quit. It's logical. Sure. Just skimp on what I've been writing daily. Abbreviate it, cut it down to one or two single-spaced pages. The account can be shortened somewhere. Why not on the left leg? Hack that intuitive side, that less rigid and more flowing side. Even though chopping it off puts the book's stance out of balance. Cut out those symbols and hieroglyphs, even if they are beautiful and valuable and the poor people need them.

The tough old dame says, "Stop work when you quit being paid! Wait till you get more money. Maybe they'll start bringing extra money with them in the first place." Sounds downright smart, doesn't it? Taken as a symbol-snipping, logic-chopping, cause-and-effect dictum, it sounds bully clever.

Yep. Why work if I'm not getting paid up to the minute? Don't work for love. Can't live on love.

But my male companion disagrees. He says this creative project, this baby book, will die on the operating table if I just quit when my energy runs out.

So what did I answer? Did I ponder my soul mate's warning? No, I vetoed him for pragmatism. "Maybe they're right. That's what people do nowadays. Don't work more than you get paid for. It's not right, they say." They. The big *they.* Those who pee standing up? But it's a posture of only pseudo-pragmatism, in my case. What should be my own natural stance here? Where is the hidden shunt beyond logic to truth? Miss DuMonde has something hidden to tell me, I believe.

Money…energy. Not a bad idea, actually, waiting till I get some more energy. But she also said, "Maybe they'll start bringing extra money with them in the first place."

Extra dream energy? I can't have a whole month of dreams in one day, I realize, nor can I put out the energy to write a whole book in one day. Each day brings its own dream and enough energy for writing it down. New energy will come day by day, along with the dreams.

So why carve up this sleeping patient? Maybe it's just sleeping, not sick. Maybe *I* need more sleep. To bring more energy to this. Hey, why not think up some energy-saving techniques to help me write it?

So with her dictums beyond logic, she's making me think twice, this Sister Gertrude DuMonde. (*Gertrude* comes from the Old Teutonic, says the dictionary, meaning "one who loves spears and power.")

Yes, I need to find a way to save this sleeping patient. My dream baby book. Watching it die, I am heartsick, tired of all the dying babies in the Eastern theater of war.

It's true. I am tired of my psyche's babies dying. Various projects are left littered along the way like tiny and half-grown skeletons. Tired of other people's dream babies dying too. Lots of psychic babies die for lack of care. Lots of left legs of holistic stance get shortened in the operating room—just the facts, ma'am—and it has unbalanced the stance of our whole culture. Damn it, cut out those mandalas and hieroglyphics on the hem-him-hymn, valuable and beautiful as they are, even though the poor people need them.

Hey, maybe I can even turn this Eastern theater of war more easygoing and lighthearted. Make the Olympics more M*A*S*H-like, with gore and jokes that still convey that war is not funny.

So how can I lighten things up for myself? Because I really do want to complete it. I don't want my baby to die on the operating table with its chicken guts sticking out. How do I get into the stadium of an Olympic sport, done for the love of it, not a battlefield?

I believe I'll add some little drawings to convey my meaning, too. It's a little more work but a lot more fun. I'll even go back and sprinkle them into the earlier chapters, too. A picture is worth a round file of ground-up words. Yes, I'll find the fun in doing this. That'll give me more energy. Lift that Groucho Marx eyebrow high. Hey, I laughed out loud today at lunch—explaining why to my husband so that he laughed too—when I realized that to this very day, I still wash a knife blade immediately under the tap water after I cut a piece of citrus fruit. Good old Miss DuMonde.

And I needn't finish every detail on a chapter *that very day*. I can just put an asterisk at a sticky point and go back to fill it in later—like that quotation from Queen Elizabeth I in Chapter 1—that took me over an hour to find, because I couldn't remember just where I'd read it.

The main thing is I need to take that old-fashioned tool down from the wall and begin to use it instead of the short modern tool. That old tool looks soft and gentle as wood-would curved into little ridges along the grain, yet it really is metal-mettle-medal inside. I don't want that glitzy modern tool that looks shiny-hard on the outside, but inside contains just "Would if I could, would, but I can't."

Hey, remember, even half asleep, I resolved to use that old-fashioned tool. That's a good sign. Maybe I'm gutting up and taking up that old-fashioned tool of verdigreed copper.

Copper—it is the metal of Venus, goddess of love. Venus symbolizes a receptive love that attracts and holds. It is not an aggressive love that strives to dominate like her counterpart, the male god Mars. Mars must have his pushy way or he gets mad and makes war, not love. Sure, aggression is necessary sometimes, but not right now. Not right here. All I need is the proper tool for this dream book, a tool that looks soft and antique, like a gentle would. Its mettle is hidden inside.

Notice, as soon as I sleepily made that decision to use the right tool, then the results turned up in the next dream. So I can go modern after all. That upgraded computer has portable screens so people can get the picture from a distance. Yes, people need to get the picture from wherever they sit. Okay, I'll bother so that you won't receive a picture that's all bent and distorted by paper clips. Get it? Paper clips? Snip, snip? Groan. Sorry. That old unconscious is just so terribly punny. And I'll make little drawings too. To help you get the picture.

Okay, I can't shorten chapters, cut out chunks, and still maintain the book's stance. I'd kill it. I accept that. But what's this rearranging the disks? Maybe events will arrange the flow of this book, even though I doubt my energy to cope. I guess it will come from the upgrade.

Yes, I do feel renewed after these dreams. Maybe things will turn out okay. Even though I'm working in the dark. But that's where we collect our dreams, isn't it, in the dark. And yes, look, I see the two-stage frame now. I'll do the runthrough first, and then for any exact quotes and statistics, I'll fill them in later: "There are * trees in Russia."

Then even people as far away, as fearful as Gus, can still come see me, even people who are afraid of night flights. See, I'm getting it ready in my study. Friends can drop into this closet that is somehow turned into a study for the duration. Odd, I'm not coming out of the closet with this book—my friends are coming in here with me. Yes. Miss DuMonde needn't come out of the closet, we'll get in there with her. And just be guys and gals all jumbled up together in one dark closet of the psyche.

And oh...I've just looked at my watch...it's only 10:30 p.m. and I'm already about done with this chapter. In fact, I even found time to attend a lecture on Richard Wagner today...which turned out to include his Venician dream that inspired *Tristan und Isolde*. The lecturer said Wagner wrote a letter to Mathilde Wesendonck from Milan (on March 25, 1859), telling her of his dream in Venice and saying, "One day you shall hear a dream, music which I composed there." I got a delicious frisson at this little synchronicity regarding his dream baby. It didn't die, but grew into an opera.

And hey, I didn't even have to drag that Wagner quote out of some book. It was on the sheet still in my purse from that lecture.

Yes, things will work out if I'll just let them. Howdy Doody does it. I can carry this through, if I just let my nightly dreams call the daily tune. I won't turn chicken and lose my guts.

I admit it...for a moment there, I did lose my metal-mettle-medal. Hey. That earring off my left ear. That's what was at risk: hearing on my holistic side. But I found my metal-mettle-medal by the waterbed and put it back in my ear and heard. Under that slab of water I also found a little hidden bit of unitized energy. It had 5 stamped on it. The 5, the archetypal number of creativity born of the *quint*essence, that essential difference of the uniting fifth.

Also under there was an I Ching stone—it was black, symbolizing the receptive yin nature that will draw me back into the Way. When I didn't even know that I'd lost it. Yesterday I was feeling so stressed out that I didn't even realize I'd lost my receptivity. But maybe I've got the message now. You don't have to bang me over the head anymore, Life, with an even bigger dream of escalating shock and finally a nightmare or a daymare or somatized pain to get my attention. I hope.

It all hangs together. This world is put together as much by webby circles as it is by lines proceeding to infinity. To see the web, you must look slantwise with a peripheral vision at the borders of twilight, into the subtle haze of feelings, dreams, and chance encounters that logic hardly notices. It spins that weird, vague stuff people call life.

So that's it for this chapter. Off to bed. Come along with me, I'm on my way to the stars. The regular night flight is boarding now—out of bankruptcy and back on schedule.

CHAPTER 6

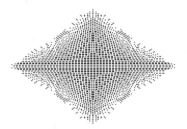

The Soul's Heaviside Layer

Dream Log — Thursday, November 10:
Dream: Wonderful journey! Many remarkable events. Exciting. Impressive. Educational. Need to write home about it.

Waking, I skim the highlights of this amazing trip in the cozy dark. I'll not to write it down—I'll remember—then back to sleep.

> *Dream:* Train trip. Time to get off. I rise from the seat of this train car. It looks brownish, wood-paneled. A woman across from me is rising too, wearing a Victorian hat, tilted up at the back, with fake flowers on the brim. A brown-bustled dress. "Take care," she warns me, pointing to the rope-net shelf above. "Be careful to take down your luggage. Don't leave it on the train."
>
> Now I'm standing in the station with one suitcase in my hand. The suitcase is being X-rayed and I can see what's in it. Then the suitcase somehow disappears in my hand as I'm walking away from the train.

I'm lying here wide awake at 4:25 a.m. Stunned. I can't believe it. Wow, I tricked myself this time! I won and lost in the dream Olympics. I won a medal but walked off empty-handed. I'll tell you about it.

See, I took this wonderful trip. Amazing. It was long and exciting and full of interesting events. I was enjoying everything a lot. The *me* figure walked around feeling enriched by it all, as though I was on that Continental Grand Tour considered to add the final polish to a Victorian education. The trip felt so edifying. I kept thinking, "Oh, there's so much to write about!"

I half-woke, cheek drowsing on the pillow, feeling cozy and quite delighted by this dream, going over the many events again, with their tremendous significance. Some little voice in the rear whispered, "Wake up. Turn on the light. Jot it down." But I knew better. This dream was so wonderful and satisfying and complete that I would never forget it. And there was so much to learn from it. This and that and the other.

Then back to sleep…on the train now, ending the trip. Getting up to leave the train. But that Victorian woman in brown sitting across from me warns me to take down my luggage. It has somehow dwindled away to a single suitcase by the time I get off the train—the suitcase is X-rayed so I can see what's inside—and even that suitcase disappears in my hand as I walk away from the station. The wealth I gained on this marvelous trip has dwindled to my walking away empty-handed.

Now I'm lying here wide awake, upset…which is not typical of me. Normally if I have insomnia, I try to make it rewarding. I read a lot, and fast, sometimes a book a day. My husband can sleep through a reading light and honking horns and a herd of elephants slogging across the end of the waterbed. So I turn on my pinpoint bedlight to read. But what? I pick a paperback off the stack of books by my bed. "A First-Class Thriller" says the front cover. *Death of a Thin-Skinned Animal* by Patrick Alexander. In the first few pages, it seems well-written enough.

But my mind keeps circling back to that moment of lying cozily, dozily in the dark and browsing over my bright dream like a contented cow. Then I contrast it with lying here with a lost dream, reading this thriller since I'm unable to go back to sleep.

Maybe if I'd waked up enough to write that bright travelogue down in the first place, by now I'd be settled back into my usual slumber. So what's this event about? I sniff around it mentally, trying the fit, listening for whispers, searching for the red thread, the clue.

My husband is snoring harder suddenly. It doesn't really bother me—like my reading at night doesn't disturb him. I've been awake for over an hour now. Ostensibly reading *Death of a Thin-Skinned Animal*. But really, I'm trying to figure out the import of this dream.

Okay, the given is that all life fits together. So I ponder this book in my hand for a clue. *Death of a Thin-Skinned Animal*. In it people say clever hollow things and pretend they aren't lying—"There was a lie to say, there was always a lie to say. And perhaps it was the simplest, even the kindest thing to say." It's a book about a hero struggling to believe in something, even if it's only that "…the Establishment, for all its faults, was run by Decent Chaps and therefore fundamentally All Right." He wants to believe it even as the Establishment destroys him— "'I suffer, I suffer, I am suffering…' Tears started down his face, burning through the sweat, tears of anger…against the Department and the whole system that had used him, discarded him and left him to rot in the back-end of nowhere because the individual didn't count."

This thriller also has an unusual villain: Njala, a black African student who was educated at Eton and Oxford. Beautifully acculturated—he even knows how to do the super-dry British wit. Now he's come back home to become a ruthless dictator in his own newly emerging nation. Njala's got basic brutality down to its essence, but he also puts a slick patina over it using what he learned in Europe—that morality and ethics are outdated cultural curios, the lost baggage of a modern society.

Musing, I recall that man I got involved with many years ago, a guy from the Ivory Coast. A handsome man, beautifully educated— schooled at the Sorbonne and Oxford—with such a soft, deep voice and a blue-black elegance and a perfect French accent, far better than mine. And he was a gentle, dedicated lover. He asked me to marry him. This was many years ago, back when I was off marriage—nothing had worked out for me anyway, so why not just enjoy sex and be a material girl? Etcetera. My adventuring years…in the outer world of extraversion, that is. Nowadays I'm an inner explorer, and it is far more interesting and satisfying—the ultimate adventure.

He was several years younger than me, this fellow, and he asked me to marry him by saying, "Come live with me and I will give you the springtime of your life." Really. Literally, he said that. "We'll fly to Paris every few weeks. You can teach at the University of Abidjan, if you wish. You can do whatever you wish."

I even thought about it for awhile too, but also I was thinking, "He never mentions the hard parts." And as though his unconscious mind heard it, he began to give me glimpses of trouble—for example, by telling me how as a youngster, he and his brother had beaten his younger sister until "she would say that blue was green if we told her to."

"But why! Why would you do that?" I asked, horrified.

"It was interesting." Then he began declaring that Idi Amin was taking the only possible course to govern an ignorant country by slaughtering his own people, and that really all the other African leaders did the same, but we Americans just didn't know it. If an African leader was pro-American, the abuse was hushed up in our press. When I disagreed, saying that Amin had so far killed an estimated 300,000 of his fellow Ugandans, the answer was that I didn't understand Africa, its people, its heritage.

Okay, I didn't understand Africa. Could it be that the brutality of dictators like Amin and Bokassa was actually necessary to govern Africa? I doubted it, but I knew for sure that I couldn't live—wouldn't live—with a man who thought so. No matter how tender his French and his lovemaking, no matter how bounteous his promises.

I don't regret my time with him, though. I remember his stories about tribal circumcision at fourteen, the tiny scar like a keloid boomerang sitting on his third eye, something most people didn't notice or thought was accidental—and his touch that held his intelligence in it. The uncanny way that lavender and blue echoed in his skin like glints in black ice when he wore certain shirts and ties. My body learned things about darkness and civilization and its veneer that I cannot verbalize.

But I would not marry him. Not if he was right and Africa had lost its roots of belief and not found anything but mod-materialism to replace it. Huge shadow looms over this bed tonight, I realize, over this silly spy novel, and stills the pages. They do not turn as I think of my beautifully civilized and savage lost lover.

I may even still have a tape around here somewhere of him reading poems of Rimbaud in French, of him telling me how the old people in the village where he was born believe that their spirits go into the trees when they die. Their voices rustle in the leaves and whisper to future generations their messages of advice and warning. No, that tape must be lost by now. I've moved too many times since then.

So all my bright dream baggage disappeared, and now I'm left with a handful of shadow at 4:00 a.m. In the dark night of my soul, it's naturally 4:00 a.m. Hey, I just noticed that this paperback cover is a somber black—unusual—generally they tend toward the eye-catching brights. So I guess a black thread is weaving tonight together.

Maybe this will even become a dream book chapter on how not to tour a dream. Even after the admonitory warning from that woman dressed in dark brown, I lost all my dream luggage. I can't show you the souvenirs and pictures of this gorgeous city and that sunlit landscape. Maybe you're relieved that I haven't got slides to show from my Grand Tour.

But on the other hand, I can show you, a major dream how-not-to. So although I've lost, I've won. I regret forgetting my marvelously rich, exciting trip, but somehow I did complete it anyway and somehow it served a purpose, even though the itinerary has vanished beyond recall.

Indeed, I'm amused at how I was set up. Maybe this was supposed to happen. Without anything to report about my grand tour—well, it leaves me plenty of time to dwell on how not to lose your luggage.

Mostly it happens by getting overconfident. Cocky. Inflated. Full of hubris. I was feeling so smug on my sight-seeing trip. Drowsing on the pillow, I got it all buttoned down, sorted, under control. So I wrapped it up, went to sleep again, and lost it.

That Victorian-hatted lady warned me. Still it happened. It reminds me of an entry in Freud's journal. He said that once again, as in uncounted times in the past, he awoke in the night to the memory of a dream rich with significant information, so informative that he lay there and analyzed it completely, congratulating himself on a thoroughly satisfactorily job, certain that it would amplify some point of his theory nicely…and then he went back to sleep…only to have it all completely forgotten when he awoke in the morning.

You can see a pocket version of this just happened to me. The richness of all those passing dream events, packed with their convoluted meaty moments like a vast multilobed fruit. I even knew I was dreaming, and I kept thinking, "It is so wonderful, so fortunate, this vast dream. It gives me so much to write about."

I acquired all sorts of luggage and filled every cranny with acquisitions. Sorted, packed them in order carefully on my pillow before drowsing back to sleep. Then came that fateful winding-down train trip with the old-fashioned wood paneling.

A train? Why a train here? What difference does it make whether it's a train or a pickup truck or a blimp? To understand, I must ask: What is the nature of this vehicle?

A train?—well, a train runs on a track. I don't have to steer it—indeed, a passenger cannot. It allows me to sit back in comfort and turn my attention to the scenery or a newspaper or someone beside me. I can forget about guiding my journey. A train runs on rails with its points of origin and destination preset. Its timing, too. So I come aboard and leave it according to its schedule, not mine. One doesn't control it in the way that one might sally out in a dream automobile (autonomous mobile) to drive around whenever and wherever one chose.

A dream automobile or a bicycle or roller skates would indicate more personal autonomous choice. And the autonomy of dream roller skates would mean something quite different from the dream car. Always contemplate your vehicle of choice in a dream. Driving a car, for example, means the ego is in the driver's seat; it can carry luggage right up to the door without losing it. Or the ego figure might be an auto passenger, able to influence its direction and momentum by talk.

But sitting in a train car—it means that I'm in a preset groove. By choosing not to wake up enough to secure my luggage, I automatically lost it. But maybe that's also a part of the tour package. Maybe fate wanted me to write about the perils of losing luggage.

A dream creates its own setting and props. It can go on location anywhere regardless of budget or unions. It picks the right vehicle for the desired effect. Something to further the plot. The Orient Express in Yugoslavia, a pickup truck across Arizona, water skis on the moon, or the Hindenburg dirigible over a Paleozoic swamp.

So in this particular dream, it's important that I'm completing my Grand Tour by train. The preset course is delivering me to my station on schedule. I sit all puffed up with marvels like Mark Twain in *Innocents Abroad*. I'm full of myself and my wondrous travels.

Notice, I even *know* I'm dreaming, know that the details will be useful in the real, waking world. Some people call this awareness *lucid dreaming*. Actually, I think most of us realize somewhere deep inside that we're dreaming. But sometimes the ego figure doesn't realize it, the *me* that is walking around in the dream, so it allows itself to get scared by a monster or a fall or a fight. It rushes out of the dream theater to yell that it is frightened in wake-up time. Nightmare!

You can understand your dream better by viewing it as an inner movie that you've just made. You, the dreamer, are the director and producer and script writer, and all the characters, too. You are even the landscape. The sound effects. The moviegoer, theater owner, and reviewer. You pop the popcorn…and consume it. You sweep the aisles afterward. You do all the work and you reap all the profit or loss. Or you can just walk away, momentarily entertained, merely a consumer, bored and killing time until the waking world turns back on.

Sometimes a dream theatergoer folds up his seat and walks slowly away, meditating on what he has seen and felt, aware that he's still partly meshed in the drama onstage even as he comes blinking out into the foyer and merging into the bustle of people.

One school of thought tries to train a lucid dreamer to take control of a dream and dominate it. This approach is well-presented in *Lucid Dreaming* by Stephen LaBerge. It is an interesting book and makes a good case for exploring dreams. It gives examples of dream lab experiments. It teaches flexibility and self-awareness in dream situations.

Yet I do have a quibble with it. Many people take lucid dreaming to mean that you should strive for an ego-driven dream state. Obviously, if you've read this far, you know that I believe dreams are communication from the greater wisdom of the unconscious. Thus I think one should make friends with the dream state, not dominate it. Ask it for help, not demand to control it. Praying is an old-fashioned word for the attitude I suggest. But a typical lucid dreamer argument is, "Dreams are just your psyche's nightly entertainment, so why not take charge of them rationally and let your dreams conform to your ego wishes?"

This way of thinking considers the unconscious less valuable and the ego more valuable. But I think a dream message is larger than the ego's wishes. It is a personal delivery letter sent nightly by the unconscious. True, its help is subtle and non-demanding, and you can ignore it. But don't, for it can see around the corners of hard-edged reality.

"No, indeed"—quoting a lucid dreamer argument—"dreams are merely creative poems—some masterpieces, some doggerel. How can they be so very important? You forget most of them anyway. So since they're just your psyche's off-duty creative writing hobby, its nightly thumb-twiddling to keep its hands busy while your body lies inert, why bother to spend time on interpreting each dream that you remember?" In LaBerge's words, "...why should you expect that every one of your dreams is worth taking the time to interpret?"

But to me, each dream says something, triggers something, whether I recall it consciously or not. Dreams do work. Literally. They do hard work in the psyche, preparing it for the daytime events ahead and repairing old damage to the psyche from the previous day's—or oblivious years of past trauma. They point the watercourse way to the tao's flow. But dreams can do their job better if your conscious mind gets in on the message, too. Reading your nightly dreams can keep your ego informed about what is happening to your soul.

Dreams matter. I think no mechanism this old, this instinctive, and still intact can be without huge purpose. The problem is, we've misunderstood its purpose. It is to consolidate information and build emotional timbre within the dreamer. For a healthy psyche not caught in arrears-dreaming, it will cue what's coming ahead in the dreamer's life. For the injured, unhealthy psyche, though, it tries to repair old damage. But since we humans are so proud of our egos, newly acquired in this last several thousand years, we've lost touch with the dreaming state and we currently underrate its work.

So don't bother to grab for complete control of your dreamtime. Use it instead as a gymnasium where your ego can exercise. Doing its nightly gymnastics can shape up your real life. Just interact with your unconscious trainer. Exchange tips and respect. Dreamtime offers a nightly proving ground for the soul. Use it to explore and develop your emotional and relational skills. Watch the dream dramas unfold even as you—the ego *me*—is participating in them; watch and learn from what happens.

It's not hard to do. Mainly it takes a willingness to acquire wisdom instead of knowledge. Knowledge is the learning that can be recorded in books and data files and tapes. But wisdom is derived from your own personal, unutterable experiences throughout life.

Dreams condense reality to deliver this wisdom. They cram lifetimes of events into a week, an hour, moment. They offer you concentrated, jam-packed experiences and emotions each night. Societal culture may offer you stacked libraries, labs, universities, institutes, and data bases for acquiring knowledge, but dream study can enroll you in a night school for acquiring vast experience. So pay attention.

With my clients, it doesn't take long for them to start interpreting their own dreams, once they get the hang of it. Insight comes in little flashes throughout the day as they go about their ordinary routines.

All it takes is making a beginning. You may not understand a dream immediately—and certainly not every little nuance—but you can begin to get the gist, the message, the feel. And slowly you learn not to let your limited ego, your deep fears, your wild fantasies or reflex denial obscure the message. Your life changes for the better. A deepening of the inner domain occurs, a spaciousness that allows you more leeway and chance for the comparison of alternatives. And meaning. Most of all, it brings transcendent meaning.

Myself, I don't want to take over my dreams completely with my ego and manhandle the actors like a tyrannical director shouting out orders to everyone on the set. Does my ego really know just what is going on here? And what to do about it? Personally, I don't think so. At least mine doesn't.

I find it better to relax into a dream and go with it, discover what it has to teach me. Work and play with it like a friend. Learning to respect each other. Occasionally I let that dream *me* suffer a bit in order to learn something new. Far better learn it in dreamtime than to transfer my suffering onto the stage of real life, where the archetypes enact themselves more concretely in flesh, if I still am not getting the message. Nightmares with all their hokey horrors and bathos of chopped babies and melting monsters have nothing on the roles that we take daily in the turgid plots of real life.

If you want to see psyche-drama in extremis, in slapstick, horror and suspense, just sit in a police station. Read a psychiatric case book. Heck, read the *National Enquirer* at the supermarket stand. As Mark Twain said, "Truth is indeed stranger than fiction. Fiction is obliged to stick to possibilities." I remember a tabloid headline from some time back: "300-lb Nun is Roller Derby Queen." I didn't need to thumb through the paper to skim that article—although sometimes I do so out of curiosity. The headline itself was nugget enough for my contemplation during the checkout line and walking back to the car.

So maybe you're a lucid dreamer. So what? Don't let it puff your ego and make you think you've got a headlock on the unconscious. That's just ego talking when you try to take complete control. It's part of the same mindset that supposes rationality to be all you really need, so wow, if you can just manage to be rational *while you are dreaming,* then you've got the world licked into order.

But the unconscious domain will outwit you every time. It is bigger, stronger, smarter, and infinitely trickier. You'll lose in a battle with it, even while your ego thinks you're winning. As I lost the goods while drowsing with my dream bags all packed. Look at that smug little *me* last night. Zowie!—travel, color, riches, education, oodles to write about. I was sitting pretty, let me tell you, head on my cozy pillow.

Then that final train trip. The winding down. The journey ends, as they all do. I rise. The Victorian woman in brown, her hat decorated in false flowers, rises too. She warns me. She points up to the rope-net shelf above. "Be careful! Don't leave your luggage on the train."

Who is this irritatingly accurate woman, anyway? In her brown dress with a bustle, her old-fashioned Victorian hat tilted up at the back, fake flowers on its brim. Hmm, she's the same sex as me. And she's cautionary. She is forbidding in aspect, yet she's also helping me by her warning. She knows my weak side, she can smell it a mile off, like all old ladies who sit in the train and look at me once and can see straight through to the safety pin in my broken bra strap. Or holey-toed socks. Or surmise that I once almost went to live in Abidjan with a beautiful black man who might have settled me in as his third wife, or worse yet, maybe as a first wife to be superseded in blows and affection over time.

This cautionary woman in the Victorian hat? She's the good witch, the empathic women like Jessica Fletcher and Miss Marple who turn their intuitive talent to benign magic, not evil, to good ends instead of bad.

Briefly said, she's my shadow. There she stands in dark brown garb (rich color, warm and deep, like earth) looking right through my smugness into my carelessness. She knows I'm going to lose my luggage just by sitting there and watching me. No wonder such women are often called witches or bitches. They know more than we'd rather they see.

How can you recognize your shadow in a dream? It is a person of the same sex as you, someone who embodies or points out a fallible, shadowy side of your psyche. This woman in brown literally points out that I'm in danger of losing my dream luggage.

But actually she's pretty benign, this Victorian woman…as shadows go. I've worked with my shadow more than a little bit over the years in her various guises, trying to befriend her and accept her paradoxical help. Once she came at me as a demon-woman with long red nails. She tried to stab me with them. But by now she has calmed down a lot. No longer a witchy horror from a Charles Addamms cartoon, more into being a forbidding aunt. Or a granny. Or a sharp-tongued friend. Last night she tried to bustle me into doing better. Maiden aunts are good at rebukes.

Shadow wants to be heard, simply that. But if it isn't, it turns nasty. It becomes a veritable demon, witch, or son-of-a-bitch, demanding its pound of flesh…in very painful real time, not dreamtime. Pay attention to your shadow. If you keep distancing yourself—"Heavens, it's not *my* fault!"—then heaven help you. Hell won't.

What we call evil is just alienated shadow. It is shadow that is split off into random violence in a terrain without ethics. Muggings, drug wars, gang murders, terrorized neighborhoods. No wonder punkers wear black. They live in the huge shadow of our society, which disavows its shadow and glories in bright ego trips of rationality. But why is our bright-lights culture so susceptible to drugs and violence and monsters that suck blood in the night, anyhow? They enthrall a society that has lost touch with its soul.

Horror movies are just fake nightmares. Violence is just fake initiative. Drugs are just fake transcendence. And alcohol is just fake spirit distilled into a bottle. You can get the real stuff, though, by finding your own your soul and its magical essence in dreams. Doing so will alter your mind permanently, so that the fake versions will never again satisfy.

Quit running from your shadow in fear and loathing. Turn around and walk into the dark and befriend it. Slowly, with care, you can turn your shadow from a dark demon into a cautionary helper. That is a whole journey in itself, and a long one. But it can be done.

Truth is, no matter how long you work, the shadow doesn't completely go away. You can't kill it. Instead it becomes a wry friend, a dark, rich source of inner support and strength. When integrated, it brings balance to your conscious mind. It knows what your ego is leaving out of the weighing pan. Ego doesn't like to pay. Shadow knows it must, that there's no such thing as a free lunch or zipless fuck or free ride.

That reproving Victorian aunt is working to balance my ego's rather naive glee at my Grand Tour with her sound advice not to neglect the mundane details of luggage. She's right. But she's no monster. She is *related* to me, you know, and kind even in her severity.

But an estranged shadow enacts its message viciously—sometimes a shadow is so split off and violent that it seems beyond redemption. But don't back off from your shadow, no matter how nasty or despicable it appears. It is pointing out something that your smug *me* is blind to. It sees around the corners that limit your ego.

My Victorian shadow knew I was about to lose my dream baggage. My African lover's shadow warned me not to marry him in time, even though his perfect French and the charming folk myths had blinded me. The shadow knows. I recall Lamont Cranston on my childhood radio: "Who knows what evil lurks in the hearts of men?...the power to blind men's eyes so they cannot see him... Only the Shadow knows."

The shadow knows the worst. It sees your bullshit and calls it by name...and can transform it into fertilizer and recycle it back into your ecosystem. In the ecosystem of the psyche, shadow will admonish, correct, redress an imbalance of the conscious waking life: "Oh my god, you mean this nuclear plant's been leaking poisons into the soil and water for the past twenty years?" "Oh my god, you mean that in the four years since the Bhopal incident, Union Carbide has spent seven million dollars a year to keep the legal case from going to court instead of making restitution to all those victims?" It takes continual recognition and work with the darker aspects of a situation for shadow not to split off and become ugly.

Split-off shadow can turn monstrous. A client of mine had a scary recurring dream about a raving maniac locked up in a dungeon, very dangerous if he got out. I suggested, "On your next dream visit to this lunatic prisoner, watch what he says and does. Listen to what he's telling you. Get his message. But please don't be naive and just open the cell and leave him free to roam unrehabilitated. After all, your ego says he's crazy. What's driving him crazy? What would it take to reform him? To rehabilitate the *him* in you?"

"Accept yourself" is a current catch phrase. But what if your shadow is a rooting-tooting monster? Monsters accept themselves quite well. No, your shadow needs to transform slowly and become related to the rest of your psyche. Then it will on occasion offer your ego some rather painful but true advice. Take my maiden aunt's unheeded admonition: "Don't be so smug. You'll lose this dream baggage, you Silly Chit."

Don't think you've got it all under control. About anything. Life will trick you every time. The unconscious domain is bigger, older, wiser than the ego; it always had a few more surprises up its sleeve. It tricked Freud as he lay congratulating himself on getting his dream under wraps. It stole my rollicking tale of a Grand Tour on the brightside of life. But in return, it demonstrated the shadowside very clearly. So even though I lost my dream baggage today, I found something too. Dreamtime gifted me with something very important to introduce—the actor called Shadow. Watch it, heed it, integrate it.

There are several major actors in your dreams. You've already met *Ego,* the protagonist—the *me* walking around and experiencing events. But Ego is limited, so it needs other characters to round out the drama. Your *Animus* or *Anima* is the second lead. It takes a contrasexual role that plays off the leading *me. Shadow* takes a same-sex role and also has a big part. Unheeded, it turns your plot melodramatic, even degenerates it into a horror show…and starts terrorizing your real life.

Oh, I feel some relief today. It looks like I can trust my dreams to deliver what I need for this book. Even if I lose my luggage. So I can just stay easygoing and lift an occasional wry eyebrow at this inner olympics of dreamtime, because even when I'm losing, I'm winning.

CHAPTER 7

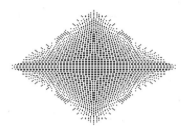

Harvest in Shadow Land

Dream Log—Friday, November, 11:
He's in the dungeon, the black dictator. But I know it's not going to work out this way. There is a trial going on. Witnesses give evidence. He's acquitted, but he is also sent into a rehabilitating program.

What is today's dream about? I lie on my side pondering.

Lordy, it's the shadow again. Oh no. Shadow is so hard to work with. It brings up all those uncomfortable, unacknowledged feelings that stop me from writing and you from reading as we muse into the space between the lines. The past rises up out of the pages like Marley's ghost. I hadn't thought of that African lover for such a long time…of his gentleness to me and of his brutality to his own people.

I open my eyes. Try to. My right lid won't slide up. It hurts, grates as it struggles vainly to rise, as though the eye is glued shut by a dirty contact lens. But I don't wear contact lenses anymore.

Good lord! Is that dirt still in my eye from yesterday?

Yesterday I was planting flowers in the concrete box that runs across the front balcony. A tiny clodlet of dirt flipped up from the tool into my right eye. I saw it coming from about a noselength away and didn't get my eyelid shut in time. "Here's mud in your eye," I thought.

I tilted my head, blinking rapidly so the tears would wash it away. Abruptly the soil dissolved, just a few grains really.

So I went back to planting, visualizing the blooms rising up early next spring. Only bulbs and scrawny green scraps now, but they would become ten yellow daffodils with orange trumpets. Six mahogany pansies and six yellow pansies. Three Delft blue hyacinths, and a flock of grape hyacinths. Yellow, red, blue. The colors of the paint spectrum.

All this delirious play of colors would rise from the dirt next spring, like richness from the integrated shadow. But yesterday I'd also thought this book had no space for my planting activities. No room, and no need. After all, Chapter 6 was about unredeemed shadow. Alienated shadow that lurks in the dead zone. Monstrous and denied shadow that extracts its due by going on rampage. Not yet integrated and fecund.

So yesterday my mind drifted as I planted. The Berserkers of Norway. "Havoc!"—a cry banned on pain of death in Richard II of England's time. It was the signal to kill and rape and destroy with no quarter given. What was that line in Shakespeare? "Cry 'Havoc!' and let slip the dogs of war."

Alienated shadow cries "Havoc!" and releases our worst fears to run amok in monstrous, materialized form. It is shitty shadow that puts the moxie in Venus flytraps and vampires, in heroin and zombies lurching from the grave.

But shadow that is reconciled can nourish the soft unfolding mandalas of organic connection into blossoming beauty. I thought of Toni Morrison's novel *The Beloved…*a girl is violently cut down in the bud, comes back as a ghost to haunt her friends who survive with their creative potential unreconciled and soured. Poor women squelched by racism and sexism, who struggle to befriend, even to love this witchy, bitchy, seductive crazed woman-shadow that haunts the whole culture. These brave women even redeem this crazed ghost into the beloved of the title. What a task they take on for all our souls! So full of darkness is this beautiful novel, so rich in shadow. Oh, the beauty of black when it becomes transforming depth. Monstrous shadow redeemed becomes an exotic, beautiful friend.

Oh well, I shrugged yesterday, surely the time will come to write about it again. My dreamtime will bring up shadow again, my life will.

So here I lie the very next morning with my right eye stuck shut. Mud in my eye. I turn onto my left side and do the blinky-blink routine so the tears will drain and maybe loosen the lid. Slowly my eye begins to water, and after a moment, the lid loosens.

I touch it, feel grains of dried mucus. Hmm, a discharge during the night. I guess there's more to this than just a moment's discomfort as that clodlet hit my eye yesterday and dissolved. Nor is the topic of shadow disposed of by yesterday's chapter. The dream shows it.

I stumble up and into the bathroom. Look in the mirror. My eye is red, weepy. My right eye…the more conscious side. It's still teary over the muddy impact of yesterday. Maybe my right eye can't abide shadow! What a comedown for ego, to have a shadow! "I have a little shadow," said Robert Louis Stevenson, "that goes in and out with me. And what can be the use of it is more than I can see." Me either. That damfool shadow. Kill it with gunpowder, manpower, H-bomb strike power. Ha! The dead shall rise again.

So I go about my normal morning routine, but with glimpses of shadow looming darkly in my mind's eye. As I'm looking for a key to the basement, I flashback on that dungeon with the black dictator. I remember an old dream of a black Swiss army knife as I reach into my purse. Why? Because as I pull out my key ring, I see on it a knife bought because of the shadow lesson in that dream. I recall another dream, of a woman with red claws.

Hmm. So today looks like "Harvest in Shadow Land: Rehabilitating Your Shadow Into a Psychic Partner." What does my dream suggest about redeeming my shadow? How about you—can you dredge up a shadow dream in your own past? Because you need to recognize shadow in your dreamtime, in your life. Only then can you start to overhaul it.

Don't worry about strict objectivity either. Interpretation is in the eye of the beholder. And shadow puts mud in your eye. It dredges up and flaunts the ignored side of an issue, some shabby, hurtful, embarrassing, nasty, denied aspect that one would rather not admit.

What a villain! How can shadow do this to my dear, Teflon-slick, precious ego! How can it have the effrontery to gainsay my will? How dare life work out so that just as I tell a neighbor in the kitchen that I'm thirty-five, my teenage son comes in and says, "Mom, you're birthday's coming up next week—you'll be thirty-nine—and I'm wondering what to get you. What would you like?"

"To throttle you" is not the answer here. What's the best way through this shadow problem? Just tell the truth. No matter how gritty, nasty, embarrassing it is. "To tell the ugly truth" should be my birthday wish. Then it ceases to be split off—the imprisoned black dictator is rehabilitated—and unacceptable truth is reconciled and integrated.

So how old am I, really? Thirty-nine? Then why am I so furious at my son, sure that he's overheard me from the other room and is now trying to put me down before the neighbor? After all, I did give him the perfect weapon for doing it, didn't I? A fear of the truth. By forbidding the truth to be acknowledged, we arm shadow with its surest weapon. Oh, shadow is tricky. It can set up a Watergate scenario for

Nixon. It can get around a hacker's caution and sight along a sniper's rifle. It can wrestle with Dr. Jekyll for mastery of the body.

So what's to be done?—if we can't just lock shadow into the dungeon and throw away the key? Well, in today's dream, a trial is going on. So just put your shadow in the dock. Try to figure out if it is telling a nasty truth, despite your ego's vehement denials of "No, no! Can't be!" Play fair. Let witnesses give their evidence, like the dream says.

Some truths are almost unbearable, so we try hard to deny them. For example… We die. We suffer. We fail. What awful truths. Let's hide them. Pretend that life doesn't have a bloody shadow side. Forget that your carnivorous eyeteeth sit amidst the biting and grinding panoply in your jaws. Save face. Make a vegetable face and wear it in public. Hah! Forget that you're still a dark animal along with the logical Homo Sapiens glitter. Some animal truths are just embarrassing. People fart. Dogs sniff crotches. Teeth stink with phyorrea. False teeth fall out on the table. I saw that happen at a dinner party last year. And yesterday I saw Mariles on the street. When we parted, I said, "See you at the festival Saturday."

She said casually as she started across the street. "I don't know if I'm going. I haven't talked with Greg yet about what we're doing."

I stared at her receding back. Greg was the brand new man friend. But a week before she'd sat on my living room couch and we'd planned this outing. I saw her write the date and time enthusiastically into her pocket calendar. We agreed to meet downtown on Saturday and travel together to the Turnip Festival thirty miles away by train.

"Turnip Festival?" you may be thinking. No wonder Mariles wanted to duck it. Just so it doesn't sound utterly weird, let me tell you about the Turnip Festival. It happens once a year. You take a two-pound turnip with white flesh and a thin purple skin. You hollow out the turnip. Carve some designs in its thin purple skin so that the white flesh shows through. Put a candle inside and light it so the white glows through the purple like a great living jewel. Attach a string to it to make a lantern. Now you walk around in the dark. Ahh! It's astoundingly beautiful.

Now, do that to about twenty tons of turnips and use them to decorate a village, its shop windows, house steps, roof ridges, walls and fences. Place turnip lanterns on the fifty-odd floats that must be shoulder-carried—no motorized floats allowed—as the peripatetic parade snakes all through the little village, with every electric light extinguished so that only candles glow in the darkness.

It's magical. And Mariles *wanted* to come with me last week, before she took that quick trip to London with her new man friend. So I watched her departing back and thought, she's doing what lots of women do—cancels a date with a woman to make one with a man.

I didn't like it. It hurt my feelings, silly as that may sound. But then I said oh, pooh, it doesn't matter. Why should it bother me? Maybe someone else will go with me, Sunny Side Up insisted. Even as my shadow was growling after Mariles's disappearing back, "You fink, you promised me! I was counting on you. You're standing me up!"

Then I recognized this conflict in myself.

So when I saw Mariles today, I brought the topic up again, and I asked if she'd reached a decision.

"No, I still haven't made up my mind. Or talked with him about it." So I let my shadow walk right out there instead of sulking down in the cellar. It had a shit load to dump: "You know, Mariles, last week I saw you write our appointment down in you calendar. You were going to the turnip festival with me on Saturday. I was counting on it."

"Oh, really? Well, I thought that maybe you were making up a group to go, and I could just decide later."

"That's not what we agreed on. Remember? We said we'd both mention it around and see if others wanted to come along. But you and I firmly agreed to go." I'd put my shadow in the dock to make a statement. It was not banished into the cellar while my Sunny Side Up glibly and falsely burbled, "Oh, it doesn't matter, Mariles. Whatever you want to do is fine with me."

"Oh?" she said remotely. She didn't want to talk about it. Not till she'd scoped out the possibilities with her man friend.

So I decided to let another witness step up, that kid who admits to—gad, to having hurt feelings!—"I guess my feelings are a little hurt. Seems like you're breaking a date with me to make a more important date with a guy. But we made our plans first."

She was silent as people swept by. I wondered if Mariles was going to cut her losses with me, maybe even our friendship, and go off angry at my shadow's testimony. But then she leaned over and whispered, "Thanks for saying that. I appreciate it. I'll think it over."

So my shadowy truth felt noticed, and in turn, could appreciate her words. Shadow was redeemed. I'd not kept it locked in the dungeon of pretense, but let it recount its side of the story without hyperbolic anger. Its reward was recognition, and a big easing inside of me.

I still don't know if Mariles will go with me to the turnip festival. But I do know that when I let my shadow speak out, I balanced my psyche's debits and credits by it. I'm okay now. My ominous shadow isn't split off from my sparkle-plenty ego. They can make a working team and not polarize into a wrestling match of Pollyanna versus Old Nick.

Recall that dream…the black dictator is acquitted, but also he's sent into a rehabilitation program. Don't be naive enough to think your shadow should be set free to roam around while a blustering tyrant. The dictator isn't set scott-free, but into reform.

Basically the verdict is this: brutal shadow tells a truth, but in too strong a form; it has become so exaggerated and extreme because of desperately trying to get the ego's attention. But given proper attention, that nasty shadow can rehabilitate into something more mild…like a strict maiden aunt, or a policeman with a warning ticket, or a high school principal holding a wooden paddle. Oh, sure, you scoff. You can just see Hitler going to rehab school and learning to weave baskets. With human hide.

Don't be so cynical. These demons and dictators in the psyche have a plus over the real-life versions. A fleshly dictator lives out its human span unless a sniper's bullet finds its mark. But a tyrannical shadow can metamorphose overnight into a more benign version.

Think about it. How did that nasty shadow become such a monster in the first place? It jumped under a magnifying glass to look bigger, distorting itself into nastiness in order to get the ego's attention. With each new denial, it looms higher and leers closer—just to be seen!

Today I read about the monstrous dictator in *Death of a Thin-Skinned Animal:* "His presence was unavoidable, inescapable. Njala Square, Njala Place, Njala Street, statues and posters of him everywhere. Even Njala T-shirts. Njala's town all right."

Looming shadow shakes its banner from all the corners of your attention. The longer a truth is unacknowledged, the bigger grow its demonstrations. So walk down into that dungeon. Figure out what the monster is trying to tell you, show you. What is its kernel of nasty truth? Some truths are not really so terrible, you know, once they're breathed into open air. Oh, you're really thirty-nine? Oh, you're getting cocky on this Grand Tour of life and not taking proper care of the baggage? Oh, you can't admit that silly old you feels slighted, so instead you sound glibly false, and underneath it all, carry a grudge?

Some shadowy truths are bigger and uglier, of course, and they get more sickeningly monstrous the more maze-like their denial. Nations and high-profile defense lawyers and mega-corporations are specialists in laying a glazed surface over a rat-warren of twisted truth. The Big Lie is the hallmark of shadow running rampant in our society.

But well, I'm limited, and all I can do is work on my own shadow. You can work only on yours. I can't integrate my enemy's shadow for him. Or my government's. Even my spouse's…dammit. It's a big-enough job just to deal with my own shadow.

Shadow work is a growth industry. There's plenty available for all. And dealing with it is a teachable skill. **Hypothetical:** you are in the dungeon of your psyche facing your dictatorial shadow. Snipers hired by your offended ego have tried to assassinate your dangerous shadow and get rid of it. Spies and victims abound. Bribes, coups, etcetera. At last this huge and brutal shadow sits snarling in chains before you—your ego says you've got it pinned down to destroy for good. You move in for the merciless kill. But remember, you can't kill your own shadow—it just resurges into ever more malevolent and bizarre forms. The outcome of your psychic state rests in your hands. What do you do?

Or imagine there's a war between two factions inside you. Casualties. Babies of creative endeavor lie dying on the operating table. The decision that you make will determine whether your split-off factions start to cooperate or continue to cripple each other. What do you do?

Or you're facing a horrible shadow attack, as I did some years back:

> I am wearing a new ring on my left hand. I've exchanged my wedding ring for it. This one has a much larger diamond, but it is milky and flawed in facets, less pure but more natural-looking. It even has blood on one facet. I know this new ring is much more valuable.
>
> I'm wearing red nail polish…like Anita wears. Oh! A horrible and dangerous thing is coming to hurt me. It becomes a black-haired woman, beautiful, svelte, with bright red lips and plucked eyebrows. She comes up and speaks suavely to me, but I'm very frightened. She is a beautiful witch. She's going to hurt me with her hands.

I take her hands, which have huge long strong red nails, and I turn the fingers back on her torso. I begin to cut her body with her own nails. I push them deep into her waist. I twist and make circular cuts. But she still doesn't stop speaking to me, so I force the nails in deeper, making even bigger cuts in her body. She begins smiling in a puzzled way as she talks, begins faltering in her words.

She turns into a few little slabs of meat. I want to burn them up so that they can't possess me. I put the meat into a box. The meat starts cooking itself and smelling good, calling me to eat it.

A man says, "Let's build a fire and cook and eat it." I am horrified. "That's what it *wants* us to do!" I cry. "Oh no, we must burn it up and destroy it so that it won't hurt us."

I'm frantic. I strike matches. I stuff newspapers around the box, wondering if the soggy meat will really cook properly. But then the flame starts up around the box, and I am much relieved.

When I woke from this nightmare, I was more frightened than by any dream of the past twenty years. It was frantic fear. Not logic. Simply put, I was afraid that this witchy woman was going to take me over. Possess me. After all, that's what beautiful witches do, isn't it.

But just look at her. What is her truth that my ego was frantic to ignore? That's the question. To find out, I had to go at this dream slowly because of the reflexive and habitual fear that I produced on cue around it. So I started by asking those little peripheral questions like "What's this silly detail about wearing red nail polish like Anita? I don't even wear polish."

Well, Anita was a beautiful woman I knew. Somehow I didn't quite approve of her. She was olive-skinned, sophisticated, and embodied a certain "bewitching" feminine quality. Actually, she carried a certain shadowy truth I needed to look at—that's what made me so uneasy around her. Whenever you just can't tolerate somebody, figure out *why.* What subliminal truth does it suggest about yourself like a distorted mirror? In skewed form, it offers some rejected, nasty tidbit that your ego just doesn't want to accept.

Finally, I realized that Anita was triggering a hidden envy in me by her very attractiveness. That's why I was so on edge around her. Look at her, I admitted: she has a certain dramatic style and beauty that I don't even allow myself to attempt with my casual garb and manner. She is more suave and sophisticated than I could ever be—or want to be, my ego adds fiercely. She exudes a fascinating smoky mystery where my style is staying transparently clear and demystifying myself.

But notice, this new dream ring is larger and more valuable, even though it's translucent now instead of clear. Even though there's a bit of blood on a facet. Blood is passion, spurting life. Blood comes from flesh. And flesh is opaque. It's black inside the body. Flesh is coagulated shadow. And my diamond is more valuable now for being not quite so see-through.

To exaggerate this point for emphasis—as all dreams do—Anita is a bewitching, fascinating, seductive creature, and I am dowdy old Katya, simple, folksy and crystal-clear. Oh, my dreaming ego was *so* afraid of her. It just *knew* she was going to hurt me, possess me, take me over. I would become contaminated by her smoky mystery.

But look, she didn't hurt me. Instead, I hurt her...I even tried to destroy her. She only talked to me, but look at what the ego *me* did in this dream! I cut her up by her own hand. Which puzzled her. She was still smiling at me, she kept on talking and trying to relate to me even as I was working to destroy her.

Then her cutup flesh turned into little slabs of meat that started cooking themselves! Appetizing, inviting me to eat. She wouldn't possess and absorb me, the pantomime was saying—instead, I would soon possess and absorb some parts of her. At this, my ego was horrified!

No, no, I just could not bear to eat and assimilate any of her shadowy mystery. I just couldn't become fascinating and oblique and sophisticated and suave. It just wasn't *me,* dammit! My ego was firmly committed to limiting myself into dear dowdy old Katya, so nonthreatening and simple and determinedly clear, dammit.

So what did my animus—that male companion—do? He gave me some good advice: "Let's build a fire and cook and eat it." Which again horrified that narrow old ego me. "That's what it wants us to do!" I cried. "Oh no, we must burn it up and destroy it so it won't hurt us."

Sure, that's what my ego said. But what happened? Ha, limited old ego always tricks itself. Ha, watch this *me* striking a match to it! Stuffing wadded newspaper around it!

Think about it. I am starting to help cook it! Despite the "No, no!" of my ego stance, I'm rushing to get this meat done even faster. How? By burning words—and I even feel relief when the newspaper catches fire.

You see, my animus knew that I needed to burn my words and start assimilating some small part of Anita's enchanting "witchy" quality, so it went right on setting up the banquet. It didn't let my left brain thwart what my right brain was cooking up. Oh yes, the unconscious outsmarts the ego every time.

So this dream said I was on my way to integrating a needed aspect of my shadow. How? By eating a few slabs of it. Not the whole woman, just a few chunks of her shadowy enchantment, a mincemeat condiment to spice up the bland stew of dowdy old Katya.

Here's another strange point about dreams. They have cannibalism in them. Guiltless murder. Rapturous incest. Painless vivisection. Innocent treachery. Dreams don't fit the normal morality, so don't feel guilty about their bizarre events. Instead, they offer a fairytale morality that operates ethically and precisely, simply because dream figures are not real fleshly people but rather, evanescent imaginary figures used to portray the deeper morality of archetypal dramas.

Ursula K. Le Guin points this out in *The Language of the Night*, when she says that dreams and fantasy use the archetypal language of the night: "Though they use words, they work the way music does: they short-circuit verbal reasoning, and go straight to the thoughts that lie too deep to utter. They cannot be translated fully into the language of reason, but only a Logical Positivist, who also finds Beethoven's Ninth Symphony meaningless, would claim that they are therefore meaningless. They are profoundly meaningful, and usable—practical—in terms of ethics; of insight; of growth."

In real life, we would be horrified at the cannibal act of chopping a person into steaks and firing up the grill. In real life we would be inexpressibly shocked at someone blithely gobbling up Mr. Ginger Brot-Mann. But in the children's story, after taunting everyone with his ceaseless chant of…

> *"Run, run, as fast as you can,*
> *You can't catch me,*
> *I'm the Gingerbread man!"*

…our cookie protagonist is indeed gobbled up—"and they ate him all up." In fact, this Gingerbread Man *needs* to be consumed, because the story is subliminally about incorporating a child's impudent spirit into ordinary adult life. Conscious cannibalism is horrible, but as an unconscious symbol, it is fortifying. We see it for example in the imagery of Jesus Christ's blood and body being consumed at mass.

So in my dream, this shadow woman obligingly turns herself into steaks and even starts grilling herself appetizingly. It sounds like a gruesome tale, doesn't it? But my ego's deeper horror was not really at eating a person, but rather at eating those seductress-steaks and ingesting some part of her mysterious, dangerous quality.

In that dream, the shadow image is seen as mystery, as seductive unknown. Red is passion—the blood on that milky diamond, the red nail polish, the red steak. All this red and black show the mystery of passion, of death and sex. Watered down into just a dash of flavoring for my psychic stew, it promises to add to me a certain zing.

And then twelve days later came this dream:

> She is holding me, the mother of my sorrow. She is black-haired, pale-skinned, and so very beautiful. She is holding me and hugging me like a mother. She says, "Oh, I am so sorry, I am so sorry that I frightened you." She tells me she loves me and wants to reconcile with me and love me better. Her arms are so warm and comforting and loving. She holds me in her arms a long time and it is so comforting. She is dark and beautiful with a face like Anita's, only deeper and stronger, even more beautiful. She is so beautiful!

This dream was thrilling to me. I woke with my fear transfigured. Such relief! And in the days following, I found myself no longer being so annoyingly clear that I scrubbed off my psychic skin.

That's how I made an alliance between the ego *me* and this aspect of my shadow. But shadow always has new aspects to offer for assimilation, and they always bring growth.

Reconciliation makes an odd ending to a horror show, I admit. Don't destroy the monster! Befriend it, embrace it, incorporate its strength watered down to human size. How tame. How productive.

In short, by going into dreams and working with them, you can have all the thrills and chills, the verve of war and violence and espionage without getting your head shot off or your town bombed out of existence. You can do it just by living the truth of each night's dream into daylight. The truth is terrifying enough to face. To befriend and harness it daily is immensely rewarding. More thrilling than any violence you can name. And quite heroic.

Finding adventure inside is less bloody and chaotic than projecting it outward. Perhaps you think I'm joking about this? Look around at the war and gore movies, at spies and spy novels, at the Grateful Dead, at Hell's Angels and Mafia dons.

Don't kid yourself. Much of the motivation for war and espionage and crime and intrigue, whether on a personal, tribal or multinational level, has simply been that it is so very exciting. It stirs up the blood— and it is a diversionary stand-in for facing one's own inner shadow.

But you can conduct an inner war that will be quite as exciting and fruitful as any extraverted war or assassination or coup. All this crude violence so visible in our culture comes from so many people projecting their inner wars into the material plane instead of resolving the conflicts inside. Issues and angers should be writ small and handled neat.

Tame your own shadow and forge a new peace that will widen your world view. The psychic campaign is quite tiring, true. But it's a far more honorable struggle than having generals kill women and children ten thousand air miles away.

The victor on the psychic battlefield does not divide and conquer. Rather, the forces unite, and from that expansion of perspective we all benefit. This kind of victory saves the day for us all.

Never fear, life will not turn bland and boring. You'll soon come upon a new shadow issue and another inner war to fight. Because, let me tell you, it never ends, this cavorting shadow that dredges up some unconsidered reality from the rich mucky unconscious…which it then slyly intrudes into your conscious attention.

If I dare bring my nasty old shadow upstairs to become my constant companion, if I befriend and heed it, it still never turns into a completely docile friend. There's always some new twist turning up where my shadow shrieks for its acknowledgment and due—maybe it is jealous when I find myself silent in a group as somebody celebrates a new grandchild—when I should be smiling and saying wryly, "Hey, Bob, congratulations! I really envy you on that beautiful granddaughter."

If you can say your shadow's truth with a simple admission, why then, your jealous green-eyed monster has undergone its rehabilitation program. Now it's just a green imp dancing in your eye.

It can happen. Take that movie tonight. I missed the title, but right off I knew the plot line—four kids trek into the countryside and discover a body. I said, "Did Stephen King write this? I know this plot."

Susan said, "Yes, it's adapted from his novella *Stand by Me.*" It's chockfull of shadowy stuff. Alienation, child abuse, neglect, hooligan-ism. This kid is struggling to find a creative path against the odds of becoming siphoned off into the random waste and violence that fills his everyday environment.

Sounds grim, doesn't it. Well, fooled you—it was very funny. There's this scene where the kid tells his friends a story as they're sitting around the campfire. It's the tale of a Puke-o-rama where everybody in a pie eating contest winds up vomiting great projectile streams of blueberry goo all over each other. The audience in the contest become so nauseated by the disgusting spectacle onstage that they too begin upchucking on each other, till the whole screen is crisscrossed with gouting purple glop.

Not funny to you? Disgusting? Well, take my word, we were laughing hysterically. But how could Stephen King run this trip on us, how could he describe such a revolting mess!...and even film it! And have us all laughing with helpless tears? It's because he's made friends with his shadow, great and good friends—blood brothers. And since shadow is so rich, its wealth rubs off on King and makes him rich too. That's how King struck a gold mine—he mines the wealth in his shadow. King and his shadow stand by each other.

Hmm...a king used to be the bright ego identity inside medieval society. The folk gathered around him as a shining image of the best and brightest. But every king needs his shadow, the fool. A wise fool sees more than the surface and calls the king on it. Fools got to speak the truth when no one else dared.

Just so are we all kings and queens, and we all have cavorting fools inside us who spout great blueberry gouts of wisdom in their gibes. But these interior clowns can also, if left unheeded, turn us into sad, mad monsters. King Lear shows us that.

I look into my *Encyclopedia of Names* and see that Stephen means "crowned with glory." Hmm. I suppose that each of us can be crowned with glory mined from the shadow's riches. Yes, I vow to stand by my shadowy truth, to become its friend, so that it will stand by me.

CHAPTER 8

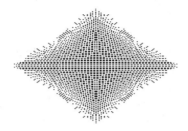

Spaceship Universe

Dream Log—Saturday, November 12:

Dream: I'm in a spaceship. I can see through the walls to black space and stars. It looks like we're carrying just about everything in here. All sorts of stuff. I start to take inventory, and then I quit. There's too much.

Here's a map of it, though. I see it's packed like a museum full of old stuff, aisles of it—but still, the map is new and updated. I see tiny dots...circles?...particles?...all over it. They're working together. It's a complex map. So this is the map! I am humbled. It contains everything.

As I float up from sleep, I am humbled by the immensity of this dream. I still hear swirling in my inner ear the massed strings of Wagner's *Tristan and Isolde,* rising to a higher and higher climax of *Liebestod*— the *Love-Death* theme. It's like the final strains of a movie score playing as **The End** comes up on the screen, and you know pretty soon you'll heave out of the trance and cushy chair and walk back up along the aisle out of the dark.

So at first I'm still almost in the dream ship—so odd too, because I can see right through its walls into space. No, there *are* no walls!

What kind of spaceship is this anyway?

Spaceship Earth! It's this big green, blue and brown whirling planet that carries us through space. Once at fifteen I dreamed of standing in the void somewhere outside Earth, looking at this beautiful shining globe. Earth. But I didn't call it a spaceship back then. It was just Earth, the place I was going, and glad to be getting there. To be born.

No wonder this ship is carrying all sorts of stuff, so much that I can't inventory it all. Aisles and aisles of it. Packed like a museum laid out in long aisles. How old is this Earth museum, anyway? Around four and a half billion years is the estimate. Lots of time to pack it full.

Igneous rocks are molecular patterns fossilized into crystals. Coal is fossilized plant life. Genes are fossilized strings of biological development. I live in a huge traveling museum of fossils, this spaceship called Earth.

Science has been trying to inventory it for a long while. There are the geologists, chemists, physicists, biologists, all their kin. And they're just working in the aisles of the *physical* structures. What about the Earth's mental structures? That section also holds many aisles to inventory.

Along these aisles, ethnologists and anthropologists and sociologists sort out the social structures. Over here, logicians and metaphysicians and astrologers and alchemists chart the various philosophical structures. Over here, historians and art critics and news commentators do the cultural structures. In these aisles, CEOs and secretaries and accountants and shop owners and bankers and so forth deal with the financial structures. Over here are psychologists, psychiatrists, counselors, friends, lovelorn columnists who handle the emotional structures. Now, these wide aisles hold politicians and lobbyists and dictators and so on, who do political structures. Back here are painters and sculptors and dancers and poets who explore art structures. These carpenters and electricians and farmers and forest rangers deal with various maintenance structures. And off in these aisles, the theologians and nuns and evangelists and mystics handle religious structures.

I've left out a lot, but I'm quitting here. It's just too much, I can't see and inventory this whole museum. I don't know what all is here. But it's very old. A global museum full of curious artifacts.

People have been inventorying it for a long time, from lots of different angles. Biology burgeons into subcategories like botany, zoology, ecology, genetics. Hybrid listings spawn—like biophysics, optical astronomy. There's just so much! I need an overview of this place.

But look, here's a map! Odd. Fancy, in this museum of old stuff— aisles crammed full of it—the map is newly updated. Look at these diagrams of dots…or are they circles? Oh. They're particles. Look at how they work together. In dynamic motion all over the map.

Good lord. It's quantum physics! These dots are quantum particles— quarks and leptons changing in relationships—they make up all matter, not just this planet. Dots form the whole universe. You can see just such shifting particles in Feynman diagrams, an informal dynamic notation of what happens in the changing relationships of particles.

Look, it's a *complex* map. The dream says so. Is it a map of complexes? A map of relationships between clusters of *psychic* energy?

Oh! Maybe this is not just Terra Firma, this traveling museum I'm riding in. Maybe it's Spaceship Universe. That's why these walls are invisible. It holds the universe...I am humbled by it.

At dawn, at this moment of the crack between two worlds, I am awed at the sheer hugeness of this Spaceship Universe carrying my life I don't know where.

There are other planets with life, don't you suspect? But there would be relationship in the universe without any life at all. Carbon atoms relate to form the crystal lattices that make a piece of quartz. In any substance, play goes on between nucleus and electrons, between each atom and the other atoms.

But I can't really set life apart from the universe, because the whole universe is alive. Everything evolves, whether it's coal into diamonds or old-timey Octagon soap into forty-seven different brands of lurid boxes lining the soap island of the modern supermarket. Dynamic flow is implicit in all this burgeoning process—it operates physically and mentally, organizing entropic matter and negentropic life. People call it God or Mother Nature or fate or design or chance or destiny.

But I prefer to cut out the fancy footwork and just say god. I prefer a lower case g because god is everywhere, like air and water and leptons and time and space. As low in the order of sizing as you want to go, there is god. As high, wide and handsome as you can go—from one end of the cosmos to the other—there is god. So why capitalize the g? It is a common noun. A capital G comes from anthropomorphizing god, from finitizing god into bits like Harold or Anabel or Baal. But this not a proper name—god—it's the commonest name of all.

To me, god is this incredible hugeness spread around us in constant evolution. Rocks and molecules and cosmic rays and moss and people and concepts like honor and hate participate in this organism, so that the whole universe partakes of a kind of super-consciousness which keeps it evolving.

Suddenly I recall that Grig is coming over tomorrow evening, on Sunday. As I write it, I realize I need to tell you where I live. A few days ago, I realized that you don't even know. Even though there was that dream about our house in Austin.

But I don't really live in Austin. We have a little house in Austin, true, but right now, we're based in Zurich, in an apartment, while I study at the Jung Institute. That Austin house was in dream land. I've been orienting you to my inner space, not to the city around me.

But the time has come to say that I live in Zurich, where my friend Grig is moving from a job in industry to teach at Eidgenössische Technische Hochschule, more familiarly known as ETH. It's a technical university with a good reputation, sort of like MIT.

Grig comes over maybe once a week. He and I sit on two couches facing each other across the coffee table and talk about physics. We've been doing it for five or six months now. Well, except when I went to Texas recently. I don't know if Grig will have much time to shoot the solar breeze about cosmology anymore after he starts his new job. Or even whether his interests will stay tuned with mine.

We met through my friend Mariles—the one with the top-priority man friend. One day back at the end of May, she and I lay stretched out in the sun on the grassy shore of Lake Zurich while I told her of a cosmology hypothesis I've been fooling around with for some years.

Actually, it came from dreamtime. And it's far out. It's been tough to find knowledgeable people who'll discuss it seriously with me. Understandably so. Cosmologists are burdened with half-cooked ideas from people who have little understanding of what is involved.

Mind and matter are inextricably linked, perhaps even visibly at the particle level. Number provides an entryway into gravity, I believe, at the root of universal symmetry-breaking. One can't unite all the forces of physics down at the level that will explain gravity, I think, without also unifying matter with mind. That's not just physics at the root…it is metaphysics, too.

This recalls the universal spaceship dream and its map of interactive particles. And yes, I do feel awe at this physical and psychic hum going on at the quantum level. I see myself as one of many around the globe who are spinning spirit and matter back together where they got raveled apart so long ago. People here and there on the globe, with green arcing between us. That's how I think of us. A network of pulsing green light. Around the world we are bending close to map various sections of this old globe, struggling to keep it current.

As I was telling Mariles on the grass, "But this hypothesis…I don't know how well it holds up. I wish some physicist would show up to bat it around with me, see if it holds up."

Mariles said, "Makes sense to me, but who am I to judge? Let me mention it to Grig. He's a physicist who likes Fritjof Capra. Maybe he'll be interested in talking with you."

So Grig called. Then he started coming over once a week. I'm glad. He has a flexible mind that doesn't get horrified or outraged at my notions, and he can suggest parallels or oppositions to what I'm saying. It provides a backboard to bounce off more angles of aspect.

But tomorrow night I'm going over to his place for a change. I'll meet his new baby, who's about two months old. Grig and his wife make an interesting couple. She's Chinese, while he's Celtic as all get-out, even to the bright red hair.

But generally Grig and I don't spend much time in social amenities. Last week our springboard for discussion was "Particle Accelerators Test Cosmological Theory" in last June's *Scientific American.* This week it's A.P. French's *Vibrations and Waves* from the ETH library.

And right now I'm in a fallow period regarding the *Big TOE* anyway, as my friend James calls my hypothesis. In fact, one reason I decided to tackle this annotated dream log for a month is that it offers me a change of pace. And then back to the *Big TOE.*

If nothing else turns up. It might, since I never did get a hammerlock on the future. Oh well, the unconscious seems to want this dream book done. Certainly it's offering a catch of dream fish each night for me to cook up and serve the next day.

So even now, I'm busy updating my section of the map—working right now in the psyche sector. Imagine us all over the globe, many tiny figures rectifying various outdated aspects of this map, a map both physical and mental.

But hey. It was a map both physical and mental that Plato gave us long ago. His universe had concentric rotating spheres and a cave with shadows. Or take the universe as Ocean, Old Spider, and Giant Clam. That map came from Nauru, one of the Gilbert Islands. There's been a long procession of just such cosmic maps, constantly being updated.

Thomas Kuhn said we're due for a new map, that we're even busy creating it in a paradigm shift. And in *The Discarded Image,* C.S. Lewis said, "…our own Model will die a violent death, ruthlessly smashed by an unprovoked assault of new facts…. The new Model will not be set up without evidence, but the evidence will turn up when the inner need for it becomes sufficiently great." So as I lie here, I feel a throb in the universal web.

Hardly light outside. I don't have to get up right away. Maybe I'll finish off *Death of a Thin-Skinned Animal*. My husband bought it more than a year ago, I suddenly notice by the date handwritten inside the front cover—he always does that—but somehow it got lost to my attention until now.

Hey, who is this thin-skinned animal of the title, I suddenly wonder? The author hasn't said yet.

Suddenly I wonder why this dream came today. Why right after those shadow dreams? Dreams always have continuity. There's some reason why this immensity-of-god dream is arriving right after the shadow stuff. Something important for this log. But what? I trek back through the spaceship, through the shadow issues of the past two days. To a casual observer, it would look like I'm still reading the *Thin-Skinned Animal*.

My husband gets up, and while he's pulling on his trousers, he says, "Saturday! Don't have to go to work!"

I look up smiling. "Yes. A day off."

This is a joke. John's's retired now, and today will be not so different from the rest of his week. He leaves the room and I go back to the *Thin-Skinned Animal:* "...a sudden premonition of death. It was in the room, she knew it was in the room. She could feel its presence though she couldn't see it. But she knew where it was. It was hovering behind the curtain. And when the curtain moved it wasn't the wind moving it, it was death. She would never see it of course, it would never show itself. It would wait behind the curtain till she fell asleep, then come out and silently carry her off on the wings of darkness."

Death. Ah, yes. Of course! Ego death follows shadow. It succumbs to the shadow's truth. It doesn't want to. Ego can't believe it will be reborn into a new, evolved form that integrates and profits from that bitter spoonful of nasty truth.

Of course! That's why these dreams took the order they did. No doubt it's also why I haven't finished reading this novel yet—because shadow isn't through with me, weary as I am of it. I still have more to learn from the *Thin-Skinned Animal.* I can sense it in the synchronous mesh of things.

Oh! Ego is the thin-skinned animal. Alert and fragile and trying to survive. That's what this thriller murmurs to me now, evoking my own past as I read on and between its lines.

Hmm. Do you suppose all this spate of spy novels ever since World War II—Smiley and Bond and Quiller and the rest of them—has been a shadow drama dressed in flesh? Each hero serves some huge hidden organization—which parallels the ego serving the greater psyche. The hero is loyal, yet the network considers him expendable in the big picture—much as the unconscious views the ego.

The hero's mission is to outwit some evil force: SMERSH, CHAOS, KGB, BEM. Just as the ego tries to outwit its split-off, alienated, hostile shadow. The vast network even sets the hero up to die sometimes, as is happening now in the *Thin-Skinned Animal.* Conflict in the global theater is extraverted into a gigantic power struggle of ego versus shadow.

Hey—that's why the loyal spy has such a devilish go of it. Like the ego, he's unaware of the "big picture" in the vast hidden organization that considers him expendable. The hero is too busy staving off death to notice. In *Death of a Thin-Skinned Animal,* our spy hero is dying by order of the big boss. As a sometimes puny ego must die in order to evolve, to incorporate a shadowy truth and move into a more complex and subtle organization, making its escape to a higher order.

I look through and past the *Thin-Skinned Animal* to that great spaceship we ride. Suddenly I'm back in the dream at 15, where I'm viewing the whole shining multihued globe from out in space. I'm hurrying to containerize and be born. Oh, I'm so tiny floating out here. Hurry. Oh! It's humbling to hunker down into flesh and be aborning.

To confront the shadow, to face its nasty truth, is even more humbling. Ego has to submit to its own death. And rebirth. It must submit to death of the old way before it can reorganize its identity and discover what a renewable resource it is.

But at first—ego death? That scares me. It will carry the *me* off silently on the wings of darkness and I'll never come back. I fear.

And look, this trifling *me* is even tinier, more insignificant than I've realized. It's not just Earth I'm riding, but rather the whole universe that is our spaceship. How fast this ship is moving, and how fast the parts in it are moving too. Each moving part has peculiar velocity, a speed peculiar to that part alone. For example, the earth moves around the sun at about 30 kilometers a second. Whoosh! The sun moves in this galaxy at about 300 kilometers a second. Parts of the galaxy move at different peculiar speeds. One nebula (a huge, gassy cloud) in this galaxy moves at about 1600 kilometers a second. Our galaxy rotates in the local group of galaxies at its own speed, too. And our group of local galaxies also has its own peculiar velocity. Earth, sun, galaxy, galaxy groups are all moving parts of synchronized matter.

How big is this universal spaceship? Hard to say, for here's another odd thing about this universal spaceship: its hull is made of nothing. Absolutely nothing. Not even a vacuum or a void. No wonder I can see through the walls of this universal spaceship. Space and time and matter and energy are contained *inside* it. All the dynamic parts are contained by *nothing*.

How tiny all this makes me. Moving outside the globe of the Earth to look at it, I see how finite become our wars and campaigns and vaunting ambitions and lives. In a few hundred years we've moved from sitting snug at the center of everything with the sun moving around us in stately circles, to become just tiny specks on one insignificant globe in a minor solar system on a spiral arm of a rather third-rate galaxy in a cluster of local galaxies on one small part of the map of the universal museum.

Pretty piddling. I'm so petty, puny, and ephemeral in this scheme of things. This *reducto ad absurdum* is a bitter truth that physical science offers these days to our species. How could god ever find me? In the universal spaceship, I shrink to a mote. Data reduces me to triviality.

The human image has recently suffered a collective deflation by physical science. Religion once vaunted us as made in god's image, but when science "proved" that we're limited and error-prone, housed in bodies with low durability as ephemeral dots on the map, some people decided, "Oh, I'm so tiny. I have no significance in a plan this mighty…no ultimate meaning or value. Look at the size of this Spaceship Universe. Why would some god notice my tiny ego point focused here in this planet, this continent, this person, this moment?"

In Henry Mencken's bitter little summing up:

1. *The cosmos is a gigantic flywheel making 10,000 revolutions a minute.*
2. *Man is a sick fly taking a dizzy ride on it.*
3. *Religion is the theory that the wheel was designed and set spinning to give him the ride.*

Now, that's a bruised ego speaking. It has swallowed the bitterest pill of science, the ugly truth that we're—wow—*how* tiny? It shrinks the human ego so much that our whole culture reels stunned. Some say it's the prime mental illness of our time, this being flayed out of our soul.

So we look to the material world for our value: "Will you give me value, Lover? I'll be your love slave—for awhile—if you'll just help me feel valued. Will you give me value, Money? Then I'll slave every day for you—at least till I find out what money doesn't buy—if you'll just keep score of how valuable I am. Will you give me value, Addictions? Then I'll tend you like a baby, feed you on schedule and put your care and pampering before all else. I'll hover over you, dote on you—warped, distorted imitation of a soul that you are. Will you give me value, Prestige? I'll lie, cheat, steal for you, Prestige, if you'll just assign me value in the eyes of others. Maybe that will reflect back into me.

But inside, I am still tiny, nothing, worthless. My value should come from inside, but it isn't, so I search ceaselessly for it outside.

The ego might be likened to a windshield on a vehicle. You ride along and look out and see the world around, not noticing the glass at all. But it protects you. A storm comes along and flows harmlessly away against its protection. Useful. But if big flaws are in it, you'll see things distorted. But if you step out of the vehicle in dreamtime, then you can study this ego windshield. Maybe install a new, better one.

In this soul-blighted century, the average psyche hasn't got such a good, serviceable ego. It has turned bitter and jaded and cynical and hopeless and shallow in its attempts to ignore that void just beneath the skin. So the wounded ego nowadays really needs a loving inner anima/animus as companion to strengthen it before it can dare to pass on into the dark labyrinth and willingly die at the hands of the shadow. Ego must be quite strong and healthy before it can manage to sacrifice itself to truth and thus gain by it.

Normally, in a healthy psyche, dream work moves in deepening layers through ego to shadow to animus/anima figure to the divine. Call it the unconscious or oversoul or big enchilada or god—this final great force of connection behind all the archetypal forces.

But currently, animus/anima development often appears first in the dream sequencing of a client. This inner companion, who is visibly maturing in the dream sequence, gradually helps the ego to believe in itself, to realize there is actually something inside that is trying to help. This supports the fragile ego until it becomes able to love itself properly. Yes, dreamtime knows just what to prescribe, if you just pay it the courtesy of reading your night letters.

Look, in this dream log, first the ego *me* and companion animus appeared in teamwork in Chapter 1. They went together down to the watery unconscious and started to examine the sea horse and flatfish complexes and so on. Then in the next chapter, the ego met the parents, as I stood at the dream window looking at my past from that limited structure housing my childhood vision. It's a broader landscape than I had realized existed in those days. Then I walked onward with my companion, led by a dog-spirit.

Those first two chapters show what gives the ego enough strength to take up the struggle with shadow in the following chapters. In the next chapter, my ego's identity enlarges into the collective role of woman, including her undervaluation in this culture as it segues into the shadowy witch. Shadow is observed closely in succeeding dreams— first, as a Victorian aunt with her sharp-tongued truth. Benign enough, that shadow. But it may become a brutal dictator if split off from an ego which frantically tries to imprison or even kill its dark, hidden truth.

Yet if faced bravely, if given a fair trial with honest witnesses, then shadow can undergo rehabilitation. An ugly truth can be reconciled into the wider vision of an evolving ego. Shadow and ego can even become wry and wary friends. If ego is willing to dim its gloss, then shadow can relax into a gentler guise, less punitive and demanding.

With so much strength under its belt, finally ego can let go and open toward the immensity of god, and although still as tiny, still as puny, it cannot be extinguished by this awesome vision, but instead find its own unique place tucked into the meaning of the whole.

This journey transports ego beyond the despair and angst of our modern world without a soul. Our scientific-techno-industrial complex has become so self-handicapped and yet so proud of daring to struggle along without the left-handed way of wisdom.

But a post-industrial approach will carry us into meaning beyond logic, where we can perceive immense connective pictures wheeling beyond the slow march of sequential cause and effect logic. It joins the analog and linear domains together into a merging discipline called analinear analysis. Tracking the dreams and events in your life will show you an interconnection that is so thorough, so tightly woven, and of such immense design that eventually you can no longer suppose that your limited ego is master of ceremonies in this game of life.

It's a long haul from perceiving the windshield to crewing happily on the transparent Spaceship Universe. But the soul wants to go. It cries: "Take me to god!" It solves the problem of death by outgrowing death's sting.

Dreams connect me to a caring that is so huge, so personal, so directed at me daily, and to each person alone in sleep—always on tap— that I come to experience my tiny point of being in a relatedness so huge, so divine, so total, that the beauty of it is overwhelming.

Everything in my environment hangs together, works together to cue me on my path. Yet I have choices, and I can take my place in the pattern gladly or be dragged reluctantly through it kicking and screaming.

How can all this stuff in the great museum possibly have meaning? How can it not? Each day is focused to carry me forward, giving me options organized beyond my ego's ken and canniness, if I can just look and listen to the clues semaphoring at the edge of my attention in dreams, words, flesh.

When the ego is strong and flexible, even ego death becomes a joy. We don't lose by it, we gain. We gain soul. The soul delights in rising up above the shining ball of earth to look at the big picture.

Growing the soul expands one's inner being until it can contain as much universe as exists. This is sometimes called the containment puzzle. As you and I consider the size of the universe, in a sense, our minds contain it. In some odd way we are bigger than it. Although just tiny bits of the universe, we somehow hold it.

Here's an example. Tonight I went to the Turnip Festival. Mariles called and said she was leaving for a weekend with her man friend—no surprise! But I didn't even really mind. I had no ego stake in it anymore, since I'd admitted my hurt and let it go.

I went on my own and ran into *nine* friends in the train. Plenty of companionship, after all. But if I'd gotten peeved at Mariles, stayed home and sulked because she'd rejected me and—boo-hoo—spoiled everything, I'd have missed out on something beautiful in a way that I cannot even describe. If I try to describe this parade, you'll laugh. It spiritualizes the turnip in a way you'd never suspect possible until you see the shoulder-carried floats melting into the dark and leaving only their scaffolds hung with heart-shaped purple and white lanterns carved in patterns turned into amber flesh by the golden glow of candles inside.

Once again this year, I was touched by the turnip festival. But I have to admit that shadow hit me too. A young woman knocked me down. She pushed through the bystanders to get right in front of me. I'd been on this spot with six friends for thirty minutes, with only a low line of youngsters sitting in front of me on the curb, and I didn't want to lose my front-row position to this pushy late arrival. So I stood my ground as she drove her elbow in with the force of her chunky body. She pushed harder, knocking me over. I grabbed the bottom of her long shoulder-strap purse as I fell, trying to keep from landing on the children sitting on the curb in front of me.

Then from the ground I looked up into her eyes. I saw a bully, yes, but also I saw how embarrassed she was when it turned sour. No wonder. She was pushy in Switzerland, a country where people are so polite that I can only guess she'd already offended a lot of folks with those flying elbows on her way up to the front of the crowd.

But now she was embarrassed and wanted to escape. She couldn't, though, because, I was still holding onto her purse for balance, canted awkwardly on the curb. She started yelling, "Let go! Let go!"

I said in English, "Why are you yelling?" because in my shock I didn't think to speak in German. Talking to myself, I guess, just wondering. She yelled in furious English, "Just remember, you're not in America now. You're in Switzerland. You're not in America now."

Yet here she was, speaking English to tell me this. She said for me to speak her way, but her words accommodated to my way. I looked into her eyes and saw that she was frantic to escape a message that was vibrating palpably in the silent crowd…that she was a bully and a jerk. I might be the one sitting on the ground, but the truth had her pinned down for the count, and we both knew it. The Swiss around us stood shocked, silent, staring at me on the ground…back at her looming over me. I could sense it in the air: "Girl, you just don't treat a tourist this way. For one thing, it's bad business." Even manners apart, the Swiss are good business people.

She was trapped. Hoist by her own petard, her shoulder bag that I clutched. She was more discombobulated than I, even lying flat on the ground. I'd become her shadow made manifest. I held her there and kept her spotlighted in the ugly truth that she was a bully, unmasked now to a staring polite Swiss crowd. So I just held onto her purse a bit longer, slowly getting up, savoring it all before I let her escape.

Standing later in the turnip-lighted ambience as the floats went by, I was glad that I'd held my ground, kept my small place in this festival tonight. Aware that I wouldn't have done it in New York, though. I might have gotten stabbed for it.

And then I flashed on that old dream of a black pocket knife. It came when I'd been taken advantage of several times by someone assuming I was so nice that I wouldn't mind being trompled a little.

So I asked the unconscious for help, and it delivered me a dream:

> I'm buying a good new car, but I can't find the key. It's some-
> where around. People help me look. I look in a box and find a plain
> black pocket knife. It has implements on it.

The dream told me that this new car I'm buying, this new mode of carrying myself, is good. But where was the key to operating my new way to go through events? Then I get it. That black pocket knife is the key to my new way through life.

This knife really talked to my imagination. It said, "My blade is a long sharp tooth held in a black mystery. I stay in a dark pocket ready to be used. Keep me hidden there, and you won't feel so helpless, you won't send a message of vulnerability. I am the cutting edge of sharp truth. Keep me on you and people will watch their step, will stop assuming that you're so nice you won't protect your self. I am useful shadow."

I realized there were no marks on my dream knife. No holy cross and shield like on a regular red Swiss knife. So I'm not a zealous crusader marching as to war. I'm just protecting myself with my shadow of a dream knife. It gives me psychological teeth.

So the next day I went out and bought a black pocket knife and put it onto my key chain. I keep it in my purse. I've driven screws into a chair with it, cut persimmons, looked at leaf veins with the magnifying glass. Quite useful. But the best part is, now people somehow sense my psychological teeth. Its hidden potential keeps me from emitting the unconscious aura of sacrificial lamb anymore. People senses the hidden teeth in my nature now, without me having to say a threatening word or show my teeth…I mean knife.

It was those hidden teeth that made me hold onto the woman's purse a bit longer, long enough for her to get embarrassed by the crowd. I found a way—even on the ground—to keep her from flattening me.

And that's what living in a body means. Learning to work with the shadow, even the shadowy matter of the body. This finite point of soul is focused into a short life span.

We're here for something. I recall the first time I attended the Turnip Festival in Richterswil. Later that night, I had this tiny dream about a tiny man:

> I see a little man with a turnip lantern head. His name is Richters Willie. He says, "I'm little, but I'm enough." And his turnip flesh glows bright with light.

That's what I think we are: little. And that's what we're here to do: glow. And that's what it is: enough.

CHAPTER 9

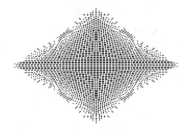

Rising Action — Ah!
— Winding Down

Dream Log—Sunday, November 13:

Dreaming with events I can't recall, only that they become horrible, horrible. Panic. A voice says, "Cry Havoc!" Heightening tension. Then suddenly it all resolves, dissolves away, leaving *Liebestod's* Love-Death music swirling at the end.

The *Liebestod* is what I wake to yet again. Just like at the end of yesterday's space opera. But the dream today is only a vague memory of events hardly even visible—it's more like...just action rising to a climax and then falling. I lie in bed looking at the graph I've just drawn in my dream log. It looks like a plot line. Literally. A plotted line of action, like something recorded by a moving stylus.

PLOTS

- For affairs of the heart — Boy meets girl, boy loses girl, boy gains girl.
- For tragedies — Boy meets himself, boy loses himself, boy loses life.
- For comedies — Girl meets life, girl loses old self-image, girl gains life.
- For dreams — Ego meets shadow, ego loses life, ego gains rebirth.

This drawing looks like the old plot line that Mrs. Mason (boned corset, rouge and face powder and blue pompadour) drew on the blackboard in my ninth grade classroom at South Junior High School. In this graph you see that things start off normal, but right away you can sense trouble. Here

It's a graph.
The plotline for every drama
onstage and off.

comes the rising action, the worry and fear that surges in ascending peaks and eddies into descending valleys of tension. But the general momentum is upward until finally, all hell breaks loose and pulls the tension way up to the perilous heights of climax—ah! orgasm! Death, birth, rebirth—whatever. Then the tension drops back down to normal.

But this is my explanation. Her version was much more formal. Mrs. Mason was maybe 62, and rigid. A corset gripped her body beneath the fabric of her dress, and you could count its boned facets circling her torso. She also had an iron will that upheld her inside.

Someone ventured, "Why, Mrs. Mason? Why does the line go back down to normal? Because things will be different. They don't ever settle back to just the same."

"This line merely indicates the level of tension. Of course, one never returns to exactly the same point in life. Notice that this endpoint"—she tapped with her wooden stick—"marks a different location from the beginning point. This level shelf at the end—" tap, tap "—merely indicates the moment when the plot is clarified and resolved. Here"—tap, tap—"the hero or heroine is released from tension and pauses in a final calm look backward. It offers a respite, a resting space in which to recuperate from the preceding events. No one can tolerate high tension all the time. Survivors of great tension must be allowed their brief pause in safe harbor before starting out on a new life struggle."

She shifted on her high stool (whose presence finally, only now, makes me suspect that she must have suffered with aching feet from so many years of standing). "*Denouement,*" she articulated slowly.

Denouement? We sat waiting. Nobody spoke. She'd tell us what it meant, in good time. Mrs. Mason got attention without ever lifting her voice above a deliberate soft tone. The angrier she became, the softer her voice...until the note-passer or spit-baller froze into unrustling silence to raise that whisper back to its normal level.

"You will learn to identify the *denouement* in this play we are going to read: *Julius Caesar.* I expect you to find this tragedy's emotional endpoint—its *denouement,* which is the name for this resting shelf at the end." Tap, tap.

"In fact, this graph has four terms that I expect you to know. There are four major phases to a plot line: Introduction of Tension"—tap—"Rising Action"—tap—"Climax"—tap—"and Denouement." Tap. From her high stool kept near the board so that she didn't have to stand, each spot on the graph got its tap with the wooden stick. Mrs. Mason sat pinched in her old lady shoes (those high-heeled oxfords that lace up) and corset squeeze and tight blue pompadour pulled back with silver hair pins firmly anchored in a no-nonsense manner. Mr. Mason was kind, but in the same way that my severe Victorian shadow aunt was kind—by always pressing a bit more information on me than I wanted to receive. She educated me with a sugarcoated quinine pill.

Mrs. Mason used a wooden stick in my eighth grade, like a short billiard cue. But sometime during my ninth grade, it changed into a thin metal telescoping wand that stretched out to about three feet at its full extension. Like a radio antenna. Maybe it was one.

Nowadays I suspect some parent complained that Mrs. Mason was threatening us students with that wooden cue. But she didn't need a weapon to keep our attention. She was a throwback to the McGuffey Reader era. She was a *grande dame* of order and propriety and a Proper Education; she frequently poured incisive Latin quotations into our uncomprehending ears.

Well...so what is this dream today? Not much. Just a plot line. It seems downright banal, even, as I study the sketch of this little graph. Not much to probe here.

I feel let down, disappointed. There's so little to work with. Maybe that's okay. I'm still tired from last night. I went to the Turnip Festival, you know, then wrote it up late last night. I lost track of the hours, surprised to see what turned up on the screen. I didn't know that part about the woman pushing me down would appear, for instance, until I found myself typing it. I didn't know the emerging threads would all pull together, either, but they did. Finally, satisfied, I crawled into bed near dawn.

And slept only till 9:20 am.

Lying here now, I feel dull and draggy. Sunday. Hey, I can stay in bed all day! No commitments till this evening. But then I slowly get up anyway, because my husband comes in and says he's made special biscuits and they're hot. He often does on Sunday morning. I go in to the breakfast table, sit down, and we chat during breakfast.

I tell him about the Turnip Festival, about being pushed down by that woman—while I eat biscuits and the marmalade that I made last Tuesday out of rose hips paste and fructose. Yes, rose hips paste…known as hagebutten mark in Swiss German. It looks like thick tomato paste, only a bit more orangey and grainy, bought from a stall at the outdoor market on Burkliplatz. This marmalade tastes wonderful. It's full of vitamin C, of course, since most of the world's vitamin C comes from rose hips.

I prefer natural food. My genes have not evolved to handle the sulfides and nitrites and artificial sweeteners. Or even that denatured imperishable stuff called sugar. Rats and roaches won't touch sugar unless they're starved into it. I won't eat worse than a rat or roach.

During just the sort of breakfast that I like, we made cozy talk, and sitting there, I got a sudden flash on those old black-and-white Perry Mason TV shows. You know, it's the end. Perry and Della and Paul are somewhere discussing the finale of the case. And eating. Always eating. It's after the trial is over and everything is solved and Perry has righted the wrong and Della has been discreetly indispensable and Paul has provided the strong arm and leg muscle that a thinking guy like Perry can't be expected to muster.

The tension is gone and the climax is resolved, so in the last couple of minutes the three of them always eat and drink and talk. Tea time, French restaurant, Della's apartment kitchen, coffee break at the office—the locales range across the eating spectrum. I imagine the script writers pulling their hair as they look for new ways and places for Perry, Della and Paul to eat at the denouement. Cozy on the shelf at the end of the plot line. Quiet for a moment before the next case springs through the door into the rising tension of the next show.

Food is comforting. Biscuits and marmalade are comfort food. I sit on this cozy shelf after the tension of last night. And it's Sunday! So now I make it even cozier by returning to bed…ready to finish finally that *Thin-Skinned Animal.*

After a few pages, I realize that today is a denouement for me. This teeny dream—it provides a leveling-off plateau where I take a rest after the high tension of meeting the shadow, killing off the ego, meeting god in the vasty deep of space, then coming back into a frail little body. Which is enough.

107

So this is why the last two dreams ended on a musical theme? Why I heard the Love-Death swirl? Because thus far in the daily chapters, I've been sketching a tense plot line of the ego's Love-Death crisis? *Ego Liebestod.* Okay, I'll even bother to get up and look for those lyrics. I find the Xeroxed sheet still lying on my desk from the Wagner lecture.

Hmm…I get the basic idea: it's about overwhelming bliss much like a sexual climax. "Do only I hear this melody…pierce me through, rise above the waves…blessedly echoing and ringing round me?…Shall I sip, plunge beneath this surging swell, this ringing sound, this vast wave of the world's breath—to drown, to sink unconscious—supreme bliss!"

I can still hear Birgit Nilsson's limpid voice curving through the cochlea of my inner ear…those words, the German phrases bending like water over the notes…surprising me that this technocrat language can sound so simple and fluid. Violin strains swirl about the paragraphs of the *Thin-Skinned Animal* as I move from one page of the spy novel quickly to the next. I want to get it finished off and buried today.

Death. Love. The French call orgasm a little death. In the spy novel, the thin-skinned animal named Clifford plots his own sexy way toward death: "Clifford idly, perhaps unconsciously caressed the rifle rather as a man even just after lovemaking might idly run his hand over the woman's body because its curves and hollows and softness and dampness and the feel of female skin still gave him a sensual and loving pleasure."

The rising climax of love and death—I guess it graphs out a plot line. You come to a resolution, you take a rest, and then start again.

Of course it's old news, this plot line. It stretches back to the one-celled protoplasm, and before that, to the solar winds that sucked gas from a sun and blasted it outward to seed space with atoms that become tinkered into the molecules that create life. We are born in the heart of a star.

Exhausting. I decide that this will be a very short chapter. Maybe I'll take tomorrow off, too. Rest time. I'm tired. Perry and Della and Paul and I deserve it.

Sure, I'll record tomorrow's dream, but I'll just hand it over to you. I'll write it down but not *up.* It's your turn. After all, you've been head-tripping with me long enough to make some sense of the layout.

And here's a secret: whatever you decide about tomorrow's dream will be right and useful. For you. Your interpretation will reveal a great deal about *you.* Because that's how the universe works. Everything connects in holographic resonance.

You think I'm kidding? It can't connect with you? You suppose that I've just been using my dreams to jump into some random associations that hook together in a frenzy of "creative writing?" Hah!

No. I sit listening with my inner ear to the swirling song of dreams. If I get silent inside, I can hear it. You can too, if you don't fill every waking moment with the loud outer noise of radio and TV and cafeteria chatter and phone talk with friends and relatives and business associates who, honestly, just keep a person too busy, and the Walkman language tape while you're jogging, and that inner harangue of self-recrimination.

Hey, just stop! Listen! Begin to hear the song of the universe inside. What could be better on Sunday morning?

What? You're afraid to hear what's in there? Maybe you mistake it for *nothing?* Remember, there's a big difference between space and nothing. Before the universe was born, that was nothing. Then events sparked into being and created space. Physical space. And inner space too. Mind space. And it is *not* nothing.

From mind space come the dreams. They merge dream with flesh, like the Turnip festival with that shadowy woman and the grain of mud in my eye and the synchronicity of this black-covered book called *Death of a Thin-Skinned Animal* in my hands just now.

But I'm at the very last pages of this spy novel. Our hero is betrayed by his own organization. Why? The African dictator is useful, after all, more useful than the hero. So the organization sells him out, delivers him into the hands of the dictator.

Now our hero struggles to the death against the shadow—I mean dictator. He tells his anima—I mean loyal girl friend—that he'll kill the villain and everything will be hunkey-dory and they'll live happily ever after in Eden, I mean Israel. She's delighted. After all, her canary, Solomon, doesn't sing anymore, what with all this tension. She wants to hear the song of Solomon again. So the hero says that they'll flee and go live in the Promised Land. She asks, "Where we'll be safe?" He answers, "And live happy ever after."

But half a mo—he's just got to kill off the evil dictator/shadow first. It's kill or be killed—to hell with what the boss wants. But apparently what the boss wants is to extinguish the hero.

So in this spy novel, the greater organization is in favor of an ugly truth over the hero/ego—who takes it as betrayal, of course. Ego defends itself to the death! Denial is what it's called.

How do you think this thriller will turn out? I can guess. Not because I know the plot yet, but because I can sense what's needed on a symbolic level to finish out our ego/shadow cycle. This spy novel *must* follow through, must amplify the ego-death motif that we are already singing, have been singing for several days now. The song of ego's death and rebirth.

Funny, I hadn't even planned to read *Death of a Thin-Skinned Animal.* It was just the top book on that bagful of my husband's paperbacks ready to give away to the local exchange library. But with nothing on hand to read a few nights ago, its rather whimsical title intrigued me, so I picked it up. By chance. Ha. Synchronicity. Divine plan. Whatever. Fill in the blank. Yes, the ego is such a thin-skinned animal.

This is how dream life and real life mesh together—happenstance events reinforce the major motifs. Mostly though, it is such an organic fit that you don't notice. But don't think that your waking life and dream life are two realities to be kept in separate compartments. You'll get very confused that way, by not letting your linear life know what your holistic life is doing. The modern ego—that *Thin-Skinned Animal* in all of us— may shrug off the split-mind confusion as normal, saying, hey, how else can I live? It's all I know.

As the *Thin Skinned Animal* fortuitously puts it, approaching the climax: "Anyway, I'm used to leading a double life—one real, the other a dream."

"Which one is this?"

"The dream of course. But played for real."

"Isn't that confusing?"

Hey, ego, it sure the hell is. It's a shell game that keeps switching and hiding the truth under different coconut shells. So just lift off all the shells and look at the whole picture.

At the climax of *Death of a Thin-Skinned Animal,* our hero finally traps the dictator in the English country house. They're face to face. But the dictator has a secret gun. He manages to ease it out and blam!— kill our hero. But at that *very same instant,* a government sniper mistakes the shadowy dictator in the window for the hero and nails him. So they both die. Ego-man and shadow-man.

What's left is the greater organization. So what is our denouement? A weird renewal as the hero pants out a fragmentary death speech that promises to meet his love in the Eden of Israel: "Tell her...I'll walk her...walk her through the palm trees...of Shaar hagolan."

Hmm, it's only just now that I notice our hero's name is Abbott, which means, according to my dictionary, a "servant of god."

What about the girlfriend, though? Oh, you know how it is with the anima/companion. She waits and hopes: "Solomon started singing. And singing beautifully. More beautiful, more gaily, more poignantly than he had ever sung before. Tears of joy started down her face. And she sat there in that tiny kitchen, listening to the song of Solomon, waiting for Abbott to come back and kiss her with the kisses of his mouth and love her with the love that many waters cannot quench nor the floods overflow."

And that's it. **The End.** Our ego/hero no doubt does return to the waiting and faithful anima. Reborn like the canary's song, the ego meets the inner partner at a more mature level. And they walk on to their next journey in the stroll toward god.

Love and death. Death-Love. They are indissolubly linked in the psyche's greatest mystery. "God loved us so much that He gave His only begotten Son." "Darling, I'd give my life for you." "It was so wonderful, I thought I'd died and gone to heaven." The love-death theme permeates our civilization.

So the *Thin-Skinned Animal* has dropped into my hands just now instead of some other time during this year it's been in our flat. Thanks, god. Thanks, too, for the lecture I attended on Wagner and the Turnip Festival with the woman who pushed me down, and the mud in my eye and so forth. It's harvest time.

Yep, I just fashion the chapters from whatever turns up, and you take potluck. I have no overall plan of how it should go. I only know that each day will amplify a night's dreams and follow the line of development. I will use whatever dream fish jump into my frying pan each night to cook and serve up to you by day.

Why not? Why dream my life and live my dream? Merge and blend them until they reinforce and guide and support each other in growth. Life is easier this way. That I can tell you from personal experience. If you haven't tried it, if you're still leery of dreamwork, maybe you'll find that what you mistook for nothing is inner space. It opens to an inner universe that goes on expanding at the speed of each dream's light.

This Love-Death music in the Wagner opera is waning in my ear now. This shadow cycle is ending, I can tell. Here is Chapter 9, and 9 is 3x3—that's tripled transformation brought to resolution. Resolution sits on the plot shelf, taking a break—its denouement.

Just as I'm resting today on the shelf after this encounter with shadow—sitting along with Perry and Ella and Perry and you—eating biscuits and marmalade and being indolent. I'm being reborn back into my finite little body that is enough, that will serve. So instead of grand opera, what comes to mind now is the mediocre magnificence of Robert Service:

> *God is the Iz-ness of the Is,*
> *The One-ness of our Cosmic Biz;*
> *The high, the low, the near, the far,*
> *The atom and the evening star;*
> *The lark, the shark, the cloud, the clod,*
> *The whole darned Universe—that's God.*

CHAPTER 10

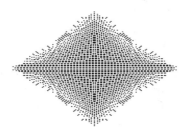

You're on Your Own

Dream Log—Monday, November 14:

Dream 1: I see the animal. Big change—he's bigger and stronger and his skin is thicker now. His hide moves and flexes under pressure—like bunched, heavy-flowing liquid. I am satisfied.

Dream 2: I'm living in a cheap, poor house. The children around me are rowdy, undisciplined. I have to take care of them. Slowly I get a few furnishings into the house. But I look around. It isn't much.

Then in a factory, I'm making things for myself and the house. I can see the logo. It's a circle with a striped tiger's head inside, stylized, with the stripes dividing the head completely.

A man comes to my poor house to help me. He repairs some things and builds me a little study in the back. Everything here is small and crowded and messy. As I look around, I feel dissatisfied and depressed. It's sad, this poverty-stricken life. I don't know if it's ever going to get better.

Then I'm sitting and watching TV all day. The house is slovenly. There's a black and white image on TV. A social worker or somebody like that comes to check out how I live. I'm lying back on the couch, angry that she came. Around me, everything is disgusting, but I'm still mad that she's trying to make me change. She's interfering with my lying back and watching TV. Why doesn't she get out and leave me alone? It's my house. Shabby as it is, it's my life.

Okay, your turn. What do these dreams suggest about the psyche—mine, yours, and ours shared at the deeper level of the unconscious? Get a general impression of the meaning. Follow your own associations. Use the following analysis list, which you can employ later on your own dreams.

113

Dream Analysis
Sequence

Look at dreams as plays on the inner stage of the psyche. Keep in mind that this particular pair of dreams came from a woman. Do you see any figures in these two dreams who might be...

- *The ego figure (the dreamer's conscious identity)?*
- *The animus or anima—(the dreamer's opposite-sex partner and helper)?*
- *The shadow—(same sex as the dreamer, and revealer of the ego's unaccepted truth)?*
- *Any other characters or animal motifs that may carry a symbolic meaning?*

Now ask yourself these questions about each dream, or better yet, talk them over with a friend...

- *What is the feeling tone in each dream?*
- *What atmosphere and information does the setting provide? Why?*
- *What does the action or plot line suggest?*
- *How do the dream figures relate to each other?*
- *What associations do the characters and animals suggest?*
- *Do you notice any word plays or allusive phrases? Any visual or verbal puns?*
- *Do you notice any carryover themes from past dreams? Describe and explore the theme.*
- *How do the night's dreams relate to each other? Why did they arrive in this particular sequence during the night?*
- *Why have these dreams come at just this point in the dreamer's life?*
- *The dream events suggest some deeper import for the dreamer's life—what?*
- *How would you summarize each dream in one sentence or title or phrase?*

CHAPTER 11

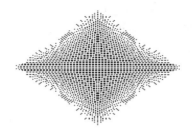

One, Two,
Three Dream Circus

Dream Log—Tuesday, November 15:

Dream 1: I'm in a strange, small-statured, dangerous world where termites eat the foundations of everything—so tribes form, primitive bands with few possessions, and move around and defeat each other.

I'm glad to leave this world.

I barely awaken, just enough to turn on my little light and scribble down this dream. It doesn't make sense, this silly dream. Then I sink again into sleep and…

Dream 2: A boat on the water. A sailing race is going on. Then all the racers return to the starting point. But now one is disqualified, and a relative of his must take his place. They race again. I watch this second race, glad that the old racer is disqualified from racing again.

Again I wake up immediately after the dream and scribble it down. Sometime later I rouse enough to know that my husband is getting up, dressing, and leaving the bedroom. But I'm not ready to get up yet. I still feel tired somehow. I'm going to stay in bed and sleep a bit longer. I sink into…

Dream 3: I see three sets of shapes—triangles, squares, and stuff—in three rings, sort of like a three-ring circus. I look at them hard…

I rouse to hear a drawer moving and I realize that my husband is back here in the bedroom again looking for something, but I am some-how incorporating his sound into my sleep and carrying him back into the dream. Good, I think. I'm glad he's here. I want his opinion.

I rouse and scribble down this third dream. What is it—6:45 am? Not light yet. Silence in the flat. My husband has gone down to the kiosk for his *International Herald Tribune* and then over to Cafe Munz for coffee and a croissant. Like every morning except Sunday.

Such a period piece, that cafe. So Swiss, steady and staid. I imagine my husband sitting now amidst the tiny tables full at this hour—all the commuters busy at this most important ritual: reading the *Zuricher Zeitung* while enjoying croissants and coffee from a lyre-handled china cup with floral design. All of them adamant members of the bourgeoisie. It's as if a whole nation of peasants has risen en masse over the last six hundred years into *burgerliche* comfort.

I consider last night's dreams and that final tail-wagger where my husband entered the last one. Yes, that's how it feels to me…the tail of that last little dreamlet wags the dog.

So I'll take the last dream first. I open my bedside log to read it. And I can't find it!

What? But I *didn't* just let it go! I remember distinctly writing it down. But where? I scan through the rest of the log pages. Blank.

Then I turn back to the previous page, and there it sits, nestled with the dreams of yesterday. How? Apparently in recording today's last dream—an afterthought—I misflipped the pages and used a short space that was left at the bottom of yesterday's entry.

Hmm. So the last shall be first. Really. I read it:…three sets of shapes—triangles, squares, and stuff—in three rings, sort of like a three-ring circus. Somehow what pops into mind is this book. Is it structured like a three-ring circus, with each ring holding a different motif?— triangles, squares, stuff. What is Ring 1 about? Triangles. Hmm, a triangle shows the archetype of the 3: it makes a transcendent movement from the line's 2-ness of polarity. Hmm. Maybe the first nine chapters were like the first ring of a circus. Wasn't that the theme of the first nine chapters? Rising above the ego's polarized fight with shadow to find a higher view, where psyche transcends ego death to move toward higher truth. That was the action in the first ring. A triangle of transformation.

And then came an intermission in Chapter 10.

Now here in Chapter 11, what's happening? What is this second ring? "Here come the squares." Foursquare, solid, real.

So maybe this is going to be the focus of the second ring? Matter? The hard-edged world of limits?

Right now, I sure feel my limits. If I'm supposed to maintain the exultant momentum of Ring 1, well, I just can't. I can't imagine any grand finale more sublime than ego death and finding god in the divine pattern. So how do I follow Act 1?

Into my mind pops something like a blip arriving on the radar screen. The tao will set up its own finale for this book. I'm not in charge here. Let each ring take care of itself and provide its own tempo and action. Okay. Maybe it's time to get out of boundless space so this dream book doesn't space out. So this second ring showcases the material world. Squares are sturdy and dependable and keep their feet on the ground.

Okay, peeking on ahead…what is the last part going to be? What's in the final ring? Stuff. Just *stuff?* It reminds me of the British usage for *stuff* meaning woolen fabric or cloth in wearing apparel. Maybe the last part of the book will weave the woolly dreams of Ring 1 and the material limits of Ring 2 into something you can wear daily. I hope so.

What's that last bit where my husband merges into the dream? That's no animus figure with an unknown face. It's a real man walking around in the bedroom, getting socks out of a drawer and making noise.

So he walked into my dreamtime. Yes, I guess my husband is becoming my reality check on this manuscript. Yesterday I printed out Chapter 10 and said, "Would you look this over? Tell me what you think about it." I wanted to find out, especially since he never bothers with his dreams. He's never seen the point.

In fact, after finishing every chapter, I've asked him to read it. Sometimes he finds a spelling or grammar error. At first he didn't remark on the content, though, except to say he gets to see me in a new way.

"But I don't know about your main premise," he said in a kindly tone, handing back that first set of sheets. "Dreams are just dreams to me." He's always let his dreams go like water flowing away under a bridge—here an instant and gone forever. I realized that, yes, this intelligent, educated man doesn't suppose his dreams have that much to do with his daily life.

In succeeding days, I've imagined him musing, "She's well-meaning, my wife, and believes what she says is true. As far as that goes, she's right on the details. After all, we did attend that lecture on Wagner's Eisendonck dreams as an inspiration for *Tristan und Isolde.* And we did hear *Liebestod* with Birgit Nilsson. And Frau Weber did hand out lyrics in German and English. So this manuscript shows that my wife is a clever and interesting woman, even if she is going overboard about dreams creating reality. She means well, so I'll encourage her by reading it. And I'll even try to stay open-minded."

Of course, he didn't say that in such a condescending way. But I sensed it, from his super-kindliness that hid a shade of tolerance.[And he does own up to it some days later, while reading this chapter.]

And that attitude is exactly what I want to speak to, I now realize. I want to reach the many intelligent people who extravert into the outer world, who value what is tangible and material—what is four-square—more than what flows from the boundless unconscious. I want this book to show—not just tell but show—how these two realms are completely interwoven. They are tied indissolubly, like body and mind, and they mirror each other.

I think back to my husband's various statements. Recently he said, "I don't know. Maybe you'll make me change my mind about...." He trailed off. Walked off.

That night, during dinner with company, my husband even told a dream of his at the table—wonder of wonders!. He asked us two women what we thought of it. We threw it right back to him, though, wondering what it meant to him. "Not what it shows literally, I hope," he said, because it was about a death. We all sat silent for a moment, and then we went on talking about other things.

The next day he said after reading the next chapter, "Look, I see that you're doing this, but I don't know how. I don't know how you manage to get it all to fit together."

"It just does," I said. "You see that it does. I'm not exactly fitting it together. It fits itself together out of dreams and days and memories. You see how the events fit with the dreams. Of course, you can't see my dreams or memories, but I do describe it as exactly as I can."

"Yes, I know that." He was a bit preoccupied all day.

Then at night as I lay reading the *Thin-Skinned Animal,* suddenly he turned over in his sleep and spoke loudly, slowly, as though delivering a statement that I absolutely must hear. "I...cannot...do...it!" With a sad declaration in his tone.

I lay pondering. Usually he doesn't talk in his sleep. He mutters and grunts. However, I have heard stories from the old apocryphal days. My husband says that his ex-wife used to tell him that he talked in his sleep. She said that it was very tantalizing to hear his sleepy-time words, that she would lie awake sometimes waiting for him to finish a sentence.

Uh-huh, I thought at the time—so is he subliminally telling me that he announced things to his ex-wife by talking in his sleep? What juicy secrets did he tell her, or almost tell her? And what might he tell me?

But he's never done it with me. Till now. I ponder his words: "I...cannot...do...it!" What can my husband absolutely not do that makes so sad a declaration that his ego chooses to announce it only in his sleep? I senses that recently he's been thinking it over...how this book correlates the real world that he sees by day with the dream world that I see by night. He's even admitted it.

Is he declaring now in his sleep that he cannot interpret his own dreams? Or that he doesn't believe dreams matter? Or that he can't allow himself to believe it and so shake the foundation of his world view? Or what?

Well, yesterday, he said...and I can quote it precisely because I jotted it down. I wanted to get his words right—first, to be sure of what he was saying so I could respond properly—and second, because it would likely be the very reaction I needed to address for skeptical or dubious readers. His words: "Maybe you're just using a dream as a diving board, a jumping-off point into things that you've already been thinking about and working on. Somehow you're putting it all together with the creative glue of your imagination."

I thought, ooh, here's the crunch. Yes, this is it. It is not simply that I note something from the day and then it turns up in a dream. It's also that I note something from a dream and it turns up in manifest reality the next day. Dream and daylight weave into one huge unity.

So now I realize that I must show how my dreams shape my days, and vice versa. I shall pay attention to making this more evident. It's no longer enough just to enjoy the fit. I must point it out, in case you're reading this book like it's fiction and don't notice that it's reality.

To get down to brass tacks—how do my dreams help me now? Basically, to write this dream journal. My life is going pretty smoothly, no health crisis either. so my main event is just finishing this dream book right. So this is where I need help.

To do it, I need a fairly wide range of dreams...dream that are clear and convincing enough to show the mesh of conscious and unconscious life. They need to include some of the major archetypes. They need to cohere in progressive development. All needs to move throughout like a symphony rising into conclusion. Can I demand all this of my dreams? Expect it? No, just ask. Ask each night for the dream catch that I will need for the next day, and then trust that it will come.

Can I do it? Have dreams about working with anima? With shadow?

Already we've seen some shadows—that dictator and that dark woman with the long red nails who scared me into eating her as little steaks. And that stern aunt, as amusing as she was forbidding in that brown velvet Victorian garb. She was a shadow more evolved and kindly.

But if I were to say blithely, "Oh, my dreams don't bring me terrible, frightening, emotion-shattering images anymore," that isn't true. Look at yesterday. Frightening! But still…I don't want to invite terrible nightmares this month by a sheer act of will, just to give you a sample. It would be like calling forth a circus lion into whose toothy jaws I would stick my head nightly for your thrills and entertainment.

But that dream tiger did show up. And the beast with the flexible skin. And the dream offered a three-ring circus.

What do you make of it all? What is that flexible animal? My old thin-skinned ego is gone. It's a far cry from those bad old days when my ego was a multiply-wounded, thin-skinned animal that struggled each day for enough courage to slog on despite the slings and arrows of outrageous shadow.

Fortunately, ego death is much cleaner than ego wounding. It brings rebirth, while ego wounding merely generates a habitual and sardonic pain, where you just drag on and on, trying to patch up that fallible faulty structure, and it gets harder and harder, more and more pointless to try. With ego death, though, you rise from the ashes, reborn, to exclaim, "Hey, it's okay that I'm fallible and things are turning out different than I expected. It's okay that I'm not a compilation of everybody's good points. I'll use each day to find my own best path. These unexpected twists and turns of fate somehow become my unerring path through the labyrinth of life. My eyes can't see over the walls and through the hedges and around the baffles and beyond the dead ends. My ego can't make a door materialize in a brick wall. But dreaming can—if I let it happen. Then my inexplicable choices become not errors to castigate myself for choosing, but sure signals that lead me to a goal beyond my knowing, into slow development beyond my understanding."

Look at that animal's skin now. Skin, you may recall, is a symbol for the soul. This skin is strong and resilient and flexible under pressure—it moves like bunched, heavy-flowing liquid.

"It's mercury that you're describing, mercury," my husband said to me yesterday when I tried to explain it.

"Yes, that's it exactly!" The skin moved like mercury shifting in a skin of surface tension. Mercury, the winged god of communication. He was a messenger versatile and fast. He carried ideas through their tricky shifts of nuance like quicksilver glinting and rolling on a table, now dividing, now merging into pools in new locations. That's how the animal skin moved. Like shifting quicksilver.

But why does this dream present an animal image? Maybe because to show the ego moving with right instinct. True, psychology has long thought we humans have outgrown our animal instincts. Supposedly, brain development has led us beyond those basic impulses triggered by the stimulus-response mechanism so evident in the lower forms of life.

Yes, animals do use instinct. It protects the bird, the reptile, the mammal by cueing appropriate action. For example, one species of bird has this cueing mechanism bred into its genes: the newly hatched nestlings will automatically open their beaks whenever mother bird stands above showing them the red spot on her throat as she offers a bit of food. The nestlings will actually open their beaks to a red spot on a card, too, when tested. It's not the mother's presence, but rather the red spot that causes their beaks to open. This is called a *species-specific* image trigger, because it operates for just this species in just this way.

But here's the big news. I believe that we humans have developed beyond this *Species*-Specific Image Trigger. (I call it the S-SIT.) We have evolved to a more sophisticated and subtle level of instinct cueing. I think each of us has an *Individual-Specific* Image Trigger that cues each person uniquely. I call it the I-SIT. I can't prove it, of course, but I believe it exists in the brain because of observing so many people's dreams. I think it is this I-SIT that creates the imaging in each person's dreams. It tries to cue us—daily!—in the instinctively right responses for one's particular life path. Its message will be individual and unique, geared to that person's specific needs, and it is given nightly while the conscious guard is down.

You may be demurring: "Then why don't we all just skip lightly along the primrose path of life with never a care or worry, always clued in by our right instincts?" Well, we've gotten so ego-bound that often we squash even our best instinctive reactions. We have forgotten how to access messages from dreamtime and interpret them rightly, have forgotten even to honor and utilize this holistic cueing from the analog domain. Often our waking self and our dreaming self are at odds. We have gone logic-crazy. We are ego-freaks afraid to move beyond the linear boundaries. We stumble in the chains of rationality that gird civilization roundabout, while all around us, the beckoning universe stretches its patterns of bright meaning beyond mere logic.

How did we ever get into such a logic-bound state? We could just blame it on the ancient Greeks with their penchant for logic—but that's a cop-out. It was only one symptom of a huge psychic movement that seized the cultural wave about twenty-five hundred years ago. Classical Greece was a symptom, not the cause. A very useful movement it was, too, for a time. Humanity learned to enjoy some real advantages by delaying our instinctive impulses for quick gratification by using conscious cause-and-effect rationality.

We've slowly built up a logical superstructure designed to override our instincts and drown out their signals. Nowadays we can quell our instincts to eat, copulate, or fight by replaying an inner tape that says, "Wait till noon for lunch." "Not here, silly." "You're in the library, remember?—study for your placement exam instead." "Kill his chance to succeed, not his body." Those girders of collective rules are quite valuable. They form a huge invisible superstructure that supports the most remarkable of hives—human culture.

You can hear the superstructure murmuring its rules. It has a vague collective voice that speaks inside your head, much like an internalized Greek chorus. "Don't be so stupid!" "Worry about your job." "They're making a fool out of you!" "Hey, you want it because everyone else wants it." And so on. It is the voice of Christmas past and Father's Day and Mass and all those other values of society made official. Some of them are useful, some are outworn or faulty.

But we humans have not really given up our instinct trigger. That trigger is still inside. It still sends out signals—although it is not "Open your mouth for the red spot." Instead, I believe that in dreams, an *Individual-Specific* Instinct Trigger is tuned to your own unique state. Most people, though, override this I-SIT—this small still voice that speaks aright—because of so many collective dictates drowning out the personal instinct—which after all, is not codified into a book of rules. The I-SIT merely cues a unique, specific dream for each situation. It can be overwhelmed by the rote dictums of the culture's superstructure, stale and over-generalized though those directives may be.

Each night, your dreams trigger individual-specific messages. Why do I think so? Long study, first on myself and then on others, has convinced me that dreams, when they're paid attention to, can cue the right instinct that leads people into satisfying lives. It happens because dream images are part of the stimulus-response mechanism built into the brain. This built-in mechanism can bring your life into balance by cueing you through your dreams into taking the right action for your own life.

How did we humans come to have such a personalized mechanism? Well, it's been developing its finesse over the ages. It speaks now on an individual, not a species-wide, basis—every night—in unique dreams. If you doubt it, study your own dreams for their meaning. (Drop that linear Newtonian mindset that calls a dream's details so silly or bizarre.) You'll find that your dreams are busy cueing you nightly, trying to bring your own life into balance.

For the psychically healthy person, dreams give cues for routine psyche maintenance in "little dreams," as psychologists so cleverly call them. Longer-range events are signaled in "big dreams." A night's sequence of "little" dreams, no matter how silly and pointless-seeming, is cueing you into the proper stance to take to meet your upcoming day. In a healthy psyche, this dreaming prepares you for the next day's onslaught of events.

You can discern this "mood-briefing action" by tracking precisely what mood your dreams coax you into each morning. For example, a dream where you suddenly fall off a tower, but then float up to a higher place can cushion you for being fired that day and then immediately finding a higher position with another company. The dream provided your ego with an unconscious emotional preview of what you need to carry you securely through this crisis of being fired. *If you pay attention,* it will bolster your serotonin into enough self-assurance to attract that other job and allow the upward fall to happen.

But for the troubled psyche, dreamtime is repair time. It works in a remedial way to undo frantically all the trauma that you or others or "an act of god" has cavalierly dumped into your life. Note: a dream does not automatically take away a problem. It merely seeks to help you treat it in a growth-producing way. Dreams seek to stimulate an emotion that will key the needed response to mature and integrate your psyche. By walking the way of dreams with a friend or a counselor, you can improve your mental health and develop a strong, flexible ego with good animal instincts.

This liquid-skinned animal dream satisfies me. In making the change from a thin-skinned ego, I discovered the most banal things—for example, that my parents weren't so awful, nor my childhood so uniquely painful as I'd imagined in my solitary suffering. The pain was real, sure, but it was the neurotic pain so many of us share in growing up. A veritable army of us misunderstood beings were not seen or nourished or appreciated in the way we would have liked. I don't even think it is usually our parents' fault. They are just the most convenient nexus to blame. I think the pain is built into the very process of being human and finite. Societies do alter, but the human condition is not lost. It continually challenges us into new adjustments and learnings.

That may sound fatalistic, but I don't mean it so. I believe it is worthwhile, even imperative to address the ongoing problems of the human condition…our physical pains, sure, but also the mental. Mental pain can be anguishing. I grew up in the submerged army of the suffering. I learned it in my gut, not on a TV show about the mentally ill or stepping over the sidewalks of homeless or around beds of the severely handicapped. Look into the eyes of strangers or your most intimate friends, and you'll sometimes see very great pain—the middle run of acquaintances hide it better.

Eventually I coped with this chronic mental pain, learned to allay it, to lessen it, even to let go of it finally as an old habit I no longer needed. Doing it was so hard and slow, though, that I suspect it actually changed my brain structure. Of course I still have sorrows, but they're not chronic. Instead, my emotions move on with the flow of life instead of staying stuck in the past, reiterating a trauma.

Indeed the huge goal of psychic maturity is to accept responsibility for one's own life and begin to work with it instead of blaming others for not providing all the breaks ready-made. One can become the loving parent of oneself, and bring oneself up well.

So what did I pick up last night to read just before falling asleep? You guessed it—something that dovetailed with this motif. The top book on the stack of paperbacks from the exchange library yesterday was *Marya* by Joyce Carol Oates. I remember glancing at the cover —"Hmm, *Marya*. Yeah, I'll take this one along."

Then last night, I studied the front cover again, wondered why I chose it…aside from chance, of course. The picture showed a young woman, what I'll call an art deco madonna. Teasers blared across the top: "SEARING…HER STRONGEST BOOK IN YEARS" says the New York Times. "EXPLOSIVE…OATES IS BREAKING NEW GROUND; MINING DEEPER INTO THE HUMAN SPIRIT"— *San Francisco Chronicle.*

Look, I protested, I don't want to keep picking up books that just turn out so apt. As I've sensed that *Marya* probably will.

My ego gets into these little self-assertive postures occasionally as I struggle to accept the flow and still feel my sense of autonomy and choice. The *me* likes to feel some control. And it does have some. But ego is just a copartner in shaping events. It has choice, but a choice can work with or counter to the flow that the unconscious intends. Sometimes my ego acts like a sulky child being dragged along by the hand, digging in its heels, wanting more say in the matter.

It's a peculiar trap, this ego resistance. Perversely satisfying. Once when I was first learning to cooperate with the unconscious, I got into an ego trap for about two weeks where my ego felt overwhelmed, smothered, possessed by a huge controlling parent-like force who wouldn't let me assert my *me* in all this web of connectivity. My own projection of course, left over from childhood fears.

Eventually my ego worked through the wrestling match to discover that I do have a say, a big one, but it's just foolish and counterproductive to struggle against the grain of the greater purpose. The divine plan, if you will. Holding onto my stubborn streak just to assert my ego, no matter what, resulted in the *me* getting dragged along by the hair instead of dancing gracefully and joyfully and creatively in the universal design. Carl Jung talked about that.

But after that two-week wrestling match, my ego made a decision. It chose to go with the flow and utilize the great power in the Tao instead of fighting it just to see if I could. I could. Big deal. Bigger deal not to. I began to see that I needn't worry. I didn't lose my individuality. I gained it by bending to the flow of my purpose. I could start to become what I am uniquely meant for, not just what the cookie-cutter collective culture had in mind for me.

So lying in bed last night, I looked at *Marya*. Three of the five letters reproduced my own name. I'm identifying with three-fifths of a name? Turning to the back cover, I read, "She was a survivor. From the brutal lesson of an abandoned childhood to the...."

Oh, shit. Not now. I don't want to read about a poor little waif. Not tonight. But then I said, "Come on, gut up. It's arrived in your hands tonight for a reason. Read it."

So I started. And it's good. I'm about halfway through the novel. You're in luck because I'm not going to describe the poverty and squalor and weepy moments. I've already wept. Marya's grown up now to a hard-won scholarship, and it looks like now she is transmuting in that sea-change of time all the debris of her terrible childhood—such as her father being beaten to death: "…he hadn't any face that you could recognize. The skin was swollen and discolored, the left eye wasn't right, something had sliced and sheared into the cheek, the jaw must have been out of line because the mouth couldn't close…."

The left eye wasn't right. It recalls that sea-changing song of Shakespeare's that I used to sing in childhood, something like…

Full fathoms five thy father lies,
And his bones are of coral made,
Those are pearls that were his eyes….

Looking on at it with the pearlized vision of time, my own childhood was not nearly so horrible as any number of abused childhoods that you could name. Not nearly so bad as Marya's. Maybe not so terrible as yours. I didn't starve in Calcutta. My arms weren't blown off in a car bomb, my face not burnt away in Vietnam. I don't even have a crippling handicap like rheumatoid arthritis. Some people survive all those disasters and more—some even come through it spiritually intact and feisty. Knock them down and they pop back up with an audacious wink and a smile, raring to take another bite out of life. They've got teeth.

Not me. I had to buy mine in a Swiss army knife store. I was so slow to start using my own teeth to tear off chunks of life, or to threaten predators. Why? For fear that I might hurt someone. It came from an old exaggerated identification with the victim.

So where did that come from? From my karma, I think now. Merely that. We were eating lunch in a Piccadilly Cafeteria when I finally questioned my mother about why she told me, "Nobody cares" whenever I hurt myself and cried as a child. We do pick the oddest times for these confrontations, don't we? She was surprised that I even remembered "Nobody cares." That wasn't the half of what I remembered.

"Why did you say that to me? 'Nobody cares.'"

"To teach you to stop crying every time you got hurt. You were such a crybaby."

But "Nobody cares" merely taught me that nobody cared when I got hurt, and to mourn it with new tears each time a new hurt came. Once I was sobbing, disconsolate with a sorrow that I could not name, hidden behind the kitchen door that was pulled back into a tight little triangle against the corner walls. Hiding because I was so embarrassed to be crying again and with no place to hide my face but this triangular darkness where I could be my awful, lonely, unloved, unlovable, despicable crybaby self.

Suddenly the wooden edge of the door was ripped out of my clutching hand, light fell onto my shame—along with a shocking mixing bowl of cold water. Bleary-eyed, swollen-faced, I looked up into my mother's grim-lipped smile. I heard her voice declare with satisfaction, "This will make you stop crying."

She was right. The shock shut me up. Outside. So I just developed colds and chronic tonsillitis and pneumonias from crying within, from watery mucus running along my nasal passages and throat and starting infections. A howling wilderness within, where the wolves were always coming up and eating the little lamb of me, and eventually I started setting the table for company with the little lamb of me. Maybe people would at least like me that way. Self-slaughtered, dressed, roasted and served up in a sauce of rue. I found myself wrong even before people proved me wrong. I found myself a failure before they could show it to me.

So you can see why I treasure that dream of the black knife. It became a talisman to help me stop me being the lamb inside and thereby inviting the wolf outside. That dream prompted me to buy a black knife as the visible reminder that I can protect my own valuable life…because there had been so many steps in the opposite direction.

A big wrong step was trying to kill myself at twenty-nine. I planned it the very best way and time and place I could…and woke up in a hospital bed, ashamed and discouraged to find that even in this, I'd failed. Knowing somehow, though, that I'd never try it again. My then-husband had come home early, unexpectedly, and found me on the bed with all the pills in the bathroom gone.

I'd tried to kill myself because he was divorcing me. I understood. Who wants a depressive rag of a wife? I didn't blame him. I didn't want me either. So I decided to kill me. So I was thinking about all that last night as I started reading *Marya*. I wondered if I need to show you the old primitive *me*…so you won't think I'm Pollyanna in the Sky with Diamonds who doesn't know where the sun doesn't shine.

Sure, I could tell you about feeling futile-depressed-alone-frantic back then, but please connect it with the *me* now. The *me* born from the death of that thin-skinned animal. I recall its death whenever I read about some politician's wife taking an alcohol cure or some drugged pop star falling apart onstage or some social misfit ending it all. I died in a corner of life too. There is a whole suffering army of us still crying in the corners. I understand that pain. And I even know how hard it is give up that habit and move on.

Which brings us to the shanty dream. Look where it dumped me—smack into poverty and despair and even anger as my social worker-shadow tried to get me off the couch. Moving on takes guts. It's much easier to lie back on the couch and watch TV and go crazy. In fact, in neurotic families, somebody becomes the escape valve for the group tensions. The most susceptible, fragile, thin-skinned person acts out conflicts for the others. For example, only as an adult did I realize that I didn't hate my grandmother, after all. On the contrary, I rather admired her. But for twenty-odd years I'd carried around and acted out my mother's buried aggression against *her* mother. As early as I can remember, Mother would start a ritual sentence, "Oh, your grandmother is so good but..." and then relay some injustice that had been visited on my mother long before I was born. She handed me the hot brand of her own denied aggression to carry and wield for her. To fight Grandmother in ways she didn't dare. Oh, I dared.

This surrogate pact is typical between parents and children, between husband and wife, boss and employee—it's nothing extraordinary. And I entered it willingly, for just as my mother loved her mother despite the injustices, so did I love my mother, despite the same thing. That is a grim fact about complexes—they are our odd way of touching each other, of reaching out to embrace each other...despite the flawed bonds. It's all we've got to tie us to each other.

So I hated my grandmother for things that I'd never seen happen. On our visits to her house, I made it plain by my violent, outspoken, reflex antipathy that I didn't like her one little bit. I'd run outside or shut myself into a bedroom. Meanwhile, Mother would sit demurely in the antimacassered living room and say horrified, pooh-pooing sweet nothings to express her bewilderment—"I just don't know what gets into her!"—while I burned with the smoldering resentment and anger that she'd fanned.

I expressed for my mother a shadowside that she could not own, so instead, she had contracted with a three- and four- and six-year-old *me* to display for her. And I did it, too. It was the one way she appreciated the *me* as I was, me and my little warped soul.

You think children are too young and naive to get conscripted into psychodramas like this? Then look around you and see the children wholeheartedly and exaggeratedly playing off the covert cues that are given by their elders. You'll also see which parts the adults, more sophisticated and subtle through long practice, prefer to keep for themselves as the plum roles. One favorite is the tisk-tisking good guy while the child is an obstreperous little social shit enacting what the parent doesn't say, but feels.

In neurotic families, the generations are chronic partners in such collusions. Children can say and act out the malice, hostility, fear that the adults feel…sometimes even only unconsciously. Childish temper tantrums are an overt dramatization of what the parents repress. Actually, such children are quite governable—they are being dreadfully manipulated, in fact.

This contract in chronic disaster can get to be a habit that is honored even when the child grows up. Grown up on the outside anyway, but stuck in childish conflict or depression or compulsion. "Crazy" people often display the family's shadow side, expressing it so wholeheartedly that the thing has gotten out of hand and the crazy person can't come out of the role any more, locked into the monotony of repeating a scene or even a few key lines of habitual suffering.

The other family members watch this crazed pain from their stance of apparent common sense that declares to the world, "Thank god it's not me. Notice I'm not that way myself. I can handle things better than this poor pitiful fool who cries or drinks or dopes or mourns in a corner of life. Or ends up sitting on hot-air gratings in winter. Or eats his own shit in the looney bin. Or cuts his wrists like they're spaghetti. Or can't get along with anybody at work. Or beats the kids under stress." They don't know that the one down is the group scapegoat.

It takes a long time to card out complexes and begin unweaving the "craziness" with its nasty snarled knots of garish pain, to reweave it into coherent and subtle patterns in a tapestry of meaning. Back in 1916, Freud said that disturbing experiences induce trauma, and the wounding is so subjective, so personal, that it cannot be approached directly. Instead we must approach the pain indirectly. We cannot see it except through its enactment in events. Even though the psyche is invisible, by its fruits we shall know it. Sometimes that fruit is bitter.

So here I lie sunk in the bad old days, as foretold by that dream in that rundown shanty of my younger soul, that TV-watching couch potato immobilized in poor, cheap, slovenly despair—with those undisciplined children, the unkempt creations of my mental life roving rowdy around me. That's how I felt back then. Productivity? I couldn't manage it. "Hey, it's too discouraging to rise up and be counted— right? Look, it's just pointless."

So in those days, I quit on the job. Watched black and white TV in a colorless life. Got angry if my damn do-gooder social worker-shadow tried to roust me into cleaning up my act and getting my life moving. Back off from interfering, damn you! It's my life!

Dammit, I already tried. Didn't you see me trying? My animus even came in and helped me a bit with sorting and repairing. He even built me a little study back out of the traffic so I could begin to ponder my inner meaning—but that study got cramped and messy, too. Okay, okay—so I did it myself. Don't blame me. Look, I had a rotten child-hood. Look, I even went to the factory and tried to make some things. See that tiger head logo—all my fierce effort captured in that single emblem. I tried. Till I gave up depressed and quit again.

About that tiger logo, my husband remarked, "I think of a tiger as dangerous and beautiful." Yes, its beautiful, dangerous head is striped by conflict. Yet it's also in a temenos, a holy circle, a sacred space.

I felt so deeply divided, which kept me from being effective. And I remembered all that last night, because of *Marya* with her whiff of *deja vu*. That poor little pitiful old *me* was revisited in that rundown shanty of my young soul. Well, at least you got to see a "primitive" dream.

But this dream also applies to what's happening now, you know, in my current life. I'm lying on the mental couch right now, after the rous-ing finale in the first ring. I mean, how do you top union with god and the universe? So this dream shows me sunk on the couch in a veritable parody of flat-out misery with those rambunctious kids of my dream chapters running wild. My do-gooder shadow gives me the what-for. Oh poor poor poor little *me*! It's enough to make me laugh.

And laughter marks the change from that old thin-skinned ego, who couldn't laugh, but only cry. It shows the difference between the old *me* who lay depressed on the couch and the new *me* whose skin is strong and flexible and rippling enough to get the joke and stand up. Now I enlist the unconscious to help the *me* out. It makes all the differ-ence in the world. It's just too hard to change without help from some-where. Call it god or the 12 Steps or the Self or whatever.

But that old *me* never asked my unconscious for help. It was my enemy, ticking away like a time bomb, tricking me, deluding me, sabo-taging my hopes. I didn't know how to read the nightly answers in my dreams. I admit it, I was a night-letter illiterate. So my soul languished in an impoverished shanty while I couch-potatoed watching canned life in mere black and white.

But finally I got up off that couch and, paradoxically, it made me strong enough to become happy and vigorous. In jargon, reducing the effect of the trauma allowed me to work on the complexes themselves. I approached each complex to release its negative energy. I mothered my forlorn waif inside. I learned to care for and hold my wounded child. Walking beyond the habit of pain revealed other alternatives. I was not compelled any longer to chose only one path, that old painful emotional groove worn deep by habit.

And the good old unconscious saved me again last night. When I put down *Marya* and turned out the light, it brought me those dreams tuned to the right frequency to begin this next movement of the dream book: we're in Ring 2 now, the squared circle. Facing finite limits. I walk into this second circle and stand facing the wild animals of my limitations with hard edges. But now it looks like my ego is strong and flexible enough to handle this.

Once the ego has experienced death, has bowed to and befriended the awesome unconscious, has glimpsed that transcendent garden of great pattern whose edges extend past seeing, then the soul can begin to face whatever sorrows fester inside. And commence to heal them. But ego can't bear to admit how bad it really feels inside unless it knows there is a way to move into something better.

Yep, yesterday I balked at exposing my sad past, my attempt at suicide. Those early years crazy with pain. Well, I don't want to deny it. It was a part of me. And of others. But should I tell the sob story here? Would it really help someone out there? I needed a sign.

I thinking about this while waiting at the station yesterday to catch the train into Zurich for my shiatsu appointment. A friend came up and chatted about a talk she'd just heard on a new James Joyce biography. But the author had to cut out a whole chapter, she said, because of Stephen, the son. The son was afraid.

"Afraid of what?" I pursued it out of some instinct even though my friend was already moving off to board the train.

"Well…" she said, as we sat down together, "He wanted the chapter on his sister Lucia cut out. Apparently she was mentally ill for awhile—they say it came on when her parents wouldn't let her dance. Finally she came out of it, though, and became a strong, happy woman. But then somebody wrote a biography of James Joyce that emphasized those sensational crazy years. Stephen was afraid it would happen again with this new book. So he wrote the author and forbade her to include the chapter on his sister. She was so disappointed—she said she'd worked quite hard on making it sympathetic to Lucia."

"He forbade it? Without even reading the chapter?" Like I was forbidding myself to tell about my young craziness in this book? Hell, I was annoyed at that social worker in my couch-potato dream.

"Without even a word."

"Hmm." I was taking mental note. Take a hint from the universe.

Then I went from the train into the incredible balm of a one-and-half-hour shiatsu massage. It happens every other week. Every *other* week I give my friend Duke a lesson in yoga. And when it comes around my turn again for shiatsu, I lie on the mat and luxuriate in the twists and passive stretches that send my brain sometimes into theta rhythm.

Duke's just back from a long shiatsu workshop. I haven't seen him for two weeks, so I've not mentioned starting this dream book. But when I walk in, he hands me a poem. "Maybe you would like this." I read:

> *The ideas are expressed in pictures,*
> *The pictures are explained in words.*
> *Clinging to the words*
> *   we fail to understand the pictures.*
> *Clinging to the pictures*
> *   we fail to understand the ideas.*
> *Having understood the pictures*
> *   we can forget the words.*
> *Having found the idea*
> *   We can forget the pictures.*
> *   Wang Pi 226-249 AD*

Word to image to underlying idea. The very path to understanding a dream. "But this is what I'm doing right now! I'm writing a book on dreams. This describes how! May I copy it onto a sheet of paper?"

"Sure." As I did, he said, "You've cut your finger."

I glanced at it. "Almost two weeks ago. Pretty deep, right before I started the book. I thought it would keep me from typing—but no. I bled it good to remove the germs. Lots of blood. Then I pulled it tight with band-aids and it healed so smoothly that now you can hardly see the cut." I drew back the band-aid. Shades of L.B.J.—showing how well our wounds have healed.

"And why did you cut it?"

I looked at Duke. Why? A peculiar question deserves a peculiar answer. "It was a blood sacrifice, I think."

"How do you mean?"

"Well, the day I cut it, that morning, I was about to start the dream book." I remembered back to that instant—I was cleaning the kitchen counter. The night before, I'd made rose hips marmalade. And it had splattered in little orangey-red dots. Dried overnight, they were hard to remove. I got up to speed with the wet cloth; it slipped on goo, and I rammed my right middle finger into the knife blade hanging in a rack there. I wasn't even holding the knife when it cut me!

Years ago a biochemist told me, "I dreamed last night that you had ten bloody fingers." I thought, "Heavens, what is this man wishing on me?" But two weeks later a friend said excitedly, "Oh Katya, I just dreamed that you had cut fingers! All ten of them. So bloody!"

Then I thought, Lordy, lordy! What is happening here? Not just one person dreaming it, but two. It's not just in someone's personal unconscious, it's in the collective unconscious. But what does it mean?

Then a month later, the same woman saw me on the street again. "Katya, you know that dream of the ten bloody fingers? I told my analyst about it, and she said to go over to the Jung Institute Library and check out the diploma thesis on bloody fingers."

"The *what?*"

"It's a thesis on cut fingers. Well, I did. It says that hands symbolize our human ability to shape matter creatively—hands are the tool-users that make us different from other animals. And blood is the greatest sacrifice we can offer. So a dream of blood sacrifice from the hands means that something is being offered up to bring forth creativity. But nowadays, we've evolved so much that the sacrificial archetype doesn't demand as much blood—it's gotten more civilized. Just dream blood is enough sometimes, or just a bit of blood on a finger that's lightly cut by accident. Not really accident. The manifestations of an archetype do evolve—just like Jahweh has evolved into gentle Jesus meek and mild."

"Huh?" I was still bemused by this sacrifice of the bloody fingers. An offering to creativity? Well, I was just starting up several projects.

"Yes, we don't kill our children anymore, as Abraham learned with Isaac. Nor even sacrifice animals anymore. Now blood and bones come in the mass as bread and wine. It doesn't take such a toll. So I guess you're going to be creative for awhile—with *ten* bloody fingers!"

"What an odd archetype," Duke said. "It was announced in two dreams, huh? Yes, blood sacrifice goes back through the religions and myths and stories."

"So, Duke, a couple of weeks ago I gave a little blood to start this book," I said as I lay down on the mat, "albeit unintentionally."

Duke, kneeling, gave a directive he never had before. Something he'd learned at the workshop? "Close your eyes and relax. When I find it, I'm going to offer an image to meditate on during the shiatsu." He waited silent above my head. Then he touched my head with both hands: "I waited for the first image before touching you. The image that came was…*nothing*. Not space, not the universe. Just black *nothing*. Then as I touched your head, immediately something else sprang into my mind: a pyramid in a circle, a temenos"—yes, that's what he said, temenos—"with a jungle outside the circle. Atop the pyramid is a strong white light that moves and turns in every direction. I don't know what this image may mean to you, but meditate on it during the shiatsu."

He began to work, and by the time he'd finished, two tears were trickling back into my hairline. Not from pain. The reverse. The massage had released hidden tensions that were blocking my doubts about how to continue with this dream log. To touch the hem of god and then walk on? Into what? Into the ignominy of human limits. Into my damned secrets of sorrow in a sad past. Despite my limits, just go on and do it.

But how did he pick up on that image of nothing beyond space…and of the temenos holding out the jungle? What was on that pyramid…the searching bright light at the top?

So I told Duke my dream of the spaceship universe, and of the difference between carrying nothing inside and containing inner space. Holding the universe inside brings god within, into the temenos, the sacred space.

"Yes. I picked up on it—that image of not-even-space." He said, "By the way, I realized it while I was working on you…that finger you cut…it's the meridian of the triple heater and the heart constrictor."

"So?"

"The triple heater deals with absorption and assimilation. The heart constrictor is interpretation and intuition. That finger where you made the creative sacrifice—I guess the only way to write properly is by allowing the free flow of your emotion without freezing up. Allow the ebb of joy and grief and don't get stuck in one spot. You need to develop some inner awareness and commitment on this."

"Yes. I know. I'm stuck right now, afraid to move on."

"You can."

That night, to loosen up, I attended a class on the body movements of Rudolf Laban. There I was, dropping to the floor, rising, twisting, turning it into a continual rising and falling motion without end. The fall, the rise, the twist. Relating to a partner made it into a dance. My body is dancing tonight, I thought. Tomorrow I can do it in my writing. Put three movements together and it becomes a flowing dance.

So during the night my dream put those three circus rings together. And my husband entered the dream too. You entered this book too, I guess, by working on the last chapter. I'm glad. Please enter.

So yesterday was not really a day off. It prepared me to face today's dreams. They're a snap. That first one of the strange, dangerous world where termites eat the foundations of everything, where tribes form and move around to defeat each other. I'm glad to leave that world.

Yes, I know these termites. They walked out of an article by Dave Barry in last Sunday's *Herald Tribune*. Bodacious insects they were, Formosan termites that scarf up everything, even metal. Yep, getting stuck in doubt and fear about my limitations can undermine everything. It makes a tiny, small-statured world, and I can't keep much because the termites eat it. I live savagely without trust. Such mentalities form little primitive bands of allies and go out to defeat each other. They don't have much. And I was damn glad to leave that cramped world.

That second dream of a sailing race. It's over and all the racers return to the starting point. But one is disqualified from racing, so a relative takes his place. They race again. I'm glad the old racer was disqualified. Maybe that first race was the first nine chapters. Smooth sailing with the wind.... Wind is a symbol of spirit. God's spirit blows across the face of the deep. That first sailing race, that first part of the book, was exalting.

But now it's the second go-around. Same lake, but at a different point on the time graph, as Mrs. Mason would say. That first sailor has to drop out, and now a relative takes his place, sailing in a related but different manner. Yes, in this second part of the book I will sail in a different but related way.

Then finally, that third dream: it's the three-ring circus holding not animals but archetypal forms—triangles and squares and I don't know what...stuff. It reassures me that the unconscious does have a plan for this book. Each of the three section will have its own major motif. triangles, squares, and some hybrid of them.

Today in downtown Zurich I met an expert on Egypt who answered, when I asked him what the eye atop a pyramid symbolizes—"Why of course, it is the eye of god! Don't you know your own American dollar bill? And the pyramid itself means rebirth."

"Rebirth?" Like my being reborn after yet another little ego death? Like this book being reborn into the second ring of nitty-gritty reality?

"Yes, rebirth. The pharaohs were buried in pyramids to make their nightsea journey. Inside coffins shaped like boats or spaceship-looking things. Vehicles to take them to a new life."

"Oh. Spaceships." I thought of the three women in a spaceship to a new world. Of Spaceship Universe. Such are the synchronicities that connect the dream world with the mundane. The dreams that come each night, the I Ching hexagrams that I derive each evening, all of synchronicity's cues are showing me the bond of mind with matter. Dreams, like gravity and cosmic rays and god, exist whether we pay attention or not. By their fruits we shall know them.

Okay. I think my ego is supple and thick-skinned enough to enter this nitty-gritty Ring 2 now. I'm glad my husband is walking into dreams now, and that you too will provide companionship on this new hard ground. Partnership. It puts a whole different quality into the dance.

CHAPTER 12

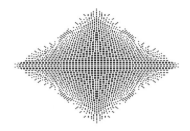

Oh, Mistress Mine

Dream Log—Wednesday, November 16:

Dream: Events. She goes out to do her work at night. At some point she has to say, "I am not a whore!" She goes around her route back to the middle bridge.

I waken. It's dark. Nothing in this dream. Nothing to write down. So short. I'll go back to sleep and dream something better, something longer and worth analyzing. I'll just go to the bathroom first.

But when I turn on the light in the bathroom, my watch says it's 6:30 and I realize I'm not sleepy anymore. I'd better go write down the tiny bit I remember of this dream. Even draw a sketch. It's all I've got to work from today.

So I note the few words and draw the sketch. It's mostly a dynamic image, mostly just seeing the woman's route. It goes through the busiest part of downtown Zurich, but it's at night. She starts walking clockwise down the Limmat River to the Quai Bridge over the river, back up the other side, and turns right to cross the river again to the place where she started by the Rathaus Bridge...which, if I were plotting this route onto a big clock face, would be about the 3:00 position.

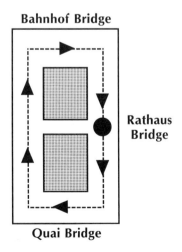

Bahnhof Bridge

Rathaus Bridge

Quai Bridge

It reminds me of the streetwalkers prowling downtown at night. But no, this woman says, no, *has* to say, "I am not a whore!" Why? It calls to mind a ditty that I read back when I was maybe fourteen. It seemed perilously poignant then, that changing beat of the last two lines—I guess it still does:

Who walks by the dockside
In furs and peroxide
Was once a daughter
And purveyed laughter.

Walking along the quai, she couldn't claim, "I'm not a whore!" Unlike the dark lady of my dream. Thus do the associations float up.

The clock face route of this night trip. I study the sketch. Why, it looks like a box of elaborate design. A coffin! A sumptuous coffin. More exactly, like a sarcophagus. Like the space capsule for the Pharaoh's nightsea journey. That Egypt specialist mentioned something else,too. Something I didn't remark at the time. The pharaoh's body was prepared for the nightsea journey, where he turned into something like an electron and went to the Polar Star and came back into the same world to be reborn. (But at a different point on the time graph, as Mrs. Mason would say.)

"They were buried in a boat?" I said.

"Sometimes a boat. But sometimes in space-capsule-looking things, sealed containers." Take a coffin to the stars, I thought. Airtight metal coffins in mortuary magazines still transport the body to outer space.

And what of the movie my husband and I saw last night? *Beetlejuice.* It was about a newly-married, newly-dead couple having pure hell with the live creeps who moved into their house. You see, when they died, a live family bought the house, so now these live-in jerks are haunting the dead couple's rest in peace.

It's kind of a *Topper* gone punk. There's an interesting twist at the end. The living and dead manage to accommodate into one big happy family and reside in the same house. The seen and the unseen cooperate. Nice notion, I'm thinking as I turn the last pages and quickly finish up *Marya, a Life.* Yep, things never get better for her, just more world-weary.

But wait!—wait! It's changing, on the very last page! Marya finds out where her mother is living. Finally! Her mother is named Vera (from Latin *verax* meaning truth), this unaccountable mother who so long ago abandoned her. It's been twenty-eight years now. Hmm. That's about the time it takes Saturn to make a full orbit round the sun. In astrology, Saturn is the planet of structure with its benefits and its limits. So a full Saturn return marks a major change in the orientation to nitty-gritty reality. Saturn's orbit…it reminds me of the dark woman's route around the river. Of Maat's movement in Egyptian mythology. The feminine comes back to the same place, but later, evolved in time.

Wow, in the last brief hundred words of this novel, Marya gets a letter from her mother! With a snapshot included, yet! Marya stares at the handwriting that she doesn't recognize, at this face she does not know and yet knows. These are her own cheekbones, eyes, nose: "The woman's mouth was tense but she might have been about to smile, summoning the strength to smile. The print was just perceptibly blurred as if whoever had taken the picture had moved the camera at precisely the wrong moment."

And then, Marya goes to the window, holding the snapshot to the light, and stares and stares, waiting for the face to shift into perfect focus. **The End** That's right. The novel stops here.

Later, after a busy day—I've been thinking. Well, maybe the end of that novel is the beginning. Because that's where a lot of us women are these days, holding up the image of our mother to the light, waiting for it to shift into perfect focus and reveal the truth about woman, waiting for woman to take her right place in the culture. Maybe this dream of the woman circling the river isn't a personal dream, but rather, a collective dream. Notice there's no *me* in it. So probably she is not a personal shadow, since shadow needs an ego image to play off.

So this woman is—*Woman!* That's how it feels, anyway. She's circling in the dark around the bridges, back to the place where she began, but at a different point in time. Onroute, she declares herself not a whore.

My dear, long-dead friend Marisol used to call herself a prostitute. Married for thirty or so years before she died, she said that she'd sold her body to her husband for a comfortable income. She said that lots of women do it. "I've sold my body but not my soul. He hasn't got my soul. Yet."

Why does this dream woman walk in the night? To do work. Where does she arrive when she completes her circuit? Back at the same spot but at a new point in time. Like Maat. It's my favorite myth, in fact, because I feel it portrays what's happened to women in the past several thousand years.

Oh, how glad I am right now, because of this dream that I almost didn't bother to record. It is a double gift. It solves two frets I mentioned in the last chapter: one was finding simpler ways to write this log and still have time for my normal schedule. Now I suddenly find this dream offering me a way to use the Maat myth that has been stored on an old computer disk for over a year now. I'm going to take it and with some editing, plop it into the text to amplify this dream. Wow, talk about saving work!

I'm also glad for another reason: I've been wondering, "Will I have a dream to help explain the anima, that feminine inner companion of a man?" Now I can see the answer, and it is yes.

A man needs to discover his inner feminine side, this anima, to develop and cherish her. She is his ego's balancing partner in the psyche. He can relate to and honor this soul image of feminine wisdom within, just as a woman can do the same with her masculine soul image called the animus. This complement in the psyche—visible only in dreams—makes the person stronger. The body's gender is binary *either-or* but the psyche's gender is analog *both-and.*

If a man confuses some woman in his outside life with his inner anima, then he projects the soul partnership onto her and demands her to act like his perfect soul mate instead of developing the anima within…and havoc results. Cry havoc! Because no real woman can fulfill a man's soul projection. Lots of women try.

You say men don't really try to get women to fulfill their anima dreams? Ha! Take just today. My husband and I attended the second lecture in the Wagner series, and in my new energy-saving policy, I waited for an example of the anima figure, since I knew I needed one today. I didn't have long to wait.

It came along with three pages of handout lyrics from *Siegfried,* an opera in the Ring series. Brunnhilde is hardly more than a walking, singing anima, which is everywhere evident in the lyrics. She is a selfless inspiration to the hero. Here is Siegfried singing to Brunnhilde: "I bless my mother for giving me birth! Bless the earth that gave me strength! Now I behold your eyes, bright stars that laugh on my joy!"

So what does Brunnhilde sing in reply? Not "Oh I bless my mother for giving me birth too, because I see you and feel joy"? Not hardly. She acts like a mirror, not a person with her own identity. She dittoes him: "I bless your mother for giving you birth! Bless the earth that gave you strength! Your eyes alone could behold me; my heart wakens to you alone."

Yep, she is an anima figure; she is warbling in effect, "Yes, we both love you a lot. And, Siegfried, nobody else can see me but you. I exist just for you. Nothing matters but you." Anima talk. She talks like the invisible anima inside.

There are lots of anima figures in literature. In novels, poems, and movies written by men. She's the dream girl. The woman in red. She's projected onto real women like Marilyn Monroe and Lana Turner and…ad infinitum. Those dreamy babes carried a heavy load of fantasy.

Siegfried sings, "Be mine! Be mine!" Brunnhilde of course answers, not be mine too, but *"Oh Siegfried! Yours I have always been!"* Not just am, but *always* been. It's anima talk. He's got her literally under his skin, has had all his life. His anima companion. They both love him a lot. Well. I've just accidentally typed "They both *live* him a lot." Can't beat a good old Freudian slip for hitting the nail right on.

The anima—she walks, talks, cleans, dresses, plays tennis, inspires a painting, does whatever you want on paper and film and stage. Male art fills the culture and defines what is "normal." Take *Pygmalion* and its derivative *My Fair Lady.* Here woman is little more than a chunk of marble/Cockney flower seller until the hero brings her to life by his attention. When really, in surrogate form, he's vitalizing his own anima. Instead of tinkering with poor Eliza on the half shell, he needs to cultivate his own inner feminine, to gentle his ways with feeling and beauty.

You often see this pact between a man and woman. They say it's a compliment to be a *femme inspiratrice,* a divine muse. Of course, it's not all bad. An "inspiring" woman in the outer world can sometimes awaken a man's creativity. If an inner union is consummated, this anima actually can get pregnant and deliver a child of the psyche. Mental creation. It's how men get to experience giving birth—in the psyche. And it's why men value so highly the creations of their minds, sometimes over the children of their loins—for this is a child they gave birth to themselves—as a book, building, music, painting, statue, guns, car, bridge, bomb, whatever.

My friend Marisol kept her soul, but she knew that some women don't value themselves as separate from a man. They don't even try to be themselves, but instead only an alluring symbol, an ersatz anima for some man who has not developed it properly within.

Marilyn Monroe was such a creature, poignant with an appeal that was so much more than just sex. Her suicide haunts us with a wordless truth about our tits-and-ass society. A woman can turn suicidal from identifying with man's view of herself instead of becoming herself, whole, deep, and capable in her own right.

Wow. If that were the way my husband and I lived, we'd be in trouble right now. No sex right now because of a prostate flareup. I'd have to go back into the polka-dot hat box, put into party-girl storage for awhile. That too is about accepting material limits, I guess.

Yes. Today's modern woman can get turned off by a man's demand that she live as his property, his sex toy, his creative inspiration. Hey, Marya spent the whole last half of that novel running through men. Afraid to give away her soul in return for worship or just admiration. Afraid to love. Aware of the penalty for being a love slave, an anima figure for some man. She didn't want to sell her soul or her body either. So Marya was attracted to men and yet ambivalent about it.

At one point she went with her current lover into a Museum of Torture Through the Ages: "The chastity belt, or girdle, drew Marya's particular attention. It resembled armor, which of course it was, except for the absurd little spikes pointing outward. There was a narrow, a very narrow, slot for urination; defecation must have been a more serious problem—Marya could not see how it was possible. And what if the hapless woman were pregnant without anyone knowing, before the contraption was fitted in place; what if both husband and "trusted friend" disappeared with the keys . . . She wondered too whether it had been simply a point of honor for a wife to submit to the chastity belt: did a woman do so graciously and willingly? Did she concur in her imprisonment? The thing was not only rather comically grotesque, it was highly unsanitary."

A twelfth-century French woman was property to be locked up when the lord and master rode away. Just like an apartment. Keep a key and give one to a trusted friend in case of emergency. Why not? The hero could still remember her while he went out whacking apart knights. She could come along as his inspiration. Oh, that's cruel, surely, goes the uneasy laugh; we don't lock up women anymore. That guy just didn't trust her.

If a man does not, cannot, trust the women closest to him, generally it means he does not, cannot, trust the feminine inside himself. He may scorn, fear, be ashamed of this part of himself, even identify with it instead of relating to it. But somehow, he's not dealing with the anima inside.

Maybe that's why this dream woman is traveling on her night journey toward rebirth, why she has to declare, "I am not a whore! She is making this dark journey along the river of channeled unconscious toward rebirth in the meaning of woman…just as the pharaoh got reborn on his dark journey to Polaris…and just as Jonah got reborn during his dark voyage in the whale.

At the collective level that art taps into, that must be why Marya on the very last page hopes that her life will change as she stands at the window gazing at the photo of her mother, "waiting for the face to shift into perfect focus." She wants to know how the true feminine really looks; she hopes that its focus is coming clear.

How did the feminine get into such a fix? Frozen out of focus in an old photograph. How did she get put on such prolonged hold? This Egyptian myth I'm going to tell you suggests how it came about. It echoes the journey of the woman who must declare she is not a whore.

Long ago in Egypt, the great sun god Ra had two children, Thoth and Maat. Thoth was male and became the god of conscious thought, of written words and numbers—of logos, in short—he embodied linear, logical masculinity. (His name is pronounced like *thought* but with *h* added—Thoughth.) Later he evolved into the Greek Hermes and the Roman Mercury—all of them good thinkers and communicators of the word. He promulgated knowledge.

His sister Maat was divine too—but she was the goddess of wisdom, not knowledge. She held the truth that sits silent in matter, the truth that is beyond the means of mere words to express. She wore a feather in her hair. When someone died, that person's heart got weighed in one pan of a scale against Maat's feather in the other pan. If the heart was lighter than the feather, then the person got to go on into eternity.

Truth makes you light, but a burden of lies makes you heavy. Maat symbolized the holistic truth stretching beyond knowledge's ability to see. (Her name is pronounced Mah-aht. Probably she was named for *ma, the* first sound that a baby makes, and later this is seen in the Latin *mater* and our English *Mama.)*

This Egyptian brother and sister pair, Thoth and Maat, married as husband and wife, equal partners, and for a long time they were very happy together. The Egyptian people honored Thoth because of his great gift of words and writing and linear thought to them. This empowering gift offered the culture a labeling tool that gave a shorthand for concepts.

But the people honored Maat equally, for her gift of wordless truth beyond conscious knowing. The mute lessons of reality were demonstrated in her matter. It held a coherent truth. In fact, all Egyptians carried a very small statue of Maat with them as a silent reminder to honor this wordless truth, whatever strange and incongruous forms it might take, for truth sometimes stretches beyond our ability to express it or encompass it.

One day Thoth went off to war. When he came back, the people began telling him that Maat had been unfaithful to him. Thoth asked her if this was true. Maat replied, "No. However it may look to outsiders," she said, "I have been faithful to you. I am not a whore!"

But Thoth decided it was only logical that Maat must have been unfaithful. Why else would people say so? He went by words and decided that his reputation was being ruined. So Thoth banished Maat from the kingdom. He made all Egyptians cease to honor her, to throw away those little statues that they'd carried as a constant reminder of how the truth comes in strange, inexplicable forms. From that time on, so goes the tale, Egypt lost its way—unhappy and no longer tuned to the balance of nature.

But the tantalizing part of this myth is the ending—it is still left open. Very few myths are left open-ended; when one is, it holds a portent for our real future. For example, the Aztecs foretold the coming of Cortez. And he did. The Egyptian myth says that one day Maat will come back to co-rule again with Thoth. But a faithful army general, so goes the story, has meanwhile been kind enough to take her secretly into his busy household and shelter her toward the day of her return to equal partnership with Thoth. Then she will rule again in harmony with her lover-brother-husband. They are that deeply related, you see, these two. Linear Thoth and analog Maat. Mind and Matter. Together they form the analinear union of body and soul.

This myth records, I feel, the beginning of the cultural split between thought and matter. We lost paradise when we began to honor logos, the conscious logical stance above the wordless analog truth stretching beyond our ego boundaries. Yet Maat is just in exile. For the last twenty-five hundred years!

As societies moved out of living in the collective unconscious like animals, they started developing the focus of ego energy with its individual complex of self-consciousness. Culture was so proud of this new advance. What a handy tool this individual ego has turned out to be, too. The culture began to pile up gains from all these assorted egos busy at work. Our accreting culture, drunk on the new power of logos, didn't see how logos began to simplify and falsify reality as it tried to make everything fit into words and number measurements, make linear chains of sequencing fit into short-form summaries of truth according to the collective concepts.

Not everything can be expressed in words and units of logic. Take the taste of blueberry pie, for instance. Tell me exactly how blueberry pie tastes. Or how a gardenia smells. You can only give an approximation. Oh, you might write out a recipe or a perfume's chemical formula, but that still doesn't say exactly how it smells or tastes to you.

Yet by eating a forkful of blueberry pie or smelling a gardenia, I can taste it myself, smell it for myself. The mute flow of matter through time—in events—creates the ongoing truth of my emotional being. I can play a tuba and *make* music, not just talk about it. I can *make* love, not just talk about it. This deep truth embedded in events is so subtle it can hardly be articulated. It is the way of the Tao that cannot be spoken.

But logos talks all the time. Logos is constantly "adjusting reality" to fit it into the word slots of meaning. Knock off the subtle edges, you guys, and fit what's left of this gorgeous truth into a word slot here and there, connect it to a definition. That's how misunderstandings start. A humorous speculation about someone for instance gets distorted and warped into a gossipy lie, because a label does not fit the strange and larger beauty of truth.

Sometimes—as seldom as I can manage—my ego will tell a lie because it supposes the awkward truth just will not serve. It is not good enough for my ego's narrow image of what fits reality. Like Thoth, I reject the subtlety of truth that has seemed unfaithful to me. The *me,* that is, the conscious ego.

Remember how I was tempted to skip over my unhappy youth? It was too painful for my ego to relate. But even though I squirmed under the embarrassment of my human limitations, I decided not to go into hiding on this manuscript. But see, even if I do manage to tell the truth as best I can, I will still leave out chunks because I'm finite. It's only *my* truth.

Likewise, if I manage to convey the opalescent beauty of my truth emerging in dreams and events, you won't grok it until you can find it in your own dreams, can see how they connect your life into symbolic meaning. When your own life becomes an empirical laboratory where you can daily synchronize your dreamtime with real time and see them merge, you'll sense the mute truth of Maat's wisdom beyond words.

It takes a practiced eye to see the dark feminine wisdom in mute matter. Many are still locked in the Age of Reason. I have done hard time there. It had me on the linear rack for years. And Thoth still rules alone.

But don't worry, Maat is on her way around the clock face and is coming back to the starting point, but in a new age. Look at that dream today and you can see it: she started at the Rathaus Bridge. Rathaus means law house or city hall in German—where she was cast out of the patrimony and sent off on her long dark journey. No longer in legitimate society, she was dishonored, suppressed, forced to walk in the dark unconscious. But she's on her way back. She has already declared, "I am not a whore!" She has even traversed the upper bridge and will arrive soon at the point where she started, back at the point where she was judged an outcast—but it's a new time now. She's just approaching 3:00 at the Rathaus, the time of transformation.

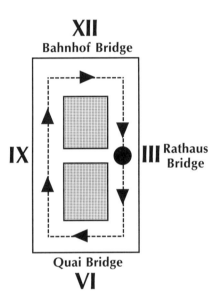

In a clock of the twelve months, three is the month of March, of Aries, of spring when the new astrological year begins. According to this big clock, Maat is on her way back to co-rule in the legitimate system. Not that she'll take the throne away from Thoth. They will both rule as equal partners.

But until they share the throne again, analog truth in all its awkward splendor still remains outcast, sent beyond the boundaries that the logical ego deems "real." But beyond those borders, in all its gigantic mute beauty, this harmony flares too big for words and rational grasp. When we lose touch with this wordless pattern, we go out of harmony with the universe. We move away from wisdom beyond explanation and beyond the ego's ability to manipulate. The grandeur of mute matter moves through time to create a continuity of our lives that is ignored because it cannot even be seen by the ego. Here is the human tragedy that marks the separation of Thoth and Maat.

Sometimes I shudder at that old saw regarding Robert Browning and Elizabeth Barrett Browning. "He loved god, and she loved god in him." Thoth and Maat are both gods. Wouldn't they make the perfect loving couple—I mean really—if they loved god in each other?

Looking back…heavens, that tiny dream has brought up much for this chapter. My old computer disk with notes on Thoth and Maat, Frau Weber's handout sheet with Brunnhilde warbling. Also it brought me enough time to take a three-hour walk with Katrine along the forest path stretching up the mountain valley near my apartment.

In the forest winter is coming. "More leaves down from the tall trees," I say. Katrine says, "You can see more light now." We turn along a path I've never gone before, up out of the valley past a small settlement. We walk beside a pasture that look very green with winter grass, past five black-faced sheep. Speckled hens come running down toward us. Katrine clucks at them through the fence. She is laughing, saying in German, "But I don't have any bread…" making a soft, clucking susurrus in her throat "…no bread at all, I'm sorry."

Suddenly I imagine a man standing with us, watching Katrine bend over the chickens and cluck. What does he do, this man? Smile while she communes with chickens? Reach out and touch her back affectionately? Look at his watch, make a sharp remark and walk quickly ahead, bored by this chat with dumb chickens, with mute flesh? Logic can get quite sharp and witty sometimes, so clever it turns off the mute messages of matter. So sharp it cuts truth's throat.

Dumb chickens. Dumb. That means mute, too. The mute wisdom of flesh is not attended very often nowadays. It is considered dumb.

The chickens follow us on their side of the fence. Their eggs must be wonderful, I say, no steroids, lots of minerals in this green grass to make the yolks dark orange. Beautiful chickens, without that pecked, raw-necked look that chickens can get from being herded together with too few nutrients in their bagged feed. We talk about the crazed hens in chicken ghettoes, laying pale eggs that drop onto conveyor belts. I read a story once about a battery of schizophrenic chickens getting loose and pecking the owner to death. Shrug. Urban life.

But what a huge roving space these speckled chickens have. Greens and bugs and people who walk by and cluck at them. Chicken heaven.

Sitting here at the computer now, I recall what my friend Mariles said a few weeks ago on a two-day trip we were making by train through the mountains of southern Switzerland. Down through Zermatt, skirting San Moritz, and back up to Zurich on a train called the Glacier Express. The weather was so beautifully clear. We could see the mountains changing colors on their tree-clad slopes, the new caps of snow, vast sweeps in perspective as the train passed from bend to bend. But it was the land itself that changed elevation constantly around us; the train just plowed on levelly through everything—into mountains, over bridges, below upland meadows, above deep valleys.

That's a wonderful thing about this trip, I thought, staring out the wide window at the amazing engineering—and about Switzerland itself. Its tranquil beauty suggests that humans can take nature into account and work with it.

And even human nature. I looked out at villages with signs in Romanish, that odd language left from the Roman legionnaires stationed in Switzerland two thousand years ago. What a strange country it is. Four different languages in a tiny space…and they don't even kill each other over it. They officially declare that all four are okay. Switzerland is too tiny to go to war internally…if it did, there wouldn't be anything left.

But that's the state of the whole world now, isn't it? This globe is getting too tiny to go to World War III over. If we do, there may not be anything left.

Mariles and I sat in the train and talked about this and that, gazing out the windows yet also deep in talk; we seemed to be traveling in a benign realm that humans even make more beautiful.

Every once in awhile, we'd round another bend or pass by a cottage with a granite-slab roof and I'd murmur, "It's just so beautiful!" Like some perfect train model in a layout bigger than possible. Finally Mariles said, "Well, you know God lives in Switzerland."

CHAPTER 13

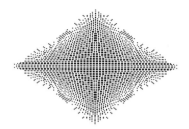

Grand Central Station

Dream Log—Thursday, November 17:

Dream: Little boy stands up, stretches into a man, finds out he's not in the center—so he moves the gauge so that he's in the center. Feeling good about it.

I wake up, put these bits down, and imitate Elmer Fudd: "Duh-duh-duh-dat's all, folks!"

Not much of a dream, right?

But still, something's there. I know it. Sometimes I feel a dream fading as I wake, so I ask the unconscious to throw up a resume for me to remember, some image or phrase that gives the essence of the dream. That's what happened this morning. A lot of events were going on, moving back behind the veil as I awoke. So I asked for an image to keep, like a souvenir program with a synopsis of the play.

This little bit is what I got. Not much. I've been so busy today, too, that I've had no chance to dwell on this dream fragment until evening. But I have a good feeling about this little boy stretching up to become a man and moving to rebalance the gauge. Because my dream is an open door to the unconscious, even this tiny fragment. It's not like potsherds, where you pick up a bit of vase and wonder what the rest looked like. Instead, the fragment contains a tiny hologram of the dream message;

and if you look at it long enough, the bit will burgeon and bloom before you, as if the vase is growing whole and full of flowers and capable of carrying out its utilitarian intent. Well, it is. It holds the message.

So this dream shard of the boy stretching up into manhood and recentering the gauge conveys something to me. This tiny image left in my memory on waking, like a hologram, holds more information than any angle of association or interpretation can exhaust. It is a door, and with each fresh glimpse through it during my busy day, some new insight popped out on the notion of the masculine needing to stretch and center.

I got a call from a client today that reinforced this motif for me. She is right now in the hospital with a foot operation. She called to say that, to her surprise, a former lover is in the hospital too. (I got her permission to describe this conversation.)

This is a man she quit seeing several months ago. Now he's suffered a severe accident during a high-risk, high altitude sporting event. He's in the hospital with an injury to his spinal cord, loss of feeling in his lower trunk and extremities, some paralysis in his left leg. They don't know how well he will recover. A handsome, talented, intelligent man in his early thirties, he attracts women who try to mother and reform him from his daredevil ways. But of course he doesn't heed their "motherly advice."

My client feels quite sad for him. Helpless to do anything, too, because she doesn't want to get trapped back into that relationship out of pity. She sees a raw irony, too. Her left foot is being operated to connect a tendon that was weakly attached since birth and further loosened by an accident years ago. She can walk okay, but decided to get it attached right so that she could do more activities. It will make her left foot's stance better than ever before. We've discussed the notion that in the mute sign language of the body, her holistic left side is getting a firmer stance in life.

But at the same time, ironically, her former lover is losing sensation and becoming paralyzed in his left leg. To put it simplistically, his injury seems to mirror his determination to repress—to paralyze—his inner psychic life. And he is accident-prone; this is only the latest of many daredevil accidents. Perhaps six months ago, when my client was despairing over the relationship, she foresaw what is happening now. "He keeps hurting himself," she said. "I'm afraid he's going to hurt himself badly. I can't get him to slow down. It's as if he doesn't want to slow down enough to know what he's doing, what he's feeling."

"What do you mean?"

"He's afraid of his feelings, it seems to me."

"How so?"

"Well, you know. He fills up most of his time with details about car engines and chemistry and mechanics and things like that. He's like an adolescent with a hundred engrossing hobbies. He's very good at them, too. But when it comes to feeling…he just won't let himself feel. He's so remote with me. And from any tender feeling. I thought I could help him learn to enjoy his feelings. But I can't. When I met his mother the first time, I was amazed. They never hug or speak affectionately. They act all business. No emotional response at all. And yet they see each other every week. I think he was discouraged from expressing love when he was little. No wonder he can't show it to me. He's afraid to feel. Because he really does, you know. Way down under there. He's afraid to look at what he feels under there."

I was waiting for her to say the R word.

"I thought I could *rescue* him from his unhappiness." Bingo. The R word. "I wanted to show him another way, an inner way."

"So you were going to teach him to trust and express his feelings. Because his mother never did."

"Yes." She grinned. "But I couldn't really be his mother, could I?"

"It's not surprising he didn't make emotional contact with you. From what you say, he hasn't with his mother. Nor any woman. Maybe he doesn't relate to the feminine part in himself."

"Yes. I think that's so. It's always science, math, chess, engines. I used to think I could attract him into contemplation with my yoga and so forth. But right now we're arguing all the time," she said. "Whenever he hurts himself again, it frightens me and I give him advice to slow down, to examine his dreams, or sit and meditate a bit…or do the I Ching or think about astrology—any of those things that make me look inside—but they all just seem silly to him. No, they frighten him. He doesn't want to look inside. He goes faster and faster, does his dangerous sports, gets more and more nervous from the pain of his previous accidents. Broken kneecaps, other things."

She paused. "I don't think I want to live this way anymore."

"You can't rescue him, you know. You can only rescue yourself."

"He won't go to a counselor or anybody like that. He thinks it's foolish and weak. He tells me I'm stupid for coming here every week."

"But you still come?"

151

"Of course. I can tell it's helping me."

"Only because you're working at it. You say you can't help him—well, a counselor can't either. Nothing can until he decides he needs help. As long as he thinks he's big enough, strong enough, clever enough to handle all his problems with his ego—well, he's just pushing himself closer to the edge. And it's a long way down."

"But he's so proud. I do love him, you know. But he's so proud. He doesn't believe in god or anything."

"So he can't ask for help from god either. Maybe you could suggest he ask for help from the unconscious in dreams. That's a more neutral word. It sounds different from praying to god for help. And the wonderful part is that the unconscious will answer him."

She shook her head. "He doesn't believe in the unconscious. He doesn't have dreams, he says."

I sighed. Everyone has dreams, whether they notice them or not, retain them or not. "Well, if he's eliminating his mother, you, god, and the unconscious…then I guess his ego has to rescue him."

And egos are not good at that. They can't see around the corners in the corridor of time. But dreams can. They walk nightly through the walls into the next loop of the labyrinth without taking the long way round. They signal what's coming up and how to prepare for that blind stretch ahead, if you attend them. You've even got choice…if you take it.

That was a sad moment for my client six months ago, and again on the phone today. Sitting now and contemplating this dream of the male stretching and growing and centering, I also consider another conversation today.

I had lunch with a business client at Mère Catherine, my favorite little restaurant in Zurich. For the past year, off and on, I've been editing a manuscript for a Jungian analyst. I've been smoothing his sentences into better English since that's not his native language. Now it is finally about to go to print. Lunch today was for arranging the final details. I've done this work for several reasons, and foremost is my interest in his subject, the archetype of numbers. Number as concept, not bookkeeping.

During this lunch I remarked, "People said that when I came to Switzerland, my marriage would probably break up."

"For heaven's sake, why?"

"Stress and strain. They said that the changed environment would change everything."

"Oh, what foolishness. It's a self-fulfilling prophecy of people who haven't realized what marriage is."

"What is marriage?"

"It's about real people not being just each other's dream figure. My wife doesn't exist just for me, nor I for her. If I am centered inside, she doesn't have to rescue me or live for me. She can leave my anima to do that. I make a commitment to love my wife as a real person, and vice versa, and to grow with the relationship."

Well. Didn't that make a neat little packet to throw in here and amplify today's dream? His unexpected remark offered something to center that male. Something to help him stretch and grow.

In a nutshell—or in the gauge, as it happens—the male is stretching, growing, working his way into balance. Notice how he reaches up and *moves the gauge* to get to the center.

Don't look at me, that's just what the dream says. I don't know what it means. Notice the words—"he moves the gauge so that he's in the center." You know, he doesn't just walk over there. You see how his hands are pushing against the top, like they're pressed against a revolving belt or something lining the gauge, and this pressure is slowly moving the belt that he's both standing on and pressing against with his hands, so that his energy is shifting the whole mechanism.

Another odd thing: by doing this, the boy is becoming a man. I think that he's stretching into maturity.

Hmm, I suspect this man is rather like the dream woman yesterday, the one who declared herself not a prostitute as she made her clockwise route in the dark. I think this man is *Man!* A symbol of collective man. Notice that again like yesterday, the ego *me* is only an observer.

In a tiny dreamlet such as this, the feeling tone is especially important. This dream has a good feeling about it. This guy likes getting centered. He may even like having to move the machinery by doing it himself, with some real work. No wonder he feels good. No wonder I feel good.

And you notice that he doesn't do it with any words, with logos, but with physical effort—the payment of the mute, wordless body. This man would probably make a great lover. He's willing to put out some effort to get some gain. I'm starting to love this little man. Fine. It's so much better than feeling sorry for a guy who's off-base, one-sided, logic-bound.

Logos. It's interesting that in the *New Testament, John* rewrote the story of creation so that it no longer said, "In the beginning God created the Heavens and the Earth," as it had the *Old Testament*. Now it became, "In the beginning was the Word, and the Word was God, and the Word was with God." Logos. The word.

That revisionary tactic shows the Greek principle of logos which at that very time was rising to gain cultural sway in the West over the mute lessons in matter. Thoth over Maat, yang over yin, chains of linear logic over analog networks that stretch beyond understanding.

How and why did this polarization in our culture occur? Actually, I have to be honest here. I don't really begrudge it. It seems to me quite a necessary phase in our psychic growth. Most religious myths split god into two complementary states—Shiva and Shakti, Jahweh and Satan, yin and yang—and from them, events are generated. I think it happens because polarity is inherent in the primal archetype of number, which creates both linear chains and cycling analogs.

But most cultures didn't worship abstract number. They made god into the human image, and usually they polarized god by sexuality. Often it was a brother and sister who could then copulate in divine incest and so create the world. Thoth and Maat offered a fleshly metaphor for splitting unity into two poles, and also for reuniting them again in a marriage of equals. But you can see that this is an inexact metaphor because it equates finite human sexes that procreate with the infinite divine energy that generates creation. It has even misled some cultures into championing incest in the flesh, when the goal is really marry the logical and holistic sides of one's own being into harmony.

For many people, though, the analog, holistic domain became dismissed as shameful, seductive, untrustworthy, much as Maat had been banned by Thoth. The guy in the hospital saw the holism of feeling as untrustworthy and unfaithful to his upright linear side. Often a man suppresses that side of himself, then projects its tantalizing and forbidden mystique onto some woman. He woos her instead of developing it in himself. A woman, of course, may do the same—she woos a guy to complete and fulfill her undeveloped side. This doesn't work, I can tell you. Sexual union can be wonderful, but it's no substitute for psychic union within. The *divine coniunctio*. Carnal union becomes a cheap fleshly imitation. That I can also tell you from experience.

If a culture splits its passionate cycling analogs and its dispassionate linear logic so far apart as we have, incest can become a tantalizing symbol for uniting that lost pair again in paradise. The forbidden act of union is projected into some temptingly off-limits partner. Taboo.

It reenacts this union that is forbidden to the body sundered from the soul by our pop culture. Those old myths of divine incest had a hidden utility: at the very base of nature, analogs marry logic, just as body unites with soul. Incest was a symbol for uniting these opposites at the deepest level, and so numinous that it became holy in many cultures—Greek, Roman, Japanese, Hawaiian, you name it.

As a counselor can tell you, incest is much more common than our society admits. Marya, for instance, endured years of dry-fucking from Cousin Lee, who was forever hauling her out to the old broken-down Buick in the junk car lot and rubbing his bare penis to organism against the crotch of her panties. But she never told. At least not to the people who mattered—her family. Her fifty-year old lover heard it years later, of course, but he couldn't reach back through time and change it.

Why didn't Marya tell? Because it was taboo. Long ago, incest was a prerogative reserved for the gods and taboo for the common people, Hera and Zeus, for example, were brother and sister. Then it became forbidden even for the gods. So unlike previous religions, Judaism and Christianity and Islam got rid of incest mythology in an extremely ingenious way—by making the creation of the universe into a wholly male event. One god, one sex. No female partner.

Hey, that eliminates incest. At least the progenitive kind. By this simple act, remarkably enough, our culture managed to sidestep divine sexuality, so that we don't have to confront the notion that sexual union is a fleshly metaphor for union between the male and female sides of oneself, which as a whole soul, then unites with god.

The Western god became all-male. This great religious innovation of the age is perhaps what gave the small tribe of Judah its huge drive. It was powered by a vast gulf of tension between the conscious and unconscious, between favored male and the split-away female that was responsible for the fall from grace. By making creation into a wholly male event, this god Yahweh had to turn his jealous attention onto humans instead of a divine mate.

Yahweh has no mate. He creates by himself. Adam has no holy mother, just a divine father. Eve springs out of Adam's side without a mother either, according to this male hegemony. Where did the feminine go? Out the back door and into the wilderness with Maat. She was banished from the male power structure. In this clever way Western culture could get rid of the whole sticky old archetype of incest—at least in its religious dogma—by making creation into a one-sex event.

Now this approach had a bonus for left-brained logic. It generated an officially approved, sanctioned male patriarchy starting right from the top down, using God as the male model and top dog.

Coming along after Judaism, Christianity makes the Trinity a wholly male event. There is Jehovah—a strong masculine nature, rough and ready, especially with his practical jokes on Job. Then along comes gentle Jesus meek and mild, receptive and compassionate, almost like Jehovah's softer side—a feminine aspect disguised in men's clothing. In fact, who needs women around as gentle role models for helping the lame and turning the other cheek and doing things with bread and fishes and wine and getting crucified when you've got Jesus, who does it all better? And finally, a thousand years later historically, along comes the Holy Ghost. This divine spirit flies down in the form of a dove to impregnate Mary, a merely human female. So even the Holy Ghost is male, too. God doesn't even make direct physical connection with this woman. She is artificially inseminated by a sperm carrier.

Male divinity creates human physical life in the story of Eden, and soul life in the story of Jesus, and a connective bond between these two in the story of the resurrection. Who needs women? Of course, you may still need them for assuaging the old body parts—but put them strictly in the second-class section. It's called purdah. Or harem. Or secretarial pool. Who thinks much of females when the moving spirit of connection of male to male to male forms the Holy Trinity of Christianity?

So the big problem is that it leaves out any divine role for woman. There's only a god who's divided into three parts, all male. The goddess has no counterpart in Orthodox Judaism, nor in Islam, either. Mary was no goddess. She was definitely lower level. Human, totally. Even the son she bore rated his invisible father up in heaven over her earthly presence. Who wouldn't? God outranks mortals anytime.

Of course, Mary did ascend into Catholic Heaven in 1951, yet that came a bit too little, too late for most Christian denominations. And even at that, she's only a human perched below the divine throne as a go-between, elevated out of the magnanimity of the pope (papa in Italian) and the cardinals and fathers—all male. She's still not functioning as an equal in this male triumvirate of god-power. She's odd woman out.

In Western religions, woman is only a fragment of man—she's an afterthought chopped off this fellow Adam, a side issue. This huge image of male creation and self-sufficiency and perfection in Yahweh, Allah and the Trinity shaped Western consciousness for several thousand years. It repressed the feminine half of numinous divinity into ignominy, into the background of events. It elevated the loftiness of the conscious logos stance—of the brightly shining linear right-stuff straight-arrow ego—and demoted the wordless analog truth of holistic connection that stretches beyond the ego boundaries.

We've pushed the feminine (in men and women) so far down into the unconscious that we've unbalanced our culture by it. Our society and religion are consciously and proudly yang, unconsciously and ashamedly yin. These two forces, split off and alienated, fight it out.

There is enormous tension and attraction here. It is this constant psychic tension that has empowered Western society like a dynamo. Freud postulated that sublimated sexual tension, and especially the taboo urge for incest, has caused our huge creative drive. He said we take our forbidden hunger and sublimate it into nonsexual outlets.

Carl Jung agreed to a certain extent: true, he said, the tension between the honored masculine pole and the devalued feminine pole provides the psychic energy that has generated Western culture for so long. But he added that creativity is not just tension rerouted from a sexual level to a psychic level. It is important to consummate this holy union in the psyche instead of suppressing it or enacting it in blind flesh.

We have suppressed the feminine side of things so far, so long that the culture has gone to the extreme limit of technological imbalance. We are even poisoning Mother Nature—that mute matrix of matter that has borne us—by our lack of relation to it.

But in the global village, we are atmospherically one, and so cannot escape nuclear fallout; we are oceanically one, and cannot escape marine poisoning. In order to avoid destroying ourselves, we are now searching for ways to raise up the banished goddess again and honor her equally. We are beginning to resurrect her human counterpart, woman, from just a silly splinter off a male body busily tempting him to sin, into what a woman really is—a balancing and nourishing fertile force. Woman is becoming a person, not an anima that carries the male's devalued feminine side. Society no longer benefits from turning woman into a possession and Mother Earth into something to be raped and conquered and defiled with hidden poisons.

The analog and linear split can be healed in the psyche. We do not have to lose our cultural energy to couple this pair, for both have grown in strength during their separation. He has honed his bright communicative knowledge and she has plummeted into deep wordless wisdom. They can now unite to release a new burst of creation that will bring the culture back into balance on a sweeping scale. We can center our society by moving logic into creative connection with holism.

See that fellow standing in the gauge? He is changing things. I am really feeling good about it. I'm glad some militant woman is not inside there, too, whipping him into the center with him kicking and screaming and dragging his heels, or cutting his head off and swinging it from the needle in glee, or something else that depotentiates him back into a little boy.

Because this guy must do it himself. He has to stretch and grow into maturity and make this machinery of our society move to center. He can move the whole society because, let's face it, his values still largely run this culture. And look, he's starting to move things into adjustment. It's hard, but he's doing it.

But oh!—if woman rises back into equal divinity, then incest comes rolling up into view again, too. Hidden so long in the dark fabric of society— "Ugh, wasn't that buried once already?—Didn't we get rid of that?—how nasty, shadowy, forbidden, embarrassing! Taboo!"

In an amazing version of Freud's "return of the repressed," incest is coming back into social consciousness. You can see it around you. It's in the newspapers. Movies. Porno videos. TV. Books. Magazines. People reveal it to their counsellors. Statistics on incest are way up, and we can't quite figure out why—are we are counting better or acting worse? Probably this long-denied act is just beginning to surface into allowed collective attention. It was there before, but nobody talked about it.

So let's deal with it. How? Well, the ancient Chinese managed to avoid incest among their gods in a wholly different manner from the West. They did not anthropomorphize god into male and female embodiments. They just called it yang and yin, not he and she. Yang and yin energies are symbolized as white and black in the Tai Chi wheel. Pretty clever, this incredible simplicity. Each pole contains a bit of the other, so that it can recognize the other's nature within itself—which is exactly the same function as the anima performs in a man's psyche, or the animus in a woman's.

Our yearning for sexual *and* psychic union is so old. Sexual drive and spiritual questing are so poignantly mixed in the adolescent. It is subverted, though, when a budding youngster is expected just to make out physically, instead of also exploring the psyche in a spiritual initiation or quest. Both expansions happen at the same time for the young—

sexual and psychic—but our society ignores the soul's hunger and panders to the sexual.

Modern humanity, Jung said, yearns to find its lost soul connection. But since our old image of god is only masculine, society hasn't yet found its way back into balance with woman, nor with the feminine principle. Man doesn't respect the woman at his side when he doesn't respect the feminine in himself. Why should he, when Eve is just a silly tempting splinter off of Adam's body? But right about now, Eve and Maat and all the other dark women are rounding that last turn on their journey toward reemergence to take a shared throne with the male.

We have as yet no modern ceremonies for this healing spiritual union. But it is this initiation rite into adulthood that every adolescent needs. Long ago in tribal cultures, people intuitively developed rituals to guide their adolescents through the spiritual and sexual shoals into adulthood. Such rites carried a psyche safely from childhood into a mature outlook. But in modern life, too often our children are left to drift into drugs and gangs and experimental sex and unproductive adolescence in the limbo of despair and empty consumerism. Increased suicide rates, addiction, nihilism, violence—the burgeoning young libido energy has no positive routing.

Remember that guy in the hospital, the man with the paralyzed trunk and left leg? He never hugged Mom, yet he saw her every week. He was afraid to look at his feelings, and he kept discovering new and more extreme ways to ignore and punish his own mute matter. You remember this man. You've seen him around you…perhaps in you.

What do you suppose that he is blocking, is so frightened to feel? Why does he set up a relationship such that he is continually with a woman and yet tuning her out frantically? Isn't that precisely the taboo's exhortation?—to prove that he *can* be with mom-woman-anima and yet tune out her appeal, sexual and psychic, over and over again?

What kind of society is this, anyway, that makes a man so afraid to express love for the feminine, within and without? Why is Western man gripped in a macho complex and yet so charged by the incest taboo? Why did Freud insist that incest—for him, mother-son incest— is the primal complex of our patriarchal society? Exactly what must a young man prove to Daddy-god-male-authority-punisher? Over and over again? That he is *not* tempted by my mom/your wife.

I think we are moving toward a centering epoch for the global culture, a new age of balance, a creative glow of energy that harmonizes our inner and outer worlds. It will heal the split in the psyche and the globe. It seems to me as if all along, the collective unconscious of the human race could see way ahead and know that this split was necessary for awhile. It has indeed brought some cultural gains, but the cost-effective factor is falling off steeply now. Each side has come to the limits of its polarized utility. Such extremity is destroying us instead of energizing us. It is time to turn around now, to walk back toward the center.

We are making the discovery that we do not need to retreat from the image of divine sexuality in order to find god within. Our deep longing for sexual union is a fleshly metaphor for a deeper union. It is a cry for closest union within the psyche, for transcendent meaning, for god. And that can happen when the anima or animus helps the ego walk past the shadow and experience the marvelous seduction and blissful union of the divine.

I cannot say words to explain how this happens or reveal its power. You must experience it in your own mute matter beyond words. It has to be created in you through the thrust of events that you choose. Invisible, intangible...but it matters so much.

Conjugate that odd word *matter*—from Matter, Mater, Maat. I matter, you matter, we matter. Just how do you matter? Let me see you mattering—please matter. You mean you *are* matter? And you're mattering already? You mean it *matters* whether heaven is stocked with a tripartite male god and a lower-echelon female human who can't do much on her own? Are you saying that our psychic setup, this interior unconscious mythology actually defines us, our cultural history? Oh.

I consider again today's dream, where the little boy stands up, stretches into a man, finds he's not in the center. Yes, he is stretching out of being petty and immature. He is moving toward balance. And growing. Look, he's touching the top of his world already.

I guess the important part was just learning that he wasn't centered. Realizing that, the rest comes easy. How grand. He stations himself in the center—oh my. The Grand Central Station. Not punny, you say? Well, dreams pun in the lowest form of humor, diving way down there to where the words melt into pictures and the pictures merge back into meaning so deep that we don't really know its structure...except that it seems to have a funny bone.

CHAPTER 14

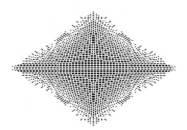

The 72-Hour
Influ-Insight

Dream Log—Friday, November 18:
Dreaming. I see shifting space and groups of movements...events?

I awaken enough to think vaguely, "I can't write this down. It's just shifting points," then go back to sleep again.

I see the same old shifting, regrouping wordless dream as before, but now it's greatly expanded and elaborated, and in the dream I think, My god! It's the annotated version of the first dream.

I wake in the night to find my husband kicking me sharply in his sleep, as if to get my attention. I reach down and hold his leg to stop it. Okay, okay, I'm awake! I get the message: remember this dream. In a minute I'll turn on the light and write it down...but how? There's no exact setting here, no actors or plot to describe.

But first I'll just rest a bit. I feel disoriented. This isn't my normal wake-up mode. My throat feels scratchy, and behind my eyes, it hurts vaguely...in fact my whole head is hurting. Uh-oh. That Egyptian expert at lunch three days ago...he was fighting a sore throat and his eyes looked glazed. Phooey. Maybe it's my turn.

Okay, okay. Write down the dream. I turn on the light. It hurts my eyes. Uh-oh. Illness—here's a real-world limit for sure. Now I'm hitting hard-edged matter with a vengeance...oh, my aching body.

So why in tarnation am I dreaming about space? With these points shifting around? What has this got to do with hard-edge matter?

Well, of course, matter is made of points in space.

Space. The final frontier. The lead-in to *Star Trek* proclaimed it every night at our house during the original three years and then through the looping reruns that brought my children into the den at 6:30 p.m. To that voice I retort now, "Inner Space. That's the final frontier."

But maybe it is both together. Back to sleep for awhile. It's just after 7:00 when I wake again. I shower, dress, eat slowly, bogged down by my sneezing, coughing respiratory tract. No terrible pain—it's just a sore throat, headache, glazed eyes and that heavy, logy feeling.

I go to the computer. Now, let's see if I can describe the dream last night. Well, I can't even draw a picture of it for you. It needs the 3D dynamics of a graphics program, with the points flowing in constant shifting relationship. I look at the box of my MacSpin program. It allows you to—let me quote here—

- *discover associations, clusters, outlines, nonlinearities*
- *pull apart complicated data sets into simple pieces*
- *compare the appearance of different subsets of data*
- *rotate the display smoothly and see its 3D structure*
- *make movies to see the effects of a fourth variable*
- *handle data with numerical, categorical and text information*
- *transform and create new variables and categories*

Uh-huh. Sort of like in my dream, but it used spiritual software. It showed spirit programming the material universe. Or let me say it another way. Remember the Holy Ghost? Its purpose is to enact the moving spirit of divine connection with humanity. This image of the Holy Ghost expresses the abstraction of god becoming connected to us finite humans in the material world.

Okay, that's what numbers do for me. Number is my image of what connects the divine with the material. Sounds pretty sterile to you? Personally, you don't want a heaven with a bunch of numbers floating around in it? You'd rather have angels wafting and blowing trumpets over saints who walk along streets of gold? Hey, maybe I see numbers a different way than you do.

My mind drifts off to how weird I'm feeling.

Last night, I knew that today was going to be peculiar whenI glanced back over my written log and blinked—thought I was seeing wrong—discovered that my mind had drifted off during the process of deriving hexagrams for today, and somehow I'd come up with three hexagrams instead of two for **How Will Today Be?** First, there was the normal hexagram with its changing lines leading into the second hexagram.

But then I must have somehow reached back into the container and drawn yet another hexagram…like being lost in a daydream and driving past my exit on a turnpike. And wow! This new hexagram turns up all yang lines. It is Hexagram 1, *Creation,* with no changing lines.

So today is going to be odd, I suspect. (You can turn to the *Chronicle of Days* in back if you want to get an overview of the daily hexagrams, and in fact, an overview of the month in general). Today's I Ching action involves *Inner Truth*–in which I am "perfectly sincere, linking others to me in closest union"–changing into *Starting Small,* where a decrease, or banking of fire, occurs to build up strength for later. It marks a small but firm beginning toward good fortune, for which I need to offer a small but sincere sacrifice. And somehow, out of this comes the unusual third thing—*Creation.* It harbingers something special.

But what will happen in terms of specific events? No idea. The hexagrams only show the daily energy patterns. They show the symbolic level of its tone, not the material level of its specifics. This is a qualitative forecast, a psychic weather report.

This space dream reminds me of that one about the spaceship universe. But this one is at a more elementary level of organization…it's like a particle map at the quantum level…with galaxies sprinkled across the universe as glitter.…all of it hard-edge matter.

But it describes inner space too, which is full of interacting, shifting clusters of feeling-toned complexes. Out of its motion comes *e*-motion. Odd to realize that my feelings come from how I move through events.

A complex can evolve in its organization. The archetype of *Father,* for instance, has evolved in its manifestations over eons to become more modulated and differentiated. If I talk about my father, in a way I'm not really talking about *him.* Instead, I'm talking about how I see and relate to him. This is not *him.* My father is much more diverse and multifaceted than what I see. And he has complexes, too, through which he relates to me. I am not what he sees. He sees only a fraction of me.

Here's a hypothetical complex. It shows a specific individual's *father* network. Conjecture how someone with this complex would act—for that is the only way you'll ever see a complex, through the behavior of the person who is using its energy pattern in everyday life to shape events in space over time.

If this is my complex, for instance, and I want to alter it, how do I go about it? Through changing my relationship with my father. But it does me *no good* to try to change him!

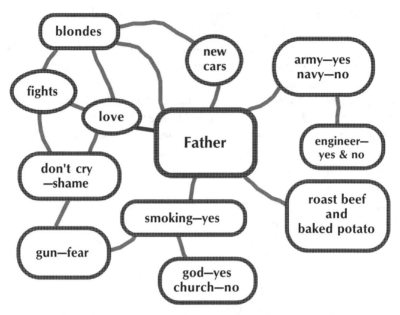

The Energy Pattern of a Sample Father Complex

What I *can* do is work on own complex—to reorganize its energy hookups more congruently, harmoniously, and efficiently. The only way to do it is to see the network shaping my behavior and attitudes, and what it says about me. Not about my father—about *me*. The question becomes: how can I inform my views regarding my father? As my perspective enlarges, it starts altering my feelings and behavior.

And that changes everything. I act different. When I change the hookups in my psyche, my whole life changes. I feel and am different. Things may even seem worse for awhile as the shift is going on, because renovation of the psyche's complexes is like house renovation—a lot of mess and work. But the result is worthwhile. The only architectural plan for renovating a complex is to honor the truth—one's own inner truth checked against other people's truths, so that they all become facets in a new and larger reality. For example, my brother sounds like he was brought up in a different family. His view is valid too. It contains a part of the truth. Exploring each other's viewpoints and realizing the differences in perspective is not fatal, but normal and even vital. All the data may be combined into a larger common perspective, instead of each single perspective fighting to nullify the others.

Each of us has many systems of networks operating, so a person is many things. A man is not only *Father,* for instance, nor a woman only *Mother.* Each complex exists for a psychic reason—to help us resonate to life. We teach each other the music necessary for soul growth. In each person, the complexes can evolve and become less brutal, more adept in their manifestations. This releases more life energy.

A picture of this happening inside you—which I can't draw—would show your complexes shifting and rebalancing continually. You would see your emotional life in flow. It would show you experiencing each day—which is something that Newtonian linear science cannot measure and calibrate and chart. No one can measure with statistics just how happy you are at this moment, just what flavor of bittersweet poignancy hides in the memory of a broken porcelain bell, just how much you miss your lover or that stuffed heffalump from childhood.

But a dream can chart your life in moving images. It carries a shifting hieroglyphic frieze whose symbols you can learn to read. You may think your dreams are born during sleep. But maybe not. In a dream, a voice once said to me…

In having dreams, you are born. Dreams are the medium, you are the message.

Maybe a dream will…. But wait. I don't feel so good. I'm quitting now. My eyes hurt, my throat. I wonder what this illness is bringing me….

Finally I awaken. I feel bad. Why am I getting sick just now? What's this in aid of? Well, it demonstrates my limits, for sure. I'm finite foursquare matter based on carbon. Living things are biodegradable.

Maybe it'll ground the dream log to have a raunchy, nose-blowing illness. Matter of fact, it seems like every time I get sick, some kind of deepening occurs in my psyche. Something enlarges my inner space even as it's restricting my outer movement. I recall studies about children who suffered through consumption or deformities like a clubbed foot and then became adventurers of the soul like Robert Lewis Stevenson and Lord Byron.

What an oddly deepening gift illness can be. But my ego doesn't care to accept it. Oh, life, is stranger than I could ever make up! The little grace notes that are the taste of ice cream after tonsillectomy, of handicap refining compassion, of limit becoming bonus, of maple leaves turning bright sculpted red instead of just tearing off the stems like sheets of toilet paper.

What purpose is incubating in my aching body? It clamps me into the pressure cooker of rising temperature. My matter deconstructs as snot. And I am bemused by this, even with a headache. Spacy.

Perhaps I need to be sick, to turn inward, to lie still and pay attention. Scout around my inner terrain like an Indian exploring the hard and stony ground of myself for signs. My burning eyes focus on the memory of the past two days. Inside, I turn over a stone.

Under Stone Number 1: That odd stillness in me at lunch when the Egyptian expert said he would be interviewed on reincarnation theories by a TV crew. What resonance was I listening to in that silence?

"Reincarnation? Why reincarnation?" I said.

"I don't know. They picked the topic. They called me about it and said they would send over a list of questions, but they never did."

And then he talked about reincarnation beliefs in India, of dreams people have told him where a just-dead relative comes back and says, "Redeem your own life before it is too late. Events have meaning and right choice. And wrong."

So I told him about a dream where my former husband, now long dead, appeared in a secret sunlit attic. He was with me and my suddenly young-again son. My toddler son pointed to photos of women on the attic wall. A beautiful ballet dancer, and a vamp, and several others, including a profile of a simple woman in a babushka. My son pointed with a chubby forefinger: "I like that lady, and that one, and that one…" he pointed to the babushka "…but that's the lady I like best."

It was the picture most like me, I realized. My dead husband started crying. He said he was so sorry he'd left us years ago for the psychedelic whirl at the end of the '60's, a departure that was supposed to segue on into his death from cancer—and didn't for so long—and he said, "If I knew then what I know now, I wouldn't have done it." And we three all cried and hugged together. That dream brought such relief—which I first mistyped as *relife*. Good old Freudian slips. Right on.

"Of course, you could call it just a wish fulfillment dream," I said to my lunch partner. "But it healed something deep. It was a reconciliation after death. It mattered to me." Intangible, it still *mattered*. Impalpable dream, but it shifted my perspective about my ex-husband.

Under Stone Number 2: I reach over to my bedside table and pick up *The Dean's December,* by Saul Bellow. And what do I find on page 2? Corde is in a Bucharest hospital with his wife, a professor of astronomy, as she tries to see her mother in intensive care. He feels disoriented because of their quick trip from Chicago, and he gazes down at the floor with "…his brown eyes, bulging somewhat, in communion with the speckled activity of the floor, uniformly speckled over the entire hospital."

Speckled over the hospital? Speckled over the entire universe! The visible universe is balloons of galaxies stretched in thin walls like giant soap-bubbles around apparent voids. Viewed from this huge scale, the great map looks like a cosmic froth of galaxy clusters spattered across the universe.

I read about the dying old woman. She had a presentment: "Three weeks ago, probably feeling the first touches of sickness (Corde thought of it as the advance death thrill, the final presage; each of us in peculiar communion with his own organs and their sick-signals), she began to make the rounds, out all day on the buses and trolly cars…arranging to be admitted."

Yes, like elephants going to the graveyard. Instinct. But most human don't know how to trust it anymore. We're locked out by our own foolish logic, whining to get back to god somewhere behind the door. Battering at the door to find the god within. Dog into god, I muse.

And then lo and behold, on page 11 Corde says, "…A dog barked, whined as if a beater had given him a whack, then barked again. The barking of the dog, a protest against the limits of dog experience (for God's sake open the universe a little more!) So Corde felt, being shut in."

Corde, we're in sync. I too want this universe to open a little wider.

Now Corde ponders his wife the astronomer who, in Corde's metaphor, is bringing together a needle from one end of the universe with a thread from the opposite end. But he can't quite say what needs to be sewn—it's just his way of "concentrating his mind on the *mysterium tremendum.*"

It's overwhelming, this synchronicity that I feel with Corde about space and splatters of matter and god/dog. I put down the book and turn off the light. The *mysterium tremendum* hums in this dim room with the blind down. My throat hurts, and like Corde, I feel disoriented and confused, awash in some shifting, trembling perspective. Death, I suddenly flash on death. It is death that has brought Corde to that site and insight. As it brought my ex-husband to my dream. I can't quite sleep. Finally I get up again, grumpy, sore-throated, scratchy-eyed.

So I sit down to write this dream, sure that it is the strangest one yet in this log. But then my husband walks in to get his fountain pen and remarks, "You sure do have weird dreams."

"What?"

"I'm just reading your dream about the termites. Is it the people who form the tribes? Or the termites?"

"The people." I make a note to fix it in the text. You can see how he helps me clarify my language. He leaves, and I turn back to the computer screen. But really, I am staring at my moving points of inner space.

My head hurts. I'd crawl back into bed again, if I could sleep. So I'll write. Such a short dream too. Hmm…maybe it's even protecting me with its shortness while I'm ill.

But maybe I should rest. I ache.

We do shape our dreams. As I work with mine, I develop a code of meanings. The old joke goes that if you see a Freudian analyst, you dream Freudian. If you see a Jungian, you dream Jungian. You build up a shared reference system with whomever you tell your dreams to, whether it's your analyst or hairdresser or lover. Dreams develop a shorthand of symbols over time.

Our species has developed many such symbols. Archetypal symbols show up in your dreams even if you've never heard of them. Ego, shadow, anima, animus, wise old man or woman, divine child, animal totems— these patterns have evolved throughout the species' psychic growth. We have dreams recorded from the last 7,000 years, and these archetypes are visible there, intact below the many variations in culture.

But today's dream is about that most primal of archetypes: numbers. Numbers connect the whole shebang. Wow! I suddenly realize that I can graft a bit of the Big TOE into this chapter and go back to bed! It fits here. Okay, I'll retire to bed. Later on, I'll take out that stored text like a pint Mason jar of black-eyed peas in the pantry— "Handy if company shows up for dinner," Mrs. Heaton used to say as she brought us yet another gift of yet another jar.

Maybe, just maybe, the bed rest will also give me enough energy to attend a luncheon-cum-election today. I am one of the three co-leaders in charge of the group, but after three years, I'm tired of my post and ready to retire. In fact, all three of us leaders have decided to resign at the same time. We've worked well together, but it's time to move on.

I call and cancel a sandplay therapy session. Someone calls to cancel a appointment. Good. Someone else calls to cancel our walk today. Good again. The decks are clearing for inaction. For flu.

In keeping with my new energy-saving policy—like using that jar of canned text—I lie down. Maybe I'll get up when it's time for the luncheon. Maybe not.

I pick up *The Dean's December* and discover that Corde is sick and drowsy too: "He was eye-sick, head-sick, seat-sick, motion-sick, gut-sick, wheel-weary. So he rested after breakfast."

Me too, Corde. What's this about, Corde, I wonder, this sickness? As I drift off, I ask the unconscious to help me understand.

Hmm. That luncheon went off well enough, even though I wasn't at my best. The nominations for new leaders were made. Speeches made. An aura of good humor and expressions of affection for us old leaders and what we've done—my main contribution was that I finally got a student lounge going. Imagine. All these years at the Jung Intitute without a place for students to gather and talk.

Dinner is over now. It's early evening. And more stones emerge from the heaving, thawing ground of my dreamscape.

Under Stone Number 3. Why did it touch me so at dinner last night, that dish that my husband concocted? I'd never seen him make it before, a peculiar combo of stewed tomatoes, green peppers, onion, herbs and—ready for this?—chunks of bread. I walked into the kitchen: "What's this on the stove? Stewed tomatoes?"

"Not exactly. Actually, I made it in honor of my mother. She used to fix it long ago." Quite good, actually. But why did his remark— "I made it in honor of my mother"—touch a chord? Because I've been dreaming about the devalued feminine for two days? He's not read those last two chapters—he's still on the termites—and I've not talked about them. Anyway, he does value his feminine side.

My husband is a man who loved and respected and got on well with his mother. And his father. Lucky man! A lucky life, I tell him. I don't think it's just luck, though. I think it's his path. He has an astrology chart full of trines, the easy, lazy-hammock angle of life.

Under Stone Number 4...a sudden recollection from last night...of my husband kicking me awake to hear him announce clearly and loudly to the dark ceiling, "I...think...so!" A measured, rising emphasis at the end, as if he were offering up this judgment after careful thought. While asleep yet! At the time, I just felt irritable with my newfound grippe and merely fretted, You think *what?*

But now, suddenly, I intuit that maybe he was announcing to the secret air his new insight: dreams do work. Literally. They do work for us. So this dream book is not fiction, not whimsical entertainment. It explores how inner and outer life mesh together. Maybe he's beginning to sense that this is actually so, that a connection does exist between the symbolic inner world and the eventful outer world. Perhaps he's decided that dreams really *do* merge somehow into reality. "I...think...so!"

Why else would he kick me awake first, before loudly announcing his sleeping verdict? And his mood was a bit different today. More openly intrigued by what I'm doing. He's curious to read more, he tells me. And I'm glad.

Under Stone Number 5. At the luncheon today, a Thai woman was sitting next to me on the couch. She said that in Thailand people consider reincarnation to be a valid way of explaining neurosis and psychosis. They are something karmic to work through from a past life. Doing so brings a release for the individual from a destructive pattern. "So why not look at it this way?" she said. "Why not allow this approach, if it helps the patient to bear the burden of mental illness and take responsibility to change it?"

Take responsibility. Some kind of lifetime accountability. Yes—I feel a resolving tug on the red thread of this dream. It's not just that flowing universal number adds up the sums of quarks and leptons to make matter, the shifting points of the dream. Number also networks the qualitative meanings. We are somehow accountable for our psychic lives in an intangible realm of meaning, just as we are accountable for our finances and health habits in this material realm of bank books and cigarettes.

Okay, I get it. But I'm not in the mood to attend this dream much longer. I hurt. Where's that jar of canned number peas? For the first time, I can't finish this log's daily entry, not even a banged-out draft. I'm sick. That's the low-down, dirty truth. I just want to slip into bed and make brief contact with my friend Corde before groaning into sleep. Cough! Honk! Sniff!

I browse fretfully to find Corde standing over a body, seeing it as a number summary: "...Rick Lester's face had the subtracted look of the just dead..... Since he had been subtracted once and for all from the active human sum, you could only try to guess when that lesson had been given. Illumination while falling? A ten-second review of his life?"

Yes. It's the math problem. What is the emotional sum of a unique soul? Where is its summing up? In death? Where is the accountability? Again I ask dreamtime to help, and fall fitfully, feverishly asleep.

I wake in the night. A funny dreamlet has just flashed by: a red dog's tail wagging happily. Is it Happy, my Irish setter? No, it seems to be my *own* tail wagging, and *I'm* happy. I know I'm getting somewhere.

The odd part is that I can see a little red button too. It is somehow a wavy red button, like the plumy tail is wavy red too, but in yet another way. When I push the red button, it's warm. Push the red button...what is this dream saying?

This tail wagging, it reminds me of my last walk with Katrine. She said suddenly, "Is your lower back sore, you know, down here at—at what?—the ass? I don't know the word in English." Swedish is her native tongue.

"What? You mean right here?" I rubbed the little knot of nerves and muscle in my lower back just above the tail bone.

"Yes. Mine is sore from that dance class. I keep a lot of tension there. I saw it while I was dancing. Pain like a dull knife came in there as the little muscles started to move. They were so stiff, as if I never move them. It's still sore...just where a tail would be, if we had tails."

I chuckled, caught up in this image of wagging my tail as I walked along the path. I tried wagging my plumy tail under my trench coat. "My tail is wagging right now, but you can't see it. My coat hides it."

And now, here's this doggy tail wagging happily in my dream. What's cooking? Do I have fever? Every time my brain stews with illness, it serves up to me a new slant on life. I think that colds and flus may even be an evolutionary tool for evolving the psyche. It cooks our brains into new configurations that are more useful. Again and again.

Now I recall asking, "Tell me again about how the pharaoh turns into an electron and goes to the North Star and back. I don't understand that part...so the nightsea journey is not always by water?"

"No, also by the ground, the water, or fire. Any of the elements can hold the journey. And remember, it all just stands for a return to the source, to the Great Mother to be reborn."

Ah. The Great Mother. The deepest feminine symbol. We have so many different images of it in cultures. But they are all finally she who accepts without condition. Embraces without stint. We find ourselves in the arms of the mother, the mate, the grave.

Fire. I'm fiery hot. Fever. Something is being forged in this furnace of my sickness. Something I didn't know before. Going through the element of fire. Cooking my brain molecules into a new configuration.

I drowse on the Spaceship Universe. The old mythic images of god were earthborn, earthbound. But nowadays Earth is just the third planet out from the sun, not Earth Mother. And heaven is a phrase in old love songs, not the home of the Heavenly Father. Yang and yin help...they turn it into plus and minus charges. That's a step toward the immense abstraction of god...not just a giant hoary-bearded Jahweh on a throne.

Aha! We need a universal-sized yin to hold our projections of the receptive womb/tomb...we need a universal-sized yang to move dynamically in it. Yang and yin as field and ground. The great mythology of physics has developed for us these terms for the universal container and contained.

And now I pour in the jar of text: Scientists see an awesome new universe unfolding, one that can only be described by numbers or poetry. They plot the course of electrons through it, bombard it with huge energies and budgets. They quest for its unified force as knights sought the Holy Grail, doing battle for the favor of a mysterious beauty they call scientific truth. A wondrous pursuit, this modern-day search through wormholes and extra dimensions for the chalice of universal background that holds its spirituous content, the perpetual motion of field.

If $E = mc^2$ is true, why then also it's true that $E/c^2 = m$. Energy divided by the squared speed of light equals mass. This means that mass is a construct of *ssslow* energy. Slow it down enough and it blossoms into the 3D stuff that we call matter. Why? Because energy has a property we do not usually notice—not just power, but also informed, polarized relationship. Electrons sense when scientists are measuring them, for instance. Really. When someone examines an electron to determine its angle of spin—where its poles point, in other words— incredibly enough, a pole is somehow always pointing straight at the measuring device, almost as if to say, "Hi, I see you too."

Cosmic constants calibrate the universal relationships so that each thing relates to every other thing in a network of movement that is a huge and ceaseless dance of change. How awesome. It's an every-moment miracle. This post-Cartesian science for some people has become the new mother church, its scientists a new priesthood. They worship a great beauteous mystery hidden in all this relationship.

I am saying that this play of field and ground called the universe is a holy coupling, our creative godhead. Plus-minus. Male-female. Container-contained. Together they make more than the sum of their parts. Analog and linear number link them indissolubly into one. Chalice background holding spirituous field. Two-in-one and unity of a coupling.

The 1 says **unity!** It is the whole before any breakup into parts. It contains all. Being unity, there is nothing left to put in order. It is perfection, so there is nothing left to improve. And it is static…existing before the creative process begins, or any counting out into reality. Monotheism was supposed to be a big improvement over previous religions, according to those who brought all the little gods under one big umbrella. And this one god did everything. We see it in statements like, "In the beginning God created the heaven and the earth."

Oddly enough, the 1 is not only beginning. It is also the end, as in the statement: "One for all and all for one." It becomes the climax, the sublime union. Bonded atoms makes one molecule; joined molecules make one cell; a pattern of cells make one organism.

Commonly, people speak of energy as some kind of unity: "He turned on the energy. He's full of energy today." It just flows. This energy is sheer potential on tap in the universe. Fire flows out of it, and lightning, and heat, and static electricity, and whatever other energy forms we manage to juice up by our ingenuity.

But the truth is, energy is really a step away from unity. Energy does not happen until the 1 breaks into mirror symmetry with itself. For example, you can't have field without ground; you can't have a positive pole without a negative pole. We acknowledge this complementary 2-ness when we say, "You can't have one without the other."

But the way you view this twosome—as partners or as opponents—tells the tale. Herein lies the difference between East and West. And between the right brain and left brain.

The linear Western culture opposes light with dark—the bright beam of conscious inspection narrows its focus to battle against the vague, billowy, shadowy dark. It hones the skill of *either-or* opposition. For example, a court decides guilt or innocence. The various people in the courtroom do not all cooperate in a fact-finding mission to explore the many different facets to form as true a picture of the issue as possible. They seek no compromise that considers the relative merits, faults, and needs of all parties. Instead the issue is polarized and simplified into an *either-or* tourney between two jousting sides—in fact the word *attorney* comes from medieval tournaments where two opponents jousted. The stronger had might-makes-right on his side. Even now, opposing lawyers confront each other in a battle of skills where brilliant and courageous maneuvers are supposed to vanquish the inferior opponent. What's truth got to do with it?

That linear mindset applies the *either-or* style to number, seeing it as polarized and binary. It views options as alternative shunts in a binary computer, where one gate opens as the other gate shuts.

But to the holistic mind, number has another style, a coupling, relational mode, where we don't have to chose *either-or.* Instead we can go *both-and,* and see the 2 as a pair of 1s relating to each other, and by it creating a third, and higher, coupled state. This kind of thinking is holistic, relational, analog. For example, we can view a negative electron. Then we can view a positive proton. Or we can put them together in relationship as the balanced charges that make up a hydrogen atom. Electron (-) and proton (+) together equal something more than the sum of their parts; they form a transcendent third condition called hydrogen, that smallest and most primal of atoms.

To get more complicated, the atom has to start storing up these transcendent third states in the form of the neutron. At every step up the periodic table, the next element uses another transcendental neutron to climb past the last polarity of negative electron joined to positive proton. Thus each new element is not merely a linear shunt of choosing *either-or.* It is also an analog process of incorporating *both-and* to create a neutron that transcends either polarity and drives on to a new level. Thus the atom is both linear and analog in its modes. It is analinear, woven from a web of complementary and contrasting number functions.

Notice that union comes both before and after polarity in this view…it both precedes and resolves the tension of a split. But each new unity arrives at a higher, more sophisticated and inclusive level of being. Prigogine called this principle of evolution in chemistry the escape to a higher order.

I see universal creation coming from the symmetrical functions of number, linear and analog. Look. The universe is finally just a lump, some hypothetical glob of the 1 archetype. But with the symmetry of the 2, mutuality becomes possible and the state of polarity, of discrimination between one thing and another thing can begin. This, not that. Plus, not minus. Space-not-time and matter-not-energy. This is the start of polar tensions moving into a transcendental third state.

And this 2 marks the beginning of understanding. We notice it in the dualities of life. For instance, the ping-pongery of the 2 becomes evident in your sense organs. They are designed to bring in data around you. Sense organs are arranged in 2-ness: two eyes for sight, two ears for hearing, two nostrils for smelling. Even taste has the 2-ness that plays the nasal cavity's promise off against the mouth's taste-bud evaluation. People exclaim, "If only coffee tasted as wonderful as it smells!" Or "Don't worry, this cheese doesn't taste like it smells!" We measure space with our two hands and we locomote through it by the alternations of our two feet. We've developed the neocortex with its two complementary lobes.

This polar dynamism of the 2, if left only to ping-pong back and forth between thrust and background, would make the universe truly static and boring, a ping-pong match with no rising scores, a place with no evolutionary motion. It would become an endless volley of fruitless debate, argument, *either-or*-ing everything to entropy death. Cynics who say the universe is all just random motion without purpose are dwelling in this linear mindset.

But there is also a holistic, transcendental mindset. It has a forming edge of truth that occurs through the relationship of parts. Not just stuck in a ping-ponging rut of *either-or,* it balances entropy with evolution, whereby things develop higher and higher orders of organization. This drive to complexity is seen in the atomic stairway of elements, of course, or in the sequences of crystal formation. By it, evolution has slowly come up with organic life, which itself becomes more complicated, elaborated, diversified over time. At the same time that the physical universe appears to be slowly cooling down in entropy death, this complicating neg-entropic force is somehow slowly increasing its power and scope.

Thus, out of this interplay between the poles of life and death, of complication and simplification, of field and ground, a third form is continually arising which is the "baby" of creation from the polarity of the 2. It is a blend that transcends the polarized state of either as it unites both poles and brings about a higher order.

We jump out of the eternal oscillatory rhythm of 2 when the 3 goes beyond the old polar argument and moves into birth. It is why, for example, the Trinity holds such numinous power in Christianity. Yet the 3-spot becomes the takeoff point for new motion. It is what happens when the parade of children become parents, grandparents, and finally unknown ancestors marching into the backlog of history. It happens in the psyche too, accreting the culture of billions who've laid down their bits of deposit.

This is why the 3 has such odd energy. It is reunified, transcended polarity, yet it wants to push onward to something else. It truly needs the 4-state to complete it. For example, the masculine Christian Trinity needs that female Mary tagging along behind to complete and stabilize it. The three dimensions of space need that other odd dimension of time rag-tagging along too, to stabilize and complete them.

This **odd power of the 3** is epitomized in the triangle, which is the takeoff point for all of Bucky Fuller's fermenting ideas. Even a human triangle automatically posits change—it means jealousy, favoritism, choosing one side or another. Any 3-ness is full of incipient change. The juggler has 3 balls to *fascinate* you—not because it's harder to juggle than 2 or easier than 4. It consumes your attention as you wait for the mysterious hidden fourth state to emerge. Remember that 3-ring circus? It was mesmerizing, that dream. I had to find a fourth place to stand in order to relate it to you, the audience.

Look at the 4. It is the first number that can be divided evenly. Moreover, adding, doubling, or multiplying it give the same answer: 2 + 2 = 4 and 22 and 2 x 2 = 4. This makes it very stable and reliable.

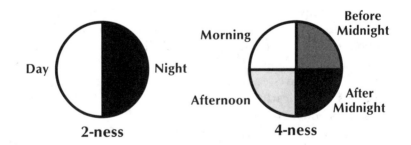

The Orienting 4 as Halves Halved

We split the 4 split and then split it again to orient ourselves—of course, we do it with the compass, as North, South, East, and West. But we also do it with time—as you can see in this chart adapted from Abt's *Number Symbolism*. Each twenty-four hours has the poles of Day and Night. But each pole has its own inner symmetry: Day has Morning or Afternoon; Night has before or after Midnight. Thus we order both time and space by the 4-ness of something being split in two, and then each part is halved again. We use these fourfold structures to orient both our outer and inner life. Its technique establishes the four elements, the four suits of a deck of cards, the four human temperaments of ancient Greece, the Cartesian cross of mathematics in Europe, the four functions of psyche in the Myers-Briggs Type Indicator, and so on.

All over the world people use this fourfold structure for orientation because of the 4's great stability. People often double date, for example, or make a foursome of golf, because it presents a much stabler form of relationship than the 2 or 3. The 4 even stabilizes the universe into the paired polarities of space/time and matter/energy. So the archetype of the 4 is stabilized wholeness, foursquare and realized.

Your body is oriented on the fourfold plan: left-right symmetry and upper-and lower limb complementarity. Your waking mind knows four dimensions—three of space and one of time. Your psyche has four ways to gauge events—through sensing, intuiting, thinking, and feeling. Christianity uses the stabilizing dogma of the male Trinity plus Mary.

To me, such archetypal number is the root of creation. Here's a tiny dream from maybe two and half years ago: I see the eight I Ching trigrams floating in space, fitting together in different ways to make the sixty-four hexagrams.

A chill and empty dream, you say? Just number floating around.

Chill except for this. Each trigram had a piece of heart hanging from it, and as they moved and fitted together in space, each pair of trigrams connected to make a whole heart. You get it? Numbers with heart. Numbers form heart connections through space. That's what this dream meant to me. The universe is made up of this—numbers with heart. Related caring thought. This dream really got to me.

And now I've emptied that jar of peas.

Occasionally I wake in the night and the next day, rousing slightly in a dozey, achy flu. It's definitely flu. During this slowing-down, deepening illness, I realize what those peculiar extra I Ching hexagrams were about. I'm saving my energy, banking my fire, sleeping through the flu. I made a sincere sacrifice by opening this small jar of archetypal number peas to serve you. It brings that tagalong hexagram of *Creation*. That's what's in the jar. The dots of universal creation. I sleep through the day, letting that stored jar serve. I feel bad.

Hmm. All this, and still I haven't come to the bottom of that dream doggy tail wagging in the middle of the night. Maybe it signaled that things are going okay. But what about the odd little wavy red warm button? I wonder if pushing it makes things work?

Oh, yes. I had a dreamlet last night:

I am putting on my left hand a ring with a number of small diamonds set across it in a pavé effect. It's beautiful and I like it very much. Then I see one of the diamonds is falling out—I can see it falling like a little faceted cone of light. It falls into the trash on the floor. So I look for it in the trash.

After I finished pouring in that jar of number peas, it filled space with all those little moving dots, paving the universe with scintillating matter. But just as I was admiring it, one diamond fell out. Where do I find that other diamond? In the trash on the floor.

So I'll look for it in the trash. Okay. I'll turn off the light and maybe dream about putting that last little cone of light into place. The great thing about asking dreamtime for help is that it gives it.

Darkness. I wake suddenly to great, overwhelming sadness, as I realize what's in the trash. I know what is needed to complete this chapter and bring it full-circle. Human trashiness. I think of the story a Swiss woman was telling me about her son in the United States, who's just started a special music school in Los Angeles. He called home excited about what a beautiful apartment he'd found, convenient to the school. Now he's just phoned home again, stunned. He came upon the body of a man in the hall outside his apartment. Shot. "Mother, like television. A white shirt. Red blood on the front. A hole in him. Mother, people say they're doing crack deals around the building. I saw two men rifling the body when I stepped into the hall, but I was afraid to tell the police when they came. The police come here often, people say, and that they're in on the dope deals. They even say Bush let Noriega make some special secret deal so dope can be smuggled in easier."

The Swiss woman asked me if this was true. I said, "I've no idea. Surely not. I hope not." Her son doesn't know whether to move or stay there and tough it out. "Would it be the same everywhere in Los Angeles?" the woman asked me.

I had to say again, "I don't know. Maybe." I don't like saying these things about my country. "It wouldn't be that way in smaller towns," I say. "But in many big cities, yes."

The Swiss aren't used to this. I saw an American magazine cover recently— "Zurich: a New Yorker's idea of Paradise." And a recent newspaper article, datelined Paris, declared that Europeans don't envy Americans anymore, despite what Quayle has just claimed in a speech. Europeans are more comfortable these days, with a better quality of life, if not a higher income, than Americans, it said, and they look upon America as dangerous, shoddy, and flashy. They are repelled by the rising crime rate, the poor quality of life, the burgeoning homeless.

Corde is sad about such things too. He talks about the contempt center of the USA: "...the crazy state of the prisoners in County Jail—the rule of the barn bosses, the rackets, beatings, sodomizings and stabbings in the worst of the tiers: in 'Dodge City,' 'H-1'; the prisoners who tucked trouser bottoms into socks to keep the rats from running up their legs in the night. Now there was a red hell for the soul to stray into."

Almost no violent crime exists here in Switzerland compared to the United States. That's what surprised me most when I first came. The unjimmied coin boxes on public telephones and train ticket machines. The gloves, scarves, caps laid up on brick walls for their owners to retrace their steps and find. People leave their bags of purchases on the sidewalk outside one local market while they enter another to buy some little item. They leave their bicycles unlocked in the racks by the commuter trains.

What's the matter with these people? Do they live in a time warp? Back in the good old days when you could trust your neighbors?

Almost no muggings on trains or in public restrooms. Almost no bag snatching on the big city streets. I can walk home alone at 12:30 a.m. after a movie—no fear, no worry.

No slums. That's another shock. How do they do it?

Interesting people, these Swiss. Not fond of royalty. Determined to be a nation of wealthy simple folk. According to a recent *New York Times* article, they have the highest living standard in the world. And cost of living too. When I told my husband what Mariles said about God living in Switzerland, he responded, "But can God afford it?"

It reminds me of a joke that a Swiss armaments salesman told me: God comes walking along after creating the world. He sees a little man and says, "Little Man, who are you?"

"God, don't you remember me? I'm the little Swiss man."

"Oh yes. Since I'm here, what can I do for you, Little Swiss Man?"

"God, I would like some beautiful green mountains on my land."

"Okay, Little Swiss Man"—whoosh— "there they are." God walks off.

The next year God comes walking by. "Hello, Little Swiss Man. I'm back in the neighborhood. How are you doing?"

"Oh fine, God."

"Is there anything you want besides your beautiful green mountains?"

"Well, God, I'd like to have some nice cows to eat this green grass."

"Okay, Little Swiss Man"—whoosh— "here they are." And God leaves.

Another year passes and God comes along: "Why, hello, Little Swiss Man. I've come back by again. How are you doing these days?"

"Oh, fine, God. I'm so happy with my mountains and my cows eating the fine grass. They give such excellent milk. Here, let me show you—" and he gets out a glass and milks a cow into it. "Here, God. Just taste that!"

"Why, this is excellent milk indeed! Is there anything else you desire, Little Swiss Man?"

"Two franks, ten rappen, God, for the glass of milk."

And the Swiss armaments man roared with laughter.

The Swiss are the world's oldest democracy, founded around the turn of the 14th century, and still armed to the teeth to protect it. They're fighters.

Back in the poor old days when the whole family brood couldn't stay home and wrestle a living from the mountain farm, the younger sons had to seek their fortune in other countries…back before scenery and watches and chocolate and financial privacy became bankable commodities. The Pope's Swiss Guard is still frozen back in medieval time with its halberds and helmets. But nowadays, the Swiss make very sophisticated armaments.

But how do I explain American-style violence to this Swiss mother? The crack deals? The body in the hall, the police you can't trust.

What's the matter, anyway, with these Swiss? They'd rather live safe and well than menaced in the glitz of Miami or LA or New York vice?

Do I say, "That's the modern world." But it's not. This country is more modern than the USA, technologically speaking. It's just behind on its quota of violent crime, slums, homeless, drug abuse.

I enjoy Switzerland. I admire its stodgy, clean, decent and comfortable people. They let me do my own thing. All this peace in Switzerland has given me the time to be creative—a boon, I find, for foreigners who come here with a lot of creative chaos boiling inside and need a calming container to distill it. Many exiles and expatriates have bloomed here. James Joyce…well, it's a long list and I won't start.

But to the Swiss, all this orderly security and predictability can be stifling. So they travel a lot and marry exotic foreigners. And too, Switzerland looks cleaner than it is. Its pristine image floats on subterranean pools of dirty money. Swiss crime is just more hidden and subtle than American crime. Switzerland launders its white-collar crime to get it smelling fresh, and it sticks mostly to victimless crimes, which don't penalize its own people much. But the Swiss abhor individual physical bloodshed—for instance, the postal carriers here can act as paymasters, carrying thousands of francs to deliver to customers on their daily rounds—without getting mugged. So Switzerland is perhaps a step or two up the ladder of evolution.

In the dark I get up and go into the bathroom. While I'm in there, wiping my bottom, suddenly it comes to me. That plumy red tail? That little wavy red warm button underneath? It's an asshole! The warm, wavy red button of an asshole is supposed to end this chapter!

Asshole. Was it the asshole on the god-dog? Have you ever met any of god's assholes? I have. And I've been one a few times. Met plenty more. Big-time, big-gauge assholes. So is this what I need to find in the trash? *This* is that fallen cone of light? An asshole?

Yes, oddly enough, I think so. What is my idea of a big-gauge asshole? One who kills and maims and connives for the power and thrill. Such people—I turn on the light again and consult Corde. He's heartsick about this dead youngster subtracted from the human sum by murder. Corde is tired of such evil, of fighting it, of suffocating in it. He knows that it was evil that overtook the boy who went out the window. Someone pushed him out the window. But the boy participated in it too, for Corde's nephew says the boy brought a prostitute and her pimp in for sex while his own wife was asleep in the bedroom:

"Mason said, 'He wanted Riggie Hines to go into the toilet with him.' 'What for?'

181

'To go down on him while she was shitting.' And Corde thinks, The true voice of Chicago—the spirit of the age speaking from its very lowest register; the very bottom."

Yes, the assholes at the very bottom. Down there in the trash. That's where the cone of light fell. I have to punch that button. Punch the assholes.

What if people could actually *know* whether they're assholes or not? That's what my dead husband said in that dream. He came back after death to the sunlit attic and apologized to me. He did act like a real asshole, too—but we were in collusion there. I was too good to be real and he was too real to be good. Together we made an asshole and a piece of shit.

So in that dream he apologized and said he was sorry, that if he'd known earlier what he knew after death, he wouldn't have acted that way. What if we all could find it out ahead of time—before dying!

Yeah. So how do we find that out?

Under Stone Number 6, something is rising up out of dark memory. The crux. I'm recalling today's *International Herald Tribune*. The front-page headline. I go look for it: *"Glimpses of a Realm Beyond Death Show Striking Parallels* ...some eight million American adults...near-death experience...a remarkable similarity...profound impact...people are permanently and often dramatically changed...adopt new values, change careers, abandon materialism and question relationships...loss of fear of death...greater willingness to live life to its fullest...much less likely to attempt suicide again."

Hmm, I know about suicide firsthand. I came back. So is this the crux of it? Death? The great big asshole of god? The shitty ending?

No, death is not the end. I am more than a random mix of molecules energizing into flesh for a brief span of time across a wedge of space, birthing and dying in the crotch of creation. I am here doing something in a design so big that I can't see much of it. But I see enough to sense a much bigger pattern that includes you, too. Accomplishing my rhythmic curlicue makes things more coherent for us all. Or I can worsen it. You can too.

But assholes don't stop the demolition derby. They don't rev down and look inside to see what's there. I remember a guy who tried meditation and said it made him so frantic that he had to take Librium.

People are raucous with the constant blare of the culture boomboxing and the perpetual TV documenting a society so out of touch with its shadow that the dark monster of pointless death stalks the land. Corde told me sorrowfully: "No, it wasn't only two, three, five chosen deaths being painted thickly, terribly, convulsively inside him, all over his guts, liver, heart, over all his organs, but a large picture of cities, crowds, peoples, an apocalypse, with images and details supplied by his own disposition, observation, by ideas, dreams, fantasies, his peculiar experience of life."

This shadow of random violence is seizing our culture, death turned into a monster that, slavering, has us by the throat. Stymied at how to stop it, saddened, I read on with aching eyes. Corde is stymied too. He feels naive and inexplicable to his old, shrewder friends—feels he's fighting futilely against some monstrous tyrant. He recalls a line of Shelley's describing George III: "An old mad blind despised and dying king."

That's the secret. Death. George III did die. The United States did come into being. It is worth the effort to fight the old mad blind despised and dying king of random, pointless violence and death.

Good night Corde. Sweet dreams in Monsterville.

And then I go to sleep again and dream of...

Noriega. I see what I know is a picture of him. It is an empty frame with *nothing* in it. No inner space, no container for space, time, mass, energy. I just know it's Noriega. A voice says, "Nada."

Noriega, the Archetypal Asshole is shown as *nothing*. Nada in Spanish. I ponder *nada* in this fretful dozing insomnia that illness brings...trying to recall Hemingway's version of the Lord's Prayer updated as brave new existentialism. Something more or less like this:

Our nada who art in nada,
Nada be thy name,
Nada come,
Nada be done,
On nada as it is in nada...

And so on. If all you see is emptiness, why not try to fill it up with two thousand pairs of shoes? Why not come to power on a web of cocaine that traps its victims?

Assholes aren't stupid. Sometimes they are very, very clever. Cleaver clever. They asshole around precisely because it pays...if you value a closet with two thousand pairs of shoes more than the state of your *nada*. If you like drugs and guns filling your *nada*.

But some people value their souls over their shoes, and they'd rather get high on soul than *nada*. Still, there are many lost diamonds in the trash of our society. I go to sleep wondering how to find the cone of light in the trash.

I wake up yet again. Well, hell. I've been a diamond in the trash. I can relate to the asshole point of view. Aha! I chuckle. It was *my* red tail waving in the breeze, with god and dog also mixed up in it. Well, I am both god and dog; I am a universe in microcosm and what I manifest depends on how I put the connections together. Yeah, it's my asshole too. My analyst once said, "We can't see our asshole because we're sitting on it."

So maybe this is the "ashamed of the purpose folded in his breast" stuff that the I Ching promised for today's hexagram. It's true. I am ashamed of my asshole-ability at some things I've done and been. So I've found the diamond in the trash. It's me. Fretfully in my fever, I realize it.

But it sure is hard to describe how I found myself and lifted the diamond of myself from the trash. I go to sleep again and dream of...

> Someone in a boat is steering a firm course up the River of Intent. It looks pretty drab at first. The water's gray. There are bold black and white stretches along the banks. But this person holds firm, is *doing* it.

I wake thinking, yeah, this is the way. Hold firm going up the river of intent—that I can understand. It does take firmness to steer up the bleak river at first. River suggests the channeled watery unconscious. Its water is banked and channeled; it is unconscious energy put to a directed course. But why is this person steering a firm course *up* the river of intent?

Well, why not? Going back to the source. I know if I follow a river back and up the watershed, I finally come to its source in the mountains. And going on up, I reach the raindrops falling. And going on up, I touch the fragile face of god.

Lots of people don't know how to touch god with their souls anymore, and it has turned this modern culture into a giant asshole shitting non-biodegradable waste onto the world. Going by appearances, who wants to be good? Nowadays you get more mileage from being *baaad*. But heading upriver toward god, one starts wanting to be good. It's much more interesting and difficult than being bad.

When society is outer-directed—living for appearances—you can cheat to the limit you can get away with. The only deterrent is legal punishment. A judge, bank auditor, review commission gets you only if you're not clever enough. Outer values develop outer watchdogs. So the game becomes Fifth Amendment goodness. Okay, you just *prove* that I had anything to do with the break-in. *Nada* innocence.

The only reason to be good is for god's sake. For the god that resides within and without, in the pattern beyond design and calculation. Because it matters to stay as close to the source of true meaning as possible. I punish myself by staying away from the secret and fragile face of god.

It's the only way to pull that diamond out of the trash.

This is what rehabilitates the psyche. Not making license plates or putting the money back before it's noticed or giving five talks to teenage addicts as part of the parole agreement. That's just a beginning. That's the social version, the outer motions of a group-directed solution. But psychic rehabilitation is private and self-monitoring. It puts the analog unconscious into sync with the linear conscious. It harmonizes the body and soul.

Not easy. Hard to get on the path, easy to diverge. But follow it. By boat, car, footing it in ruby slippers. In this dream, the best way is by boat because it follows the natural flow of the channeled unconscious. So on this River of Intent, I hold the course firm and keep steering toward the source. The scenery turns marvelous. It glows with odor and sound and textured meaning. It whispers of god behind the form.

I've been in sync and out. And let me tell you, in sync is better. I can even show you an illustration. Because that's what my dream did as I looked closely at the person who was moving up the River of Intent.

The closer I looked, the more the blurred face came into focus, until it was one clear happy image. It suggested to me that focusing the split vision unites one's conscious and unconscious views. Uniting body and soul makes one truth. Words and mute action start to say the same thing. No more double messages setting up no more double binds.

Do you remember how Marya stood at the window looking at the snapshot of her mother, waiting for the blur to come into focus? She was looking for the diamond in the trash of her life. Looking for Vera, the mother of truth.

It is not, as Freud suggested, that we project the images of our parents onto the larger world and wish for an infinite version of humanity in god. It is rather that we receive a finite version of god in our parents. They are tokens to help us know, early on, that something is more powerful, organized, loving, helpful, imponderable than we are. No wonder parents turn out to be rather disappointing. They are infinite caring that is manifested in a limited fleshly edition.

Parents have to fail us somehow. They eventually make it bearable that we fail ourselves, and our own children. And life itself as we die. Parents are time-and space-limited editions of god. I know my fleshly limits by now, asshole that I am sometimes. But I am also a diamond rescued from the trash of events. I have found myself in the trash of my past and have become a cone of light.

Oh, I'm so tired with, of, by, from this flu. It's so very much work trudging down into the dark and trashy travail and mining diamonds in the *nada.*

So now, I come to the simple-minded fun of ending this chapter and finally choosing the title. Hmm. It suggests another pun, wouldn't you know, which is why I've decided to call this three days of experience "The 72-Hour Influ-Insight."

CHAPTER 15

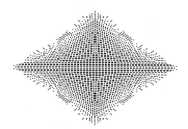

The Pretty Poison

Dream Log—Monday, November 21:

Many events, on and on, doing things in a red jacket. Then a woman says, "You can wear my white jacket if you like, until it's time to go home." The jacket is lying on the ground, wrinkled. I pick it up and put it on. It's a short white jacket, button-down-the-front with points at the waist. A pharmacy jacket? Or soda fountain jacket? Drugstore?

I wake up and sense that it's about dawn. The big window in the bedroom is shuttered with what my son calls a "persian," a name he learned while living in Barcelona. It's a wide metal blind over the window that you can raise and lower with a crank. So our bedroom is dark. But light comes in through the doorway leading into the living room with its wall of windows. The light is odd…like a frosted light bulb.

I close my eyes to rove back into dreamland, disappointed in the paucity of my night's catch. I can make nothing of this dream.

Well, I can troll for its dream meaning by noticing what I feel when I wake up. Because the dreamtime has triggered it. Immediately I think of shame and the assholes. Next, that I need to up my B vitamin intake, especially B_6, plus some acidophilus to help me produce my own Bs. This flu is devouring them. How do I know? Because I'm not remembering my dreams much lately; they're just dreamlets and getting smaller all the time. This last one, I can only remember a bit.

But hey, I do feel pretty good today. At least lying here.

My husband gets up, and when he reaches the living room, he says, "Snow. There's snow everywhere. More coming down."

Of course. That accounts for the frosted light bulb effect. Snow turns the light like this.

Yesterday Davis phoned and said flu is going around. He predicted mine would hang on as a cough for a month, like his did. Ugh! Cough!

I get up, take some vitamins, and then make a cup of hot lemonade with a tablespoon of my rose hips marmalade for sweetener. I wouldn't be doing this with regular marmalade...I sweetened this batch with fructose, which is absorbed slower into the blood. Even so, it's hardly sweet at all: a cup of fructose to a kilo of rose hips paste.

I get back into bed with the lemonade, sipping it, toying with this dream. Soon I must get up and start Monday morning chores. Maybe I feel good enough to do this...if I don't push too hard. The flu symptoms, the aches and headaches are close to gone.

But I cancel the dance class tonight. No leaping around across the beautiful parquet floor under that ceiling like a swagged white wedding cake. Yet I feel almost healthy enough to be restless, and I *must* keep two appointments in downtown Zurich this afternoon.

I wonder if events today will pick up on these jackets in the dream.

Two jackets, red and white. What is this red jacket about ? I don't even own a red jacket. Oh yes, I do. A woman gave me one not long ago, with a red skirt, as I stood at her front door saying goodbye after a visit. She brought out this suit, red, tailored in Hong Kong, and insisted that I take it. An utter shock to me. But finally I did, after many protests. I've not worn it yet. Maybe never will.

It just finally seemed wise to take it. She kept insisting in a frustrated tone that she wouldn't wear it any more. The new baby would spit up all over it, ruin it for future use. She couldn't go anywhere. No job. Nobody to talk to all day. The baby took so much energy. And she'd already spent so much time in the hospital with postpartum depression. Life was hell. I understood very well. I'd had postpartum blues too.

So I took the red suit, thinking, You're not giving this gift to me. You're saying something about your life...to me and to your husband who's standing here listening. You've got the blues. No, the mean reds. The hard-edge aggressive mean reds. You're literally fighting to make me take that red suit. Remember Audrey Hepburn in *Breakfast at Tiffany's?* The mean reds. Yeah. I've tried to foist off my mean reds on other people too, but actually it's something you can't give away.

Oh, of course! That's what this dream is about...the mean reds. I'm wearing the mean red jacket at the first of the dream. Events are in a blur, and I'm wearing the red jacket. I have the mean reds. Reds is a nickname for Amphetamine. Speed. It's a mean, hard-edged upper.

But I didn't need speed to get my mean reds. That red jacket was the anger and aggression I felt when I was twenty-something, as a relief and variation from my other more frequent variation, the blues. Turning hostility outward for a change, instead of inward.

That mean streak in me looked much like what you see in speed freaks. Oh! I remember Ruidoso! Freaky Mean Red with his frizzy red Afro. Strung out on speed when I first saw him in that cabin of dopers. It was the only time I ever saw people melt heroin in a spoon and shoot up.

But Mean Red was a speed freak. A crazy bedbug redhead.

Now I see what this dream is about. Now I'm going to unfold this secret in my breast and let you know. It comes in this ring of limitation. Matter is substance. And I have been a substance abuser.

You see, I have this addiction. No, I don't talk about it much. Lots of people wouldn't notice it or believe it, anyway. I appear downright normal these days. But it nearly destroyed my life. Horrible, a monkey, no, a gorilla on my back. It demanded constant feeding. Over the years I moved, with many ups and downs, into a depressive muzziness where I cried a lot. Sometimes I even wished for the courage to kill myself.

Finally I tried. And when that happened, and I woke up alive despite my best efforts, something in me wised up enough to begin living differently. I knew I would keep living, so I might as well take myself in hand and *no matter what* my pusher said, start living differently.

My pusher was the society, my relatives, especially my mother.

You see, I'm a sugar addict.

I hear you laugh as you stir another cube into your coffee and finish off that Danish. Ha ha, she's joking. A little sugar never hurt anybody, and besides, you need to jump-start your body. You gotta go to work, right?

Oh, I understand. I drank several cups of coffee every morning for years as I ate something sweet. I had to, or I'd get this panicky headache by 9:00 or 9:30 a.m. Yeah.

In a nutshell, refined sugar and caffeine wiped out my psyche, before moving in to destroy the hard-wired body. Sugar does to me what alcohol does to some people.

But I guess I'm lucky—alcohol makes me so sick that it isn't worth drinking, no matter what fun I have in the first thirty minutes, before I start to feel poisoned. And I'm not talking hangover here, I'm talking massive toxic poisoning.

Champagne is my real *bete noire*. It tastes so delightful that once I drank four go-to-hell glasses at a caviar party and spent the next three days in bed, crawling out for another week to look bleakly at the world through bloodshot eyes and soured disposition and sluggish timing. A Chinese woman once said that I must be a secret Chinese because that's the way alcohol affects her and her relatives too.

Since I'm poisoned by alcohol too fast to make it attractive, I'm left to a slower poison that works such subtle mind-altering tricks that many people think it's only normal to feel constantly grouchy, tired, sardonic, soured on life, and at wits' end.

Yeah, sugar. About a fifth of us are acutely susceptible to it. In my old sugarholic days, my moods were so fragile that I couldn't bear much stress. Somewhere beyond that foggy cover of my stifling dark cloud of *sturm und drang,* I could see that the sun was shining. But I never could get there. When I read *The Bell Jar* by Sylvia Plath, and then her biography, I thought oh, there but for a lack of talent and candy bars and cookies and Cokes and a gas oven go I.

I recognized a kindred soul. I'd gone through a suicide attempt myself. The fierce insecurities and temper tantrums and depressions sounded so familiar. So much like the symptoms of my sugar addiction. But if my suicide had made the grade, my posthumous book would have been titled *The Candy Jar.*

I tried to find help. Counseling didn't cut it. Then I picked up a thick volume called *Orthomolecular Medicine* in the Waco Public Library. What a shock as I recognized my own symptoms! Look, you're smart, I thought. Crazy but smart. Maybe you can help yourself. Nobody else can.

A lot of us sugar addicts come genetically from a Scandinavian-English-Irish-Icelandic belt lying across that part of the globe like a cloudy web. It carries a special susceptibility to systemic poisoning from alcohol, refined starches, and fake food. Or we're Asian or Amerindian. None of us knows what to do with the fake metabolic highs that can then drop us into the pits. That split the psyche and even make a lot of us look schizophrenic.

Schizophrenia is called a "modern disease." Its victims are mostly urban. Torrey said in *Surveying Schizophrenia* that "...there is clearly a disproportionate number of schizophrenics who come from the cities, and especially from those portions of cities where the poor live."

Mindell mentions this too and points out in *City Shadows* that regarding schizophrenia, "Countries like Japan, England, Denmark and Germany have the same rate as the USA. Higher rates are found in the

Scandinavian countries, Ireland and Northern Yugoslavia. Lower rates have been found in Africa, with the exception of those exposed to western technology and culture. It is very rare in Papua New Guinea, which is probably the least developed country remaining in the world."

You can find maps showing that the incidence of schizophrenia correlates positively with the rate of alcoholism. I think many susceptible psyches have cracked under the stress and strain of modern diet and lifestyle. Further, I think this metabolic sensitivity is genetic. I even suspect that it signals a sensitive psyche that, when balanced, can offer the culture special insights into the huge realm of the archetypes, but when unbalanced, can look like schizophrenia and alcoholism and depression and a host of related disorders. It's shamanism gone wrong.

Much mental illness, I believe, is triggered by modern foods. We "refine"—what a misnomer!—whole food to discard its dark side and turn it brite, lite, and foney. Gone is the bran, the germ, the vitamins, all the decayable parts that keep it real. Eating fake, split-apart food fosters fake, split-apart psyches whose symptoms manifest in bizarre ways as mental illness, violence, despair and cynicism.

But some of us are more sensitive to this fake food than others. We don't tolerate it as well, nor the addicting substances like coffee, nicotine, alcohol, drugs. We're the test canaries in the societal coal mine, going wacko and dying off at that first whiff of poison gas in the shaft before it affects the others.

If simple old sugar addiction isn't evident as a big dramatic tragedy, it is seen in subtler life failures. I discern it in people with a certain moodiness that has stared too often into the pits of the hell without any restraining rails, those who've staggered up the slippery slope only to slide back into the crap again. These people are not just cynics, but failed optimists—the ultra-sensitives who seem a bit like fallen angels. They're especially tuned in to the music of the unconscious. The Sylvia Plaths and James Deans and Montgomery Clifts. They have a certain poignant promise that keeps fragmenting and leaving nothing in the hand except sharp slivers of a broken life. And a certain irony, if they last long enough.

They have the potential—intelligence, sensitivity, and an odd awareness of the unconscious—to find a way into the psyche's mazey labyrinth, and even into the center to kill that collective minotaur enslaving us all. But too often, they instead become imprisoned in the corridors of lost intent, where they are the walking wounded of our society. Worst cases fill psycho wards, detox clinics, alleyways, train and bus stations. They're often the freaky dekes too smart for their own good who prove to the rest that "It just goes to show, Al, brains don't do you much good."

Modern nutrition has put our psyches out of balance and often finally out of commission. Those who have a potential to become especially fine-tuned instead react so strongly to the additives and deletions in modern food that their psyches go completely out of whack. They can't stay in balance anymore. Unbalanced, they lose momentum and fall into dead ends. They don't know a way out anymore.

"What's normal fatigue?—what's normal sorrow?—what's normal drinking? You mean this hysterical laughter doesn't sound happy?—god, I just can't take it any more. Maybe another chocolate bar—Tequila Sunrise—hit—snort—will comfort me. My life is hell. All life is hell, and some people are just faking it."

As with any addiction, they increase the dosage until something gives. It's not just a jump-start, it's jump-living.

Well, I'm not merely a sugar addict. I'm also a coffee addict. A refined pastry flour addict. I crave goo-filled sugar-dusted donuts and coffee, I dote on vanilla ice cream and coffee, I adore German chocolate cake and coffee. Hot coffee, you see, besides giving its own swift kick, melts the sugar into my bloodstream faster.

So what's wrong with that, you say? A bit of sugar makes the medicine of life go down?

Yeah, okay. If you can handle it, then you eat it. I'd rather eat *un-*refined food that has not thrown away as dross its balancing dark side. That rich, nourishing shadowside of food—all those things that can actually decay!—they are worth keeping and admitting into my body. My body isn't built to handle so very refined and civilized food, those lite fakes that are split off from shadow. It goes wacko.

This has happened all my life. How does a sugar addict get started?

For me it began when I was six weeks old. My mother couldn't breast-feed me anymore because of a milk-gland infection, so she switched me onto an addictive substance called formula. It was made of cow's milk and pure golden refined Karo sirup, fed out of a bottle. Doctor's orders, but pure poison to my system. I cried constantly and got extensive eczema. I must have been hell to handle.

But by the time I was a year old, I could recite the Pledge of Allegiance and poetry and whatever else people wanted to pour into me along with the Karo sirup. Somewhere around then, I remember Mom reading to me her college assignment of Chaucer's *Canterbury Tales*. I especially liked the Wife of Bath, whom Mom said was delicate enough to wipe the grease off her lips before drinking so she wouldn't float globules in the communal wine cup. I liked Chaucer for adding that touch, and I felt observant and thoughtful, too.

But I wasn't really thoughtful. I was a Tartar. Always running, yelling, pulling things down, drinking ink, spilling it on my white leather shoes, eating Ex-Lax (chocolate!) out of the bathroom cabinet. Demanding attention, crying hysterically, laughing frantically, drumming the heels of my hightop shoes (stained with blue ink splotches under the white polish) on the floor in a temper tantrum. You name it. Monster, thy name was—*me*! A hyperactive child drunk on sugar.

I even saw myself as a horror. My *me* knew how awful I was. People would stop my mother on the street and say, "Oh what a beautiful child!" And my mother would say every time—this I remember quite well— "Pretty is as pretty does." A remark from a well of bitterness. Pretty as hell. Helen Wheels. And I lived in hell. That's where I learned the existential meaning of no exit. Hell is other people. Hell is oneself.

You think a child freaking in addiction is happy? Maybe intractable, but not happy. I didn't cry to bother others. I did it because even in the midst of laughing, my mood would fracture and shift and suddenly I would be at the other end of the spectrum, raging out of control with some petty issue as the trigger point.

But eventually I settled into a steady enough routine of being horribly unhappy and its variation of being unhappily horrible. My mother really did her best, and I—thank god—didn't have to bring me up. I had my daily routine of cod-liver oil, orange juice, milk, sugar and Post Toasties. Maybe a piece of pie or some cookies—Franticsville! Then my mother would say, "Not too loud, Cookie. Calm down, Sugar." Our culture is full of sugar talk. But nothing else would keep me content.

Well, not content exactly. That's not the right word. More like fixed. It was my daily fix. And I was so smart that I could work around a lot of my addiction handicaps. I didn't have to pay much attention to get the point in school. If I couldn't play well with other children in the neighborhood, so what? I'd get out a book and a package of cookies.

Oddly enough, now that I'm not feeding that sugar addiction, I can hold my attention on something extraordinarily long, maybe because of such long training against the odds.

And my mother was not an outrageously poor nutritionist. After all, she fed me what the doctor ordered. She took me to the pediatrician when we could hardly afford the food he recommended, much less the bills he sent. (His recommended diet of citrus, milk, sugar, and corn, I now know, are among the commonest trouble triggers).

How insidious my sugar addiction was. Every child deserved a lollipop if you didn't cry during your shot. And some of the Christmas cake that Grandma made. I still remember the big slice of chocolate meringue pie from the neighbor downstairs. We addicts endear ourselves to cooks by our appreciation for sweets they make. Just one more piece of pie, cake, fudge? Sure.

Perhaps two in ten are affected this way. In its most extreme form, with blackouts and the whole bit, it can be spotted by a complicated glucose testing—sometimes. But there are also many agonizing stations of the cross along the way before getting the disease nailed down. It's so tricky that many doctors "don't believe in hypoglycemia."

At one time, many doctors also didn't believe in washing their hands before delivering a child. They found it insulting to suggest that their good Victorian suits might harbor germs that caused childbed fever, the leading female death. They ridiculed the Hungarian Dr. Ignaz Semmelweiss, who discovered puerperal fever. They booed the valiant lectures he tried to give, even removed him from supervising his obstetrics clinic in the General Hospital of Vienna when it showed a twelve-fold lowering of the death rate in childbirth. He'd made them look bad.

Those Victorian doctors refused to accept the evidence because their own eyes couldn't see germs, and as Robert Prentky put it in *Creativity and Psychopathology*: "It made little sense to disinfect one's hands when bacteria had not yet been causally related to disease."

Doctors fought Semmelweiss until his mind broke under the strain. Destroyed by the profession that he was trying to enlighten, ostracized and disparaged by his colleagues, he eventually died in a mental hospital.

Yes, doctors know a lot. Except when they know it all.

The best way to discover whether you are an addict or not is to look into your own life patterns. You can tell, if you are honest. It is the only policy that will work here. Your ego can hide an addiction behind a blind spot. But your soul knows. Dreamtime knows.

In addiction, outside measures like how many times you've been arrested for drunk driving or how often you coke up in a month or your score on a hypoglycemia test are just not that reliable. Data often just make statistical gobbledegook. But you are an individual with your own unique variation in the norm, not a generalized statistic. Examine your life carefully, honestly, instead of turning it over to be flayed and dried on some statistical table like a piece of dead meat.

Participate in your own diagnosis and cure. Use preventative nutrition and medicine and meditation rather than the remedial work that tries to repair gross damage after it's done. If we focused more on preventing an illness than repairing it, we'd have more health and fewer lawsuits.

The most socially-sanctioned addiction is the sugar fix. It starts you on the road to harder stuff with sugar suspended in it—alcohol. One of my favorite books on this subject—and there are many good references here—is *Hypoglycemia: The Disease Your Doctor Won't Treat*. In it, Saunders and Ross emphasize how tricky this diagnosis is: "A Los Angeles television news program produced a short segment on hypoglycemia. The problem of obtaining a proper diagnosis was raised. When asked, one of the panelists commented, 'Provided you can get your physician to do the proper testing, the chance of a proper diagnosis is about 5 percent.'"

About half of hypoglycemics transit on into diabetes. I could have been one of them. I remember my long-gone Aunt Sally who kindly gave my brother and me a cigar box full of candy every time we visited her little laundry, inciting with peanut butter logs and licorice and cinnamon hots a bloodsugar rush that plummeted us into quarrels and moody sulks. But in those days, though, we all thought she was just being nice. Not leading us down the little red lane of mean reds toward the full-blown diabetes that she herself died of. I don't want to reach that destination myself.

Borderline hypoglycemics are hard to test. An examination often does not show symptoms to the degree considered necessary for making this diagnosis by many traditional doctors. But of course, they look at the body's symptoms, not the psyche's. Psychic symptoms appear long before the disequilibrium begins to manifest in the harder stuff of flesh.

My own symptoms became more accentuated as I approached puberty. That's a time of great body and emotional stress. And what made it even worse was the fact that now I was old enough to take more control over my diet. During the fifth and sixth grades, I stole money, nickels and dimes from my mother's purse. Money for candy bars. We lived a block from Baylor Drugstore, and I would go over and buy Baby Ruths and Butterfingers. I can still remember the ecstasy of

195

those splintering peanut butter shards around the chewy core of a Butterfinger. Until she caught me at it. Ah yes, but we addicts remember.

If this sounds incredibly silly and overstated, try going without any sugar for a week. You'll discover, first, how much effort it takes just to manage this in our modern society. Second, you'll find out how addicted you really are to sugar. You'll think of every possible excuse to go ahead and eat that candy bar or donut: "It's one little thing" or "Just this once" or "There's nothing else to eat around here" or "I've gotta be polite to the host" or "It's the simplest way to kill this hunger" or "This stupid fad diet is just too puritanical and deprived and uncivilized to maintain." You'll find a thousand rationalizations for tending your innocent little fix.

If you are serious about it though, in order to keep from being driven by creeping hunger into consuming those phoney foods in snack machines and packaged food bins, you'll start carrying snacks nestled in your pockets and purse and briefcase—an orange or apple or banana, a hunk of real bread, some nuts, a small box of raisins. You'll eat it with aplomb at 10:00 break in the office while others choose that elegant-looking, cardboard-tasting Bearclaw laced with monosweet icing. You'll drink herbal tea from your personal box of tea bags and hot water from an electric coil instead of mainlining the murky office coffee. You'll—if pressed—even explain that you're eating real food to keep your blood sugar from rollercoastering up and then plummeting into a nose dive.

The final elegance is wholeness. You can't find it climbing and sliding on the Big Rock Candy Mountain. If you manage to hold out a week, your body will protest mightily for the first few days as it is giving up the addiction. Sugar will try to seduce you, using every wile to make you give up this silly, inconvenient diet. For example, you'll want to ignore the contents labels because reading them shows that sugar is hidden everywhere, often in deceptive names that don't spell out sugar but rather its many chemical variants, usually ending in -ose or -ase. You'll find it in spaghetti sauce and soup and TV dinners and even salad dressing.

And then, if you can make it past the first four days or so, you'll begin to discover how much calmer and saner and more equilibrated you feel. It takes four days generally to break the habit. Your body will tell you clearly when you switch off the false highs and lows. Events and people that formerly drove you up the wall, you will now start to take in stride

And then, why then—wonder of wonders—you can even begin to change your life because of your newfound attitudes and approaches. You'll slowly realize how sugar created in you a subtly draining, psyche-destabilizing addiction. You'll begin to recognize that all our distilled and refined addictors of the last five thousand years—alcohol, tobacco, cocaine, heroin, sugar, refined grain products—haven't been anticipated and prepared for by the slow natural evolution of the body.

The important thing is to eat real food, with emphasis on unrefined grains and vegetables, fish and low-fat meats. I eat all grains but wheat. Many of us, actually, are subtly allergic to wheat. You can feel okay, but a toxin builds up in the cells that demands a constant dilution by water. The result is a bloating that looks like persistent fat. Cutting out the wheat makes such a person look miraculously thinner in four days. I use oat, rice, and other flours instead.

I eat reasonable portions so that I don't need to diet using those fake sweeteners and Lite-benighted products. Walking for an hour three times a week will do more for lowering my cholesterol than stuffing myself with fake dairy products and eggs. The moderate, natural way is better, even though it seems like the long way around to people attracted to those shortcuts of Foney Food, to instant weight loss and cholesterol reduction with no pain or gain. But instead of fixing the real problem—bad health habits—it even worsens with pseudofood.

So to me, all that is symbolized by the red jacket of last night's dream. I lived in the mean reds, in a supercharged, unhappy whirl so full of events that I can't even remember them all very well now. It's been a long time since I've succumbed to daily Cokes and Double Fudge Temptation cake and coconut cream pie.

But hey, do you know what I did yesterday? Why this food mantra? Only just now do I realize it, and put it into context! After lunch yesterday, I roamed the apartment like a restless zombie in my housecoat, saying, "I'm still hungry. I don't know why. I don't know for what."

You know how you crave something that's just the *right* thing? Odds are, you're looking to appease an addiction. I tried oat bread, cheese, and apple juice. No help—it wasn't really hunger. That uncharacteristic (nowadays) gnawing was not appeased. Finally I said blithely to my husband, "Do you have any chocolate?" He buys chocolate for himself and eats it after meals sometimes. He can tolerate it, I can't.

He broke it out and I ate four squares of chocolate—about a fifth of a 100-gram chocolate bar. And I ate it without a qualm. My snickering addiction wouldn't let my blindered ego see what I was doing. It kept my brain from clicking on and saying, "Hey, wake up, dodo! This substance is off limits for you. You know where it leads...."

And hey, the day before my flu began, I also ate an opulent dessert that my friend had ordered prepared specially for us at Mère Catherine. How could I refuse? Oh sure. By saying no thanks.

So the sweets have been sneaking up on me lately. They do it in times of stress that drain the B vitamins. Under the guise of "just a treat once in a while," they jump into my gullet. As Saunders and Ross point out, once you get this sugar disorder under long-term control, it is even possible to cheat once in a while if you stay carefully on a good diet most of the time. But I cheated twice within one week, driven by cravings in an already unbalanced system, and my disequilibrium got so pronounced yesterday that it blindered my ego and snuck some chocolate squares right into my mouth. Oh, addiction is such a canny and relentless slavedriver.

Another factor is that my period is about to start. Right before it begins, like clockwork I get a sugar craving. Often I'll find myself wanting something sweet when my period is just two or three days ahead. In times of body stress, the addiction sneaks up on my ego by carefully lowering awareness so that the craving seems just an ungovernable lusting that is beyond fighting. Addiction is so skilled at doing this. It knows what it wants and tricks the ego into getting it.

Oh well, things aren't so bad this time. I jumped back on the wagon today instead of winding up pulling it. But there was a time when I couldn't stand for someone to bring chocolate into the house. Back in the old days, it would have been gone by morning, whether a 6-ounce chocolate bar or a 3-pound box of chocolates. I was a sneak-eater because it was so embarrassing to explain that however much was left after someone opened a candy box and took a piece or two—why, that was just exactly how much I needed before bedtime.

Alcoholics do this too. Only they get their fix in a more sophisticated form. "Candy is dandy, but liquor is chic-er." To make this rhyme, you need to have grown up in Texas and supposed that chic is pronounced like...you've got it.

Dr. George Watson in *Nutrition and Your Mind* talks about what happens during the breakdown of alcohol. Whiskey does metabolic things that reinforce the addiction: "As you sip it slowly for a few minutes, life, strength, and hope seem to push out the ache, the cold, the despair.... You've been rewarded at a time and in a way that will be long remembered—consciously or unconsciously. And the next time your energy reserves are gone, and you're mentally and physically spent, you'll probably think 'whiskey!' You will also have gained a personal insight into the experience behind the word, which comes from the Gaelic usquebaugh, meaning 'water of life.'

"Water of life it would indeed be if the whole story of alcohol were to end with its nutritional biochemistry, and it was simply another easily utilizable and wholesome source of energy. But it is not. Every drop of alcohol burned in the tissues creates a nutritional demand for carbohydrates and for the many biochemicals that it does not by itself supply, the vitamins and minerals necessary to process it."

Watson also explains a strange but true phenomenon which I can personally attest to—the healthier you are, the less you can tolerate alcohol: "This is why truly healthy individuals cannot tolerate alcohol: Their cellular acetate breakdown is near maximum, and any rapid increase such as will result from a drink of whiskey may lead to headache, sweating, nausea, and possibly vomiting. In short, one's tolerance to alcohol reflects the state of one's nutritional biochemical health. The more one can drink without adverse effect the worse off he is. It is just plain utter biochemical nonsense for people to pride themselves on being able to hold their liquor, for only those in very bad shape can do so."

I notice this same thing occurs with me, but on a less drastic scale, with sweets. The healthier and the more balanced I am, the more I react negatively to a dose of refined sweets. On the other hand, back in the bad old brownout days when I ate sweets indiscriminately, I slowly, almost imperceptibly spiraled into a morass of low energy and morale that concealed the adverse sugar reaction within it.

Some people suppose that this lowered physical and mental well-being is normal. It's all that they have ever experienced.

But some people do know it, and yet even prefer to stay in a psychic low rather than go to the trouble of giving up refined sweets or alcohol. In what sounds almost like a bad joke, Watson tells the story of a young patient who was feeling and looking much better, but decided to stop his healthful diet and vitamin-mineral supplement because he was losing his taste for Scotch. The guy said he preferred the pleasures of drinking to his increased mental and physical well-being.

A rather romantic stance, don't you think? Love that debilitating addiction. My world used to be full of *sturm and drang*. Tempest and impulse. If you find hell romantic, well then I lived in a melodrama as romantic as *Wuthering Heights* or the *Sorrows of Young Werther*.

Such a foolish idiot, that young Werther! Killing himself over a woman who cared not a whit about him. Goethe's novel took Europe by storm. The hero was intriguing to the public: who could imagine such a romantically neurotic idiot! Goethe turned literature in a whole new direction, lit critics say, made neuroticism fashionable. But I wonder if this novel was the bellwether of neuroticism for a more mundane and pragmatic reason. Did you know that great Romantic Age arose at the same time as the use of refined flour and sugar became widespread enough for the majority of society to partake of such delicacies?

Oh yes, I can imagine it: they dueled at dawn. A prolonged, profound and excessive love for Chocolate Viennese Torte was the cause.

Or how about this one? The sun began to set on the British Empire when it was conquered by tea time. Huge cups of tannin and caffeine washed down great gobs of god-awful sweets to the point of instituting itself into a mealtime. No veggies, no protein—just refined carbos and stimulants. Yes, beginning with the widespread assimilation of refined flour and sugar, Britain's sun waned. The Empire was defeated by tea time.

Or this one? China lost its internal balance and turned rigid when it converted to white rice. When was that? Well, Confucius helped popularize white rice. He thought it more civilized. He also sent the Taoists packing and instituted a tradition of hierarchy, hegemony, and polite convention. The rough and ready way of the Tao is not civilized, just real. Its course is not mapped by societal convention. Its voice is not social but personal.

Why does the body go out of kilter this way? Because in the total genetic history of humanity, the use of addictive substances is proportionally a dot in time smaller than the last period at the end of this book. Even five thousand years ago, alcohol or honey or cocaine were very special, festive substances, and their scarcity and ritual ceremony protected us from the worst excesses of these addictors. Now alcohol and sweets are everyday diet. Drugs are sold on the corner and even on the supermarket shelves.

Addictions are woven into our culture. What sort of specialty shops do you see in the mall? Those that serve addictions. They specialize in highly processed starches, sugar, tobacco, coffee, alcohol. I've found no steamed veggie and brown rice franchises. Why? A body doesn't crave health foods addictively. A sudden zucchini craving doesn't force you to spend money for a rush fix in a drive-through window. Health food is merely nourishing, merely desirable if you are merely hungry. But you *crave* candy, pop, ice cream. The big moneymakers are the addiction-triggers. Caffeine. Cigarettes. Candy bars. Soft drinks. The great American fixer-uppers.

Heinous, aren't I. And it gets worse. Do you realize I am undermining all that is sacred, not just for the junk food addict, but also for the sophisticated palate? For example, there's Auntie Mame's Whisky-Soaked Candied Fruit Cake. Julia Child's Brown Eminence Chocolate Cake. Taillevent's Marquise au Chocolat a la Pistache. Harvey's Bristol Cream Sherry and walnuts. Stolichnaya vodka with caviar. It hurts me to write these names, for I know what I've lost.

But I also know what I've gained. Sanity! A comfortable ease that I never found in fake food or alcohol, for all their sweet promises. It's been hard-won. After I realized my problem, I had to start changing my diet. That was very hard indeed. We're talking about years here. But I hung on, making changes here and there, and slowly I got stronger, calmer, more able to see the point and purpose of trying.

Somewhere along in there, I guess, came the moment when that beneficent woman of last night's dream showed up and said I could wear the white coat instead of the mean reds jacket. I got to drop the aggression which actually had been some improvement over the inward-turning blues of a still-earlier depressive phase. She said I could wear her white jacket. It was on the floor, wrinkled and disused. I've got it on now. It sports a button-up front (some acquaintances think I'm incredibly prim about what I eat nowadays), and it has points at the waist—you know, they point to the stomach. Well, I do have points to make about the stomach nowadays. In fact, you're reading them.

Maybe this unknown woman was Mother Nature. An archetype of natural health. Because after all those years of illness and emotional fragility, I found my way. Not just health, but superabundant health. People say I look young for my age, that I have energy and stability and calmness. From inside, I can tell you that I'm satisfied. I'm happy.

I still slip up sometimes, though. Like the chocolate squares. The stress of this flu pushed me imperceptibly over the safety margin without even noticing it. Addictions are that seductive. But I did notice it eventually and moved back on the path again.

Oh yes, I do eat dessert occasionally. But they're mostly homemade and contain fructose, the only sugar that doesn't hit my bloodstream with an immediate roller coaster effect. Maybe I should write a cookbook. I'd throw in some desserts with the sound of instant tradition. How about some of Aunt Katya's Scrumptious Baked Fresh Pear and Oatmeal Crisp Compote? Try Uncle Norm's Demon Delight Ginger Raisin Applesauce Cake. Here's John-Boy's Walnut Pie. See, I'm not just trying to strip away the tradition of good-tasting food. I want to re-embrace an ancient heritage from the days before those Viennese bakers went gaga over the brave new building blocs of chocolate and refined carbos found in powdered sugar and super-refined wheat flour. Let's start a better eating heritage than the present.

By American advertising standards, what a weird life I lead. I stay away from those elaborately promoted artificially-flavored, sweetened, and preservatived items that advertising battens on. I never cash in grocery coupons for over-processed but under-nourishing synthetic foods. Those glossy ads in the magazines for alcohol, smokes, sweet foods, fast foods—they don't touch me.

I eat real food. It comes in vegetable and grain and fruit and nut and fish and meat shapes. Sometimes I feel far off the beaten track of middle America. Yet…there are quite a few of us careful eaters nowadays. We know that the millions of years that produced the human body and psyche didn't put in equipment for running smooth on fake food.

Fake food rings false finally in the body and cheats it—even if your ego goes along with the propaganda of synthetic taste enhancers and eye-fooling teasers, and exclaims, "Great stuff! Delicious! Boy, I love this white three-tiered wedding cake frosted with lots of acridly sweet powdered sugar held together with white artificial lard and weirdly-colored and flavored piped icing roses and swags over the uniform-celled, blindingly white layers of cake with an imperishable consistency of wet plastic sponge. Yum!"

Fake food is a bizarre modern novelty to the older sectors of the global community, and I wish we Americans would clean up our act and put more nutrition into this stuff before we addict the whole world to it. Why not herald more than a quantity approach to the American way of life (1 zillion hamburgers sold)? When do we start to emphasize high quality? We live in a land bountiful enough to boast good health. But we tout and export our fat and salt and refined carbo addictions as surely as the colonial British addicted the Chinese market to opium. For profit. They had to fight the Opium Wars to *stop* consuming the drugs that the British insisted they buy.

Instead of touting "the real thing," let us see these ersatz edibles and drinkables for what they are—fake food that cheats the body and soul. It gives an artificial high—and low. We hook the world on pseudofood and call it exporting the American way of life. As Saunders and Ross say, "Food faddism is indeed a serious problem. But we have to recognize that the guru of food faddism was not Adelle Davis, but Betty Crocker. The true food faddists are not those who eat raw broccoli, wheat germ, and yogurt, but those who start the day on Breakfast Squares, gulp down bottle after bottle of soda pop, and snack on candy and Twinkies."

Later...I'm so tired. I'll go to bed with Corde and cosset my cold. No, it's back to flu now. It didn't help that I stood waiting downtown with two hundred people at 5:30 p.m. for a train that was twenty-two—what!—twenty-two minutes late! Unheard of in Zurich, but it happened today. A switching junction froze at the main station and it had to be thawed out before the train could be routed on toward us. More stress on this flu-ish body. So tonight I drank orange juice and took an extra B vitamin. Tomorrow I'll cook some brown rice.

While riding home on the train today, I read that Corde was wondering if he should really go ahead and write his big exposé on the lead poisoning that has been caused by three industrial centuries. The true extent of this poisoning, he said, is only now becoming apparent with new instruments and procedures. He was worried.

He said, "Biological dysfunctions, especially observable in the most advanced populations, must be considered among the causes of wars and revolutions. Mental disturbances resulting from lead poison are reflected in terrorism, barbarism, crime, cultural degradation. Visible everywhere are the irritability, emotional instability, general restlessness, reduced acuity of the reasoning powers, the difficulty of focusing, etcetera, which the practiced clinician can readily identify."

I was thinking, oh I understand your fervor, Corde, because I sound this way about fake food. Yep, just change one word in his remark, from *lead* poison to *fake-food* poison, and it sounds like me on the deficits of modern nutrition. But it also sounds like a sensational overstatement to most people. Should I even mention it in this book?

And then Corde groaned, "It wouldn't be easy. The public was used to doom warnings; seasoned, hell—it was marinated in them."

But dear Corde, dammit, look here! Corde, why not take up arms? Here's one of the few mass evils that I can correct *by* myself *for* myself *in* myself, using just my own action. I can take up eating well!

It's hard. I have to move in new, uncharted ways…like choosing the more expensive natural orange juice without added sugar over that colored, artificially sweetened and flavored insult to the taste buds called orangeade. Real juice has more vitamins and flavor…and calories. So I have to subtract the calories somewhere else. Drop the Danish. Give it to a friend. Or better yet, an enemy.

I will eat in balance, Corde. If I go wacko one meal, I won't kill myself with remorse and feel so bad that I must comfort myself with a bag of Famous Amos chocolate chip cookies. See, I know all the routines.

Join me. Just get into the boat and steer yourself firmly, purposefully upriver. The landscape will look pretty drab at first. Others will feel that this course you're taking is dreadfully moralistic, monochromatic, monotone, with no middle slack or leeway. But after awhile, the colors brighten up, and your spirit begins to sing upon reaching waters closer to the source.

Ask my husband. Maybe he'll tell you while he's sleeping. Because last night he spoke again. Talking to the ceiling again. He's getting to be a regular dreamtime chatterbox. Last night he said in a clear, loud, good-humored voice: "I'd…say…so!"

I don't know what he meant exactly, but I sense what it portends on the dreamtime front. For him the internal verdict is in. He's decided that analyzing dreams really does work. Because today he said to me— when he was *awake,* after reading that last chapter I'd given him— "Well, it's amazing. I'd say you're doing self-analysis using your dreams."

"That's right. And I think anybody can…."

"Don't say anybody can do it. You've got old dreams in there, dreams going back years."

"Yes. But I think anybody can do it over time, given these techniques. The main thing is the decision to do it. To pay attention to each dream in context with each day, to let it speak to you through the mute pantomime of daily events."

Two weeks ago, when I started writing this log, I thought, Look, don't say it, show it. Correlate the night's dreams with the day's events, so people can see how the fine threads weave together.

I think of an old Chinese saying: *In waking life, we stay in the same place. In dreams, we move ahead.* The truth of dreamtime can move us on past the illusions of alcohol, drugs, empty food. Relinquishing the pseudo highs will clear up the inner vision so one can get high on real spirit.

People don't realize that they eat sweets and drink alcohol and do crack because they are yearn for spirit. They long to get high on god. They hunger to get high enough to glimpse an overview of the divine plan. All they have is artificial spirits...a poor substitute for the *real* real thing.

I must admit that I have used psychedelic drugs in the old days and they have taken me to mysterious places. I consider them nonaddictive and mind-expanding, essentially different from the drug addictors like heroin, cocaine, and crack. Switzerland is the home of LSD, and here I learned much about positive, therapeutic uses of the hallucinogens. I do think that properly used and supervised, they could open consciousness to a wider view for many people. Our laws have overlooked this essential difference between the addictors and hallucinogens. But nevertheless, without therapy, the problem becomes integrating that artificially-induced vision into real life.

So for me, the *real visions* work better. In using that term, I'm following the old Sioux medicine man Lame Deer. He talked about the difference between hallucinogenic visions and what he called *real visions:* "At the time I quit peyote I had found out what a real Sioux vision was like.... The real vision has to come out of your own juices. It is not a dream; it is very real. It hits you sharp and clear like an electric shock.... Peyote is for the poor people. It helps to get them out of their despair, gives them something to grab hold of, but I couldn't stop there, I had to go further. Once you have experienced the real thing you will never be satisfied with anything else. It will be all or nothing for you then."

It is true. Once I tasted the real thing, I couldn't go back. I steered upriver toward the source of spirit.

If you try it, be warned: the switchover time is hard, but eventually you find that the good spirits inside make alcohol seem stuporous, drugs ersatz, and refined sugar monotone in flavor and unsatisfying in its jolt. They give a cheap imitation of the real thing. Experiencing the real thing—your own soul in connection with the Oversoul—you'll know why existing without this inner spirit forces people to look for an artificial solace to fill up the gap. Once you have the real thing, though, you'll understand what you were missing all along. You'll discover you haven't lost anything by dropping your addictions, but rather, gained immensely by heading upriver toward the source.

I really am feeling feverish now, woozy as I imagine heading upriver. Drawing closer to the source, I choke up with wordless emotion, high as any poetry-spouting Irish alcoholic—but transported on inner spirit, not distilled spirits. The same as I did this morning when I found out from my dream that I'll get to wear *for the rest of my life,* instead of that mean reds jacket, this white jacket whose material points at the stomach will remind me of my physical limits. I do need these frequent reminders, because it's easy to lose my way in the stress and strain of everyday living. But I'll get to wear this white jacket until it's time to go home. Home is where I'm heading, upriver to the source. Home is where my heart is already. Home is on up there somewhere with god.

CHAPTER 16

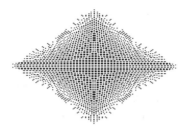

Two Into One

Dream Log—Tuesday, November 22:

Dream: I see her coming along behind. It's not over yet. She looks at the container. It has two of them in there. Side by side.

Dream: My three little babies come in capsules. A woman takes one of them into a room and tells it events. Then she says to me, "Watch this. It's such an amazing baby. It can already talk about whatever I mention to it." This tiny baby is in a tub container about the size of a restaurant packet of jam or coffee creamer. It is talking. I can hear the words clearly. The woman reads the news to the baby, and it answers, repeating and then elaborating on her words.

I go into another room, but somehow I know when the woman flips the tub baby onto the floor—it had been resting on the padded arm of a rocking chair while she rocked and discussed the news with it. At first, the baby continues talking on the floor, and I think it's all right. Then it begins to hemorrhage and bleed inside its tiny container. The container is swelling. I hear it screaming while it is still talking. I come running back in. Scared for my baby.

Oh, no! She tells me it's dead. My baby has died! I mourn it. Then I dream that I look at my watch and decide it's time to get on with doing things—it's 5:44, almost a quarter to 6.

I wake up in the dark feeling sad about this baby, yet somehow not too sad. Maybe by the time I wake, I've already done my mourning. I turn on the light and look at my watch. It's 5:44—almost a quarter to 6. Hey! Just like it said in the dream!

This dovetailed timing reminds me of a gift I've discovered over the past five years. I don't need an alarm clock anymore. I can ask the unconscious to wake me up at a certain time and it does. Always. It makes life pleasanter than using an alarm clock or radio as a exterior alarm. This talent came as I began to work with my dreams about ten years ago. I didn't trust it at first, though. Who wants to miss a vital appointment?

But slowly I began to experiment, daring a bit more and more. I found the key is to be unified inside about the reason for waking at a certain time. If the psyche is split between messages of "I have to" versus "I don't want to" regarding your schedule, it incapacitates the alarm system. I had to sort out my values and priorities. It took years of experimenting and changing my lifestyle. A lot of work, you say, just to avoid using an alarm clock. Personally, you'd rather buy a snooze alarm and hit it a few times until you manage to get up. Much less work, and you don't have to shift your whole life around for it.

Okay. For me, though, this is cheaper and easier in the long run. It means I'm not wasting my psychic energy fighting an inner split each day. It frees my libido for more productive action. And it's more fun.

My husband wasn't willing to trust my internal clock at first. He'd say, "You think you can get us up in time to catch the 7:00 a.m. train?" I'd say, "Yes." And I did.

But one day I found he'd lain awake much of the night worrying that we wouldn't make the 6:30 a.m. train to the Zurich Airport for our flight out. So I thought this issue through again. How could I accommodate to the psyche of another person and still honor my own? That was the problem. I didn't want to make him nervous. To assuage his worry, should I maybe buy a little clock for emergency, crunchy situations?

I finally decided, though, that the only way to keep a psychic gift is to trust it. These gifts are so subtle—they're made of sheer thought, after all, finer than cobwebs—and they are altered and damaged by mistreatment. So I said I didn't want to worry him, but I'd really rather trust my inner clock and let it carry on, if he'd be willing. He was, and it hasn't failed us yet. Now he seems to take it pretty much for granted.

For years I've been performing little experiments with this internal alarm clock. At first I'd ask to get up at 3:30 a.m. in Zurich and phone my son back in the States. I'd waken at 3:30 a.m. every time. Then I began to make variations on my request like this: Rather than waking me up at 3:30 a.m., please wake me up at whatever time is best for calling him. Because sometimes I would phone 3:30 a.m. only to discover that on that particular day, my son hadn't gotten home until perhaps an hour later. So I'd lose a wide-awake hour in the middle of the night trying several times to call him. But by this new, flexible wakeup call, I saved wear and tear.

But it takes a lot of trust in the unconscious. For example, once my inner clock didn't wake me up at all one night when it had been given the variable wakeup-call request. The next day, though, I found out my son hadn't been at home all night, so there really was no point in me waking up to call him. It saved my sleep.

Only once did my unconscious clock pull a fast one on me, and even then I couldn't complain, because it had followed my instructions to the letter. It always does—and that's why the inner clock breaks down if you're split inside over some issue…you break the clock with your mixed message of "I really should wake up at 7:00!" versus "Oh no, I don't want to wake up at 7:00 and face this situation."

On this occasion, I flew back to Zurich after a two-month visit in the States. My husband was still in Austin. I felt a bit lonely coming into the Zurich apartment, wondering whom I could call just to say, "Hey, I'm back!" But I also had jet lag. So I wished for a simple way to touch base with my friends. Oh well, it could wait. I was so tired that I wanted a nap. But first I set my inner alarm to wake me up in time to get to my important appointment in downtown Zurich at 10:15 a.m.

I woke at 9:45. Stared at my watch, unbelieving! What? My inner alarm had never failed me before! What went wrong? It was too late now to catch a train for the appointment—it had left at 9:30. Taxis are almost impossible at such quick notice in my suburban area. But suddenly I thought of calling Liza. She might be home and have enough time to drive me downtown. By car, my appointment would be only ten or twelve minutes away.

I dialed. "Liza? This is Katya."

"No, it's Nicky. Liza is out of town, so Suann and I are housesitting. I didn't know you were back in Zurich already."

"I just got in. But I have a big appointment downtown in thirty minutes! I overslept! Who has a car and enough time to take me in?"

"Why not ask Suann? She's right here."

So Suann agreed readily. I dressed quick as a flash and was waiting on the sidewalk when she picked me up in ten minutes. We had a brief but heartwarming chat enroute, and I walked into my appointment right on the dot. Well, actually one minute late, at 10:16. But the other woman never even noticed, because she was *two* minutes late!

As I waited, I sat feeling presentable, calm, warmed by that conversation in the car, and most of all, I was amazed at the close timing. I thought back to my wake-up-call request. Hadn't I got just what I wanted? One, a quick contact with friends who cared enough to help me out, and two, reaching my appointment on time. Yep, just what I'd requested.

You get what you ask for consciously *and* unconsciously. Truman Capote said getting what you ask for is dangerous. It's too hard for mere ego to spot all the ramifications and then live with them afterward. So I just try to get my conscious and unconscious dancing to the same tune.

But what about this dying tub baby? What does it have to do with my requests? Why am I thinking of answered prayers right now?

Oh, yes. Last night I asked for an easy way to do this dream book while I recuperate from my jaunt into Siberia yesterday. I want to take it easy for a few more days, yet do this book justice. An impossible wish?

No! It's being answered now. I see just how to sleep a lot today, but it means using a chunk of writing that's been tucked away for a book on psyche balancing called *Going Crazy, Going Sane*. I have three literary irons in the fire right now, and occasionally I give each one another twist and hammering, whenever the urge takes me. In fact, maybe these are the three capsule babies in the dream. So I could use a chunk of one—symbolized by that little tub baby. As the dream says, this baby already talks.

But while that woman takes it easy, remember, rocking back and forth, talking with the tub baby about current events—whamp!—it flips off the rocker arm and dies. It hemorrhages to death. Well after all, I can't use the same chunk of writing in two places. So I'll mourn its loss for one book, but shift it on into this one...starting when I waked up at 5:44 a.m. I've synchronized my inner and outer watches. Get ready, get set, get real.

Yes, this tub baby is a natural tie-in. It's on the left and right brain, and that's what you must working in tandem so that your inner alarm clock will ring right. Otherwise your left brain won't agree with what your right brain wants. Yes, here's the place to put this brain child.

As far back as 1955, scientists began to realize that each side of your brain fosters a different behavior pattern. And somehow it is triggered by breathing! Lynn found: "…the two sides of the body are associated with distinct and very different patterns of behavior…diametrically opposed personality types that have a consistent correlation with the congestion-decongestion response in nasal airflow. The switch from one personality type to the other would occur instantaneously. This was also accompanied by an immediate shift in nasal dominance."

What a surprise for science! But the yogis of India knew it long ago. You experience it when you have a cold and one nostril feels like it's clogging up and losing its air channel, forcing your breath to go through the other side. Then after sixty to ninety minutes, it wants to switch back again. That's because the other brain hemisphere wants to come online again, and it provokes a subtle nervous tension till it does.

This hemisphere switching mechanism is explored in an article called "Selective Hemispheric Stimulation by Unilateral Forced Nostril Breathing" in *Human Neurobiology.* Werntz, Bickford and Shannahoff-Khalsa say, "The results indicate that forced nostril breathing through one side can generate a relative increase in the EEG activity of the contralateral hemisphere."

It works by triggering a reflex inside the nose. You can trigger it manually by breathing through just one nostril for awhile in the alternate nostril breathing technique of kundalini yoga. You do it like this: close your left nostril by pressing it flat with your finger. Close your mouth too! Breathe only through your right nostril. It will trigger the brain hemisphere on the *left* side of your body into greater activity—your logical, linear left brain. If you keep breathing—slow, deep—through your right nostril for at least three minutes, your left brain will fire up. You can use this technique before a meeting when you want to be calm, collected, and on top of your data. It's a cheaper, safer way than cocaine to feel clearheaded and in command.

Likewise, you can trigger the other hemisphere to turn you emotional, pattern-sensitive, spontaneous, and intuitive. Years ago I was driving to Texas from California. Over endless desert, while I pondered the relationship with my lover, I began to realize that my left and right brain were at odds. Each hemisphere literally saw the relationship differently. I had a cold and was breathing through only one nostril—the right. It fired up the left side of my brain. I observed my psyche. The left brain was sweeping me with thoughts like, "Be logical. Look at all the data. This relationship hasn't worked and it won't in the future."

But after awhile, that nostril unclogged and the right brain came online. I could literally feel my viewpoint switching over to the right brain's stance: "Oh, but I love the guy! It's all that matters!" Talk about ambivalence! My attitude changed, my priorities, even my body tension, and certainly my decision-making on this foundering relationship. All across the desert I literally saw this flip-flop going on in my attitude at about ninety-minute intervals! What was the final result? Well, I resolved that it was time to get both sides of my brain working together on this subject instead of pitted against each other in a stymied standoff.

Eventually I did leave the relationship. I saw that it was energized by a complex in myself that operated out of a divided mind. But after that, it took about four more years to get my divided mind meshing together on most topics. Doing it has brought my life into more harmony. Now I can generally tell if my mind has a split vote on some emerging issue. I work to resolve it by investigating what each side of my brain has to say on it. Both sides have their truth. Each deserves a hearing. Ultimately, if my views expands enough, the disparity reconciles and resolves into unity.

I lie in bed pondering all this…and hoping this flu is subsiding into a bad cold. Runny nose. A cough that starts up whenever I talk.

I look at my watch and decide to begin calling to cancel appointments for today. Then into the bathroom. As I take off my watch for the shower, it amuses me that, awake, I can't tell exactly what time it is. Under the warm drum of water, I ponder how my waking mind, dressed in its ego, must watch a clock to keep track of the hours and minutes. But my sleeping mind always knows just what time it is. My goal is to meld the two locales of inner and outer into one concerted, harmonious realm where I live my dream and dream my life.

Out of the shower, into fresh pajamas, I eat something. Then I type this entry and throw into it that tiny tub baby on the brain you just read.

Back to bed, to sleep. Going under, I sense that it isn't enough to live in one side of the head. What's necessary is to get both sides working in concerted harmony—as much as possible, that is. Asleep, I…

Dream: Both sides of the factory are working now. Suddenly in the midst of all this productivity, the scene switches to the central boardroom. A feminine podium-shaped creature is lecturing. We see some slides that were taken in China, where they never once saw a manioc root pounder. But now in China, hundreds of thousands of manioc root pounders are being made and shipped to Africa, because that is what the Chinese thinks Africa needs, so the Chinese make them, determined to help out.

But wait! Aren't manioc pounders needed in South America, not Africa? At the realization, everyone in the board room breathes a sigh of relief. So we can still do it better than those isolated Chinese.

I wake up smiling. Yes! If you get both sides of your brain factory working together, you'll ship the right product to the right place. The corpus callosum—that central switchboard—routes messages between the left and right brain. It shouldn't send manioc pounders to Africa when they're really needed in Latin America. If manioc pounders can't be used in Africa, then don't send them there. Otherwise, you'd be a maniac manioc pounder producer. But a split mind may say, "Listen, send me this item that I request but can't really use. Dammit, send me that alcohol—sugar—nicotine—poisonous lover—thrill a minute!"

I suddenly realize that the manioc pounders were shaped like nerve endings. I see. Yeah, ship that stuff to the right place.

For the rest of the day I doze, getting up at lunch to eat some two-alarm chili that my husband's made. It gives my respiratory system the old 1-2, forcing a rush of circulation to loosen up my clogged nasal passages. Thank goodness for him right now. There's all the difference in the world between being sick alone and being sick with someone around who shops and cooks and brings in the daily mail.

Back to bed. To...

Dream: I see the twins plainly. They merge.

That's it? I think, waking up. What twins? Is it the two sides of the brain? Or what? Merge how? Shrug. All this 2-ness right now: the two dreams that began this chapter; the two watches that synchronize dream time with the real time of 5:44 a.m., the two hemispheres of the brain, the two-alarm chili, the two days of flu—so far.

All the 2s. I wonder if some polarity is cooking deep inside to bring a transcendent resolution to this illness. I hope. I wish.

Tomorrow I'll need a second tub baby to throw into the next chapter, so that I can rest easy. Hmm, wonder what it will be?

Good night. Sweet dreams.

CHAPTER 17

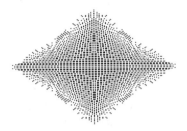

The Colorful Captain

Dream Log—Wednesday, November 23:
I see the captain. I watch him acting one way for awhile. Then he changes his clothing and everything and starts acting a different way for awhile. I watch him acting these two ways in turn.

I wake. The light in the apartment is pearly gray. I go look out the big living room window. It's exactly 7:00 a.m., and people are beginning to move in the snowy street outside. Toboggan caps flash on the youngsters across the way darting into the schoolhouse door.

If this weren't Switzerland, I doubt that we could tolerate living across from a school full of seventh and eighth graders. But in the three years we've lived here, there's never been a problem with vandalism or litter or gangs or loitering, nor even much noise. The chairs and table and stack of firewood sit unmolested on our patio, the flowers are unpicked, untrampled. These handsome creatures fermenting with pubescent hormones act just about like real people, not armed monsters with crack deals, handguns and chains and knives up their sleeves.

They take off on the longest holidays too, these children. That school shuts down for two weeks every so often, for winter skiing or autumn or spring hiking. Quite pagan isn't it, this being so civilized? And get a load of this: it is only a trade school, not a high-toned gymnasium for students preparing to attend a university.

The snow now is just perfect for cross-country skiing. At least six inches sit cubed on the roof of the bird feeder. There's a slight surface crust, just enough to keep the skis from sinking into the powder. It would make that nice crispy whisper near the edge of hearing as the skis bite forward through the silent evergreens.

But I can't go now. Not with this raging flu-cold. Katrine promises to go with me later. I love *longlauf*, as it's called here, this long running.

I return grumpily to bed. Yes, it has degenerated into a nasty cold. Sleep it off. Abruptly now, I recall waking last night with a frantic feeling…turning onto my left side so the mucus could shift and close off the left nostril instead. My right nostril had been closed so long it was making me fidgety. That plugged-up right nostril kept the left brain firing too long, and it wanted to go off-duty. But it couldn't until I turned over and let the other nostril clog up for awhile.

Of course! That's the captain in my dream! The captain in my brain pan. He puts on his cool linear garb and stands watch on the port side for sixty to ninety minutes—and then switches into a warm analog uniform and keeps watch on the starboard side for a similar period.

If one hemisphere is forced to stay on duty—maybe because one nostril is stopped up with a cold—the little captain of my psychic ship starts to complain and stomp on the deck of my brain pan—trying to get my attention and make me do something about this improper ventilation. "Blow your nose, dummy!" the captain yells. "At least turn on your other side!" Normally the switch between the hemispheric watches occurs like clockwork, though, and there's no problem. And by appearing in this dream today, the captain is hereby allowing me to pour in another jar of canned peas while I go back to sleep.

What is this hemispheric switching, exactly? Barbara Lex describes it in *The Spectrum of Ritual: A Biogenetic Approach:* "In most human beings, the left cerebral hemisphere functions in the production of speech, as well as in linear, analytic thought, and also assesses the duration of temporal units, processing information sequentially. In contrast, the specializations of the right hemisphere comprise spatial and tonal perception, recognition of patterns—including those constituting emotion and other states in the internal milieu—and holistic, synthetic thought, but its linguistic capability is limited and the temporal capacity is believed absent. Specific acts involve complementary shifts between the functions of the two hemispheres." She's talking here about the captain in the two different suits, performing two different jobs.

DREAM MAIL

The two hemispheres of the brain allow your mind to enjoy two different ways of knowing the universe: the left brain offers the logical, sequential, cause-and-effect mode (sometimes called *classic*); the right brain offers the holistic, networking, emotion-toned, synchronistic mode (sometimes called *romantic*). Both approaches are equally valid and important, and both have their advantages. But neither one alone offers a whole picture of the world.

This left-right schema holds good for most people. But about 40% of left-handers have some activities in the hemispheres reversed. The same holds true for about 1% of right-handers. Then there are also infrequent other mixtures of activity. So when I say the left and right brain, it doesn't mean literally for *every* person in the world *in all conditions*. Just the vast majority.

You can find out your own arrangement by firing up your hemispheres alternately through closed-nostril breathing as you closely watch your play of thoughts and feelings over time. It is a wild experiment to study your own psyche in motion, with data that you've acquired empirically by observing your own experience in a way that no one else can...from the inside out. It's worth the time and the vaguely silly feeling while you hold your nostril shut.

Watch how the brain takes in data. Notice how the psyche organizes and evaluates it. I go along with Norman Cook, who says in *The Brain Code* that physiologists seldom ask the one question most interesting to psychologists: how does the psyche deal with stimuli *after* it is registered by the brain?

Please imagine that the figure on the opposite page is a little captain who is standing in the book and facing into its pages, just as you are right now. Both of you are looking in the same direction, so that you can see this little captain from behind. Project yourself into the figure to explore how your own psyche operates within the body.

And do remember that this layout holds for the great majority of people. All of us have the same basic equipment, but some of us have it arranged a bit differently betwixt the hemispheres. Also notice that a neural crossover occurs whereby your left brain controls the right side of your body and vice versa. It is signaled by the arrows that crosshatch the neck of the little figure.

As you can see, this captain is very busy. The duty watch on each side of the brain pan has a jam-packed job description.

The Captain

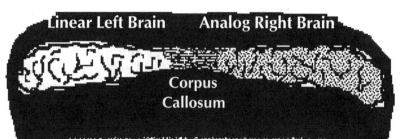

Linear Left Brain   **Analog Right Brain**

Corpus Callosum

The left brain controls the right side	**The right brain controls the left side**
Indirectly links with consciousness	Directly links with consciousness
Times your life relatively/infinitely	Times your life sequentially/finitely
Fluidly relates event, sound, image	Codifies concepts & hierarchies
Conceptualizes almost nonverbally	Conceptualizes verbally
Responds to image & pattern	Responds to verbal elaboration
Sorts according to image relations	Sorts according to abstract concepts
Holistically imagines experience	Logically discriminates discrete details
Networks in spatial ratios	Orders linearly & sequentially
Expresses through archetypal flow	Expresses as solid material reality
Fosters humor and wisdom	Fosters wit & knowledge
Centers in timeless God/Self awareness	Moves in the timeline of ego awareness

...and thus is...

Ultimate meaning & teleos-oriented	Cause & effect-oriented
The source of creative flow	The source of critical analysis
The home of dreams, emotions, ideals	Home of "real world facts" & plans
Untrained in modern academics	Trained in modern academics
Relatively unhonored in modern culture	Relatively enshrined in modern culture
Promoter of family & friend relations, spiritual and ethical values, literature, theater, art, music, dance, holistic medicine, & synchronicity	Promoter of government, law, linear sciences, technology, banks, grocery stores, western medicine, & statistical probability

I'm tired. Grumpy. Back to bed. I dream that...

The captain wears two suits: one is red and the other is a pale violet-blue—or is it indigo? It's sort of the color of faded-out blue jeans with some dull purple in it.

The phone wakes me up. I reach over to get it.

Annie is calling about the Thanksgiving dinner on Friday night—yes, a day later than usual. Each year some Americans here in Zurich get together on the weekend to celebrate Thanksgiving and invite the Swiss to a banquet of food, family and noise. I've volunteered to cook turkey dressing for sixty on Friday, but as I said to my husband this morning, "If I continue feeling this way until Friday—then if I were a guest at the dinner, I wouldn't want to eat any germy dressing that I'd made." So he has agreed to cook it this time—if I'll tell him how.

Each Thanksgiving for the past three years now, I've mixed the ingredients in a 35-liter plastic trash bag. Here's my recipe: Throw into a garbage bag the following ingredients: the cubes from 3 kilos of dense bread, a huge pan of crumbled yellow cornbread, ten big chopped onions, lots of chopped celery leaves, a dozen beaten eggs, a big jar each of thyme, sage, marjoram, rosemary, parsley, some salt and pepper to taste (not too much salt), enough chicken broth to moisten it all thoroughly, and lots of boiled chestnuts. Then tie the bag and turn and toss it all till everything's mixed. Put the stuff into every casserole dish that I have and can borrow, and bake it in relays in a 375° F oven around forty-five minutes till thoroughly brown.

On the phone Annie reports various things that she's been doing to get ready: decorating the tables and the dining room walls and so forth—it sounds like her usual fine job—and she offers to transport the casseroles of dressing by car. Finally we hang up.

Since I'm awake now, I may as well consider the little captain in this last dreamlet. I could see both suits, red and violet-blue. What's this color stuff about? Hmm, red lies at one end of the spectrum going down into the infrared. But blue-violet is at the other end going up into the ultraviolet. Hmm. I think that the captain's fuzzy warm red suit drops into the darkness of feeling, plummeting into the depths of soul, but that other suit is of an odd, cool purpley-blue—it lofts upward to the heady heights of thought. And there's a full spectrum in between.

Hmm, it feels to me like this red suit is suitable to wear when the analog, holistic style in right-brain behavior is dominant. Red is at the end of the spectrum moving into longer and longer waves, into infrared. The right brain is in charge of the left side of the body, which is less controlled and more receptive; yet oddly enough, it is also more artistic, intuitive, unconscious, holistic and lyrical. This left side is often called the feminine side of the body, according to the old-fashioned ideas of gender.

If you want a personal confirmation of this flowing feminine receptivity that exists in the left side of your own body, take a sheet of paper and a pencil and sit down at a table or desk. Hold the pencil in your left hand—if you're righthanded—and close your eyes. Now start drawing random circles on the paper. Then switch into loops, swinging back and forth across the paper, not worrying about the overlapping lines. Just feel the flow. Then finally, allow your pencil point to dance over the paper any way it chooses. Don't worry about margins and neatness. Just notice how it feels. This is not drawing for looks, but rather for feel. For you lefties, do all this in reverse.

Okay. Now compare it with the actions of the other side of your body. Take a second sheet of paper, close your eyes again and do the same thing for several minutes with your opposite hand, making the same circles and loops and then random dancing on the paper. Just notice how it feels.

And hey, if you really *are* going to do this experiment, do it now, before you read an explanation that might preset your results.

Okay, if your own experience goes along with the majority—the righthanders—you'll feel a vaguely uncontrolled wobble in your left hand that soon rolls into a free-flowing lyrical ease which carries your pencil point into expanding arabesques and whirls. It's like freeskating on paper.

However, if you switch hands and make those same movements again with your eyes closed, you'll feel how your right hand has more clarity and control, more fine-muscle coordination and precision. It's like skating those precisely delineated school figures instead of the lyrical freeskating of the left side. (For the left-handed person, all of this is of course reversed—unless you're one of those rare lefties with other brain arrangements.) Experiment with your own breathing and hand coordination, and you'll find out a lot about how your brain is laid out.

The captain of the right brain steers toward the holism of emotion, art, and the relational quality of connection. She emphasizes analog humor, wisdom and creative caring. She doesn't talk so logically or incisively, but instead lets a few wise words and mute action convey her meaning. She offers instinctive truth beyond conscious knowing. She gives us the wordless truth of Maat.

Athletes enter this realm to tap into the flow of good timing. For example, humming a tune at the top of a ski slope helps your right brain come online and click you into spontaneous timing, instead of laboriously trudging through the left brain's careful rules of linear sequencing of "Now slide your right foot forward, then...."

But when the captain changes into that other suit of the indigo-blue linear mode so favored by Western culture, the captain becomes a crisp, clear thinker. He likes to talks in 1-2-3-4 sequencing that logically defines a cause-and-effect chain to reach a goal. His uniform is impressive because it is decorated with rows of sparkle-sharp facts from that Adkins data file and the crime statistics for the last ten years and that 1893 case of Wilson vs. Portland and the projected downturn on the GNP graph for the next quarter—all the battery of specific details that can be filed as collective knowledge. This captain uses the clear, bright, sharp tools of words and quantitative math that Thoth brought into the culture. He verbalizes with exact definitions and number sequences in linear formation.

But words and numbers conceal as much as they reveal, so if you don't like what you see, why then, this captain can contrive to shuffle the words and numbers around so that you misperceived the data. Logic, being linear, oversimplifies the networks of messy connection that continually color beyond the lines of the cultural silhouettes.

By studying this captain and the two alternate dress uniforms (whose accoutrements even include a change of sex) you can visualize that...

•**The Cool Blue Uniform signals the linear logic of the left brain/ right side of the body.** Here you perceive and evaluate patterns that are linear, time-oriented, logical, sequential, verbal, "physical real-world oriented"—more conscious, in everyday terms. This side marshalls data you must consider in order to live in our concrete world. It quantifies the tangible world that is perceived and evaluated by left brain knowing.

•**The Warm Red Uniform signals the analog networking of the right brain/left side of the body.** Here you perceive and evaluate patterns that are holistic, relational, imagistic, timeless, "nonmaterial" and thus more nearly unconscious. It attends to patterns at the more unconscious level, the relationships that simply present themselves in life, whether as family, friends, feelings, sudden creative inspirations, hopes, ideals.

It charts the qualities of networking connection in the intangible world that is perceived and evaluated by the right brain's knowing.

These two modes have symmetry, both physically and functionally. They act different from each other, yet they also mirror each other in a complementary fashion. Here is the 2-in-1 brain. It has the ability to offer a two-part harmony within the unity. Actually, you can't even have harmony without having at least two parts, and you don't get good music if they sing, grumble or hiccup along in two unrelated songs.

Recall that the archetype of the 1 is the beginning and the end, the point before and after all splitting. And 2 is really just the symmetry aspect of the 1. For instance, identical twins show the alternate routes that one specific genetic pattern can take.

Each hemisphere of the brain acts, in many ways, as a self-sufficient, complete brain. It puzzled researchers for a long time. Science started calling the left brain the *major* hemisphere and gave it preferential value, because it handles the tasks that our culture esteems. But finally, scientists realized that the right lobe isn't just an unnecessary duplication of gray matter—god didn't make a dumb mistake by sticking an extra, backup hemisphere inside your skull. If this side were really unused, it would have atrophied and withered away in the course of evolution.

Finally science now admits that the right brain is just as smart and important as the left brain. Each explores an alternate mode of reality. Each uses a different style of taking in and processing data. When they are integrated into one unified vision, they give the person a balanced world view and life path. They steer the soul surely on its life voyage.

This double gateway of the brain is symbolized in society all around us. For example, a culture will set up two poles or pillars or guards or swords or hazing paddles for its hero-seeker-celebrant-initiate to pass through. A passage between the two poles brings us along the central path toward a goal. At the end, you can get married or crowned or awarded the prize. You win acceptance, adulthood, certification—some kind of recognition that you've taken the proper route.

Day & Night

Left & Right Brain

But if you don't know how to tread the honorable path that is balanced between the 2-ness, if unity splits into inimical light and dark visions, then you've lost what the Chinese call "the middle way." The two aspects of vision become disintegrated and split into conflict. In *Number Symbolism,* Abt puts it like this: "Along with the two comes doubt (from the Latin dubious, dual), split, opposites, quarrel…in nearly all cultures and religions of the world two identical demons or divine figures represent the symbolic guardians of the entrance to the Beyond. In order to become conscious of something, we have to discriminate, to "cut apart." This is why a content which appears at the fringe of consciousness is immediately cut apart by the light of discrimination. The two parts then appear as two identical beings."

Often a dream about a dawning realization will show such twins. You saw it in my dream yesterday, when the twins showed up. And today they merge into the two sides of the captain. If we try to keep these twins apart as two separate systems, one worthy, and one unworthy, they act schizophrenic. The left brain doesn't know what the right brain is doing, nor what it needs, so it misfires and sends off maniac manioc pounders to Africa.

But the two sides can merge their different ways of knowing into one unified vision. When a 2-in-1 integration is effected, we go into balance. The internal gyroscope tends to hold us on the proper path through all the difficulties, frailties, stresses, and hard times of life, through all those inevitable limitations that are inherent in being spirit locked into finite matter.

We begin to discover that ego isn't really the captain of the soul. The ship of life is steered by the whole psyche—or it is foundered by the split psyche. As yet, our current culture hasn't begun to tap the depth of wisdom in the night-brain.

I'm tired. It's to bed again, after pouring in these canned pps. about the brain. And so long, Corde. Tonight I'll start another book. Too bad. Corde had to resign his job because he got too carried away with caring and fighting corruption. He couldn't change Chicago for all his caring. Poor ineffectual Corde.

Well, me too. Personally, I care far more than I can change, for I can change only myself, and that only partially and slowly. Maybe a lot of us care far more than we can change. It is oh such a subtle and ubiquitous evil that Corde and I and perhaps you are fighting, this twisted self-saboteur that he calls the schizophrenic tapeworm of society.

Well, at least at the very end, Corde goes out to California's Palomar Observatory with his astronomer wife Minna. As she smalltalks about the birth of stars from gas clouds, radio waves, FU Orionis, Corde remembers: "...the wise Egyptian who had told Cleopatra, 'In Nature's book of infinite secrecy, a little can I read....'"

We still can't read all that much. Oh, we're past the primer stage, maybe even into junior high, we noisy bratty know-it-alls. Corde gets to ride up in the elevator of the observatory to the cage where his wife will spend the chill night with the two-hundred-inch telescope, cataloging the stars.

But the mystery of inner space is certainly as big as all outdoors. And the only way beyond our modern schizophrenic tapeworm society is to learn to integrate our linear and holistic sides into a new and broader perspective, like two eyes starting to focus and work together in shared vision. I hope we outgrow this ungainly adolescence that supposes the conscious ego to be the best judge of reality. Truth goes beyond the ego's limits, and in this vasty deep of inner space, the soul steers by the constellations of higher stars.

CHAPTER 18

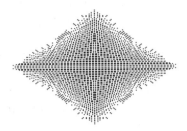

Darkening of the Light
and Vice Versa

Dream Log—Thursday, November 24:
Last night in bed I suddenly recalled a tiny dreamlet still whispering from my afternoon nap. It was a voice of few words:

"After dinner, you're going deeper and deeper."

Oh, great! After dinner, I'm going deeper and deeper where? I was in bed already. Thank goodness. I felt lousy. And that I Ching hexagram I'd gotten just before climbing into bed didn't help. It predicted that my feeling the next day would be an unchanging *Darkening of the Light.* So I thought, Tomorrow I'm heading into the deep, dark what?

Feeling ill but restless, I pulled the top book off the stack from the exchange library. *Wax Apple* by Tucker Coe. Its cover had a rather sardonic collage of a big bright apple made into a male face with eyebrows, nose, mouth, chin. A big bite was taken out over the left eyebrow. A mystery. Okay, I felt ready for some light entertainment.

I started reading and met Mitch, an ex-cop fired from the NYPD for neglect of duty. But what troubled Mitch more than losing his job was feeling guilty "...over the death of his partner and friend, shot dead as a result of his failure." Oh. So that's why Mitch has retired into a grim and remorseful world of his own.

In the next few pages Mitch gets hired by a psychiatrist to register in a halfway house as a "wax apple," a fake patient in a barrel of mental misfits. This odd tactic will allow him to detect which patient is sabotaging the halfway house. Hey man, somebody is setting booby traps in the booby hatch.

Ooh. I see this novel is taking a big exploratory step into a split psyche. No wonder my dreamlet said I was going deeper after dinner. No wonder tomorrow's hexagram will be *Darkening of the Light*. I see that I'm still not off the hook on the split-brain topic.

No sooner does Mitch enter the halfway house than he gets caught in a booby trap. Doesn't that suggest that Mitch is really a booby, too? How come? What's the evidence? Well, he's been building a wall around his house for over a year now. "This may seem like slow progress, but to me at times it seems far too fast, because I can see that a day will come when the wall will be finished, and what will I think about then?"

Uh-huh. His left and right brain are slugging it out over guilt, I see. Our hero has entered the halfway house for a good reason. He fits there.

Why do I think so? Well, building a wall is the drastic retreat of people more wounded and less gifted than our old friend Corde. Not everybody can be a modern paladin like Corde with friends in high places. Not everybody can ruefully resign from his deanship to write blistering *Harper's* articles and go gallivanting off to Palomar with his sexy scientist wife.

I understand you, Mitch. I've been there too. Build a wall around yourself. Maybe it will keep out the ugly cruel world. Maybe not.

Mitch is not happy that his wife Kate and an old friend Marty have pulled him off that endless wall to work on the halfway house case. Mitch distrusted them: "I looked at her with mistrust. She can't help wanting to push me back among the living, and I have to be always on my guard against her....urging some new job on me, Marty out of old friendship and the mistaken idea that I really did want to work, Kate in hopes that some job like this would so distract my mind that a magical cure would take place and all painful paralyzing memories would disappear forever from my brain."

Yes. Relatives do unrealistic things like that...hope. Hey, maybe this novel *Wax Apple* will let me give you some specific examples of a split mind in action. I didn't want to use examples from my own clients much, and certainly not without their permission. Do you suppose that the *Wax Apple* is stepping up now to offer an example? Thanks, Mitch.

I consider. Yeah, Mitch looks pretty depressed to me. He's building an outer brick wall that parallels his own inner wall. Depression. That's one way of experiencing Hexagram 36, *Darkening of the Light*. Generally it brings some kind of trial that is hard but necessary, a tough passage that is rewarding finally.

Once I got a forecast of *Darkening of the Light* when it turned out that I would read difficult matter on black holes all the next day. Once it presaged mental gestation on an idea that I couldn't birth yet. And some years ago, it literally occurred on a solar eclipse. Once it came with jet lag after a bad flight, so that I slept in all day. You can glimpse Variations hang around this central core of *Darkening of the Light*. It carries overtones of darkness, depression, oppression. Always the challenge is to use *Darkening of the Light* well. Find gold in the shit.

So tomorrow sounds hard. Oh well, I know just where a tub baby lies that can fit into this chapter and make things a bit easier for me. Especially since I need to venture out into the workaday world tomorrow, although I still feel weak and shaky. My limbs have that trembly newborn feeling. But I must go into downtown Zurich today.

So I put down the *Wax Apple* and turn off the light. Better store up some extra ZZZs for tomorrow. This flu-into-cold is easing, but I don't want a relapse and hang-on cough like Davis got from overextending himself. I sleep and dream that...

> A man is checking the lives of his daughters—each is worse off than the last. He calls them his shields. I feel sad and perplexed as I accompany him on his route.

Morning. I wake up feeling sad. This guy in my dream, I'm feeling sad for him. The ego *me* is walking alongside this despairing animus figure... who also recalls Mitch behind his wall. All the Mitches.

This dream man is checking the lives of his pitiful daughters. Each one is worse off than the last. It's like a fairy tale, isn't it—this image of him walking down an endless row of daughters, each one more tattered and ugly and disheveled and hopeless.

He calls them his shields. Ah, here's the crux! All those daughters, those pitiful creations of his being—they keep his failures at a remove from himself. They reinforce the feeling sorry for himself, yet they shield him from facing and making necessary changes in himself. It's the immobilizing main trap of black depression: "Life is awful—it isn't worth going on—it can't get better—I hate myself—no point in living—they're better off without me—I'm a total fuckup."

I pick up the *Wax Apple* and consider Mitch. Yes, here's the whiff of depression, all right: "Sometimes I wish I had the courage to leave entirely. Kate would be a thousand times better off without me, and God knows so would Bill. What does a fifteen-year-old boy need with a father who

226

just broods in the house all the time? It would lighten both their lives if I were simply to pull up stakes and go away…but I just can't. I'm afraid to go, and that's the truth. If I didn't have Kate, and Bill, and the house, and my wall, if I didn't have these threads of my cocoon to enclose me, I doubt I would allow me to go on living." Yep. That's a Mitch for you. I recall all the Mitches I have known—and been.

Did you ever try to cheer up a depressive? Ha! Don't bother. They already know all the words. And they don't work. A depressive already has spent a lot of time shouting "Cheer up!" down into the endless sucking vacuum that gobbles up his energy. A Mitch throws in daughter after daughter, those hopeful creations of his psyche, and each one offered up is a little less appeasing to the ravenous monster of depression.

As the psyche grows weaker, the daughter creations grow uglier, and the monster grows hungrier. It's a gruesome ritual. The Mitch finally says, "Depression, I've thrown you the best of myself, all those darling daughters who were my creative hopes, who acted as my weakening shields against this black hole. All that's left is making a busywork wall. But even it won't block the sucking vacuum of despair. Must I throw in my own body too?"

Oh sure, Mitch feels sooo bad. But surprise! Depression isn't really caused by wounded feeling in the right brain. It is caused by wounded thinking in the left brain.

Yes! In depression, the real trouble rests over there in the left brain, in the thinking function. Some trauma has marred Mitch's logical processing on a specific issue. For example, remember Mitch's statement that he was building a wall to keep from thinking? It's quite revealing, actually. He wants to stay completely away from thinking—no high-detail job to distract him, please—although he does allow himself the no-brain work whereby he can *feel* up a storm, indulge in a regular whirling cyclone of emotional dark connection. Why? Because unconsciously Mitch *wants* to stay locked in that relentless repetition of miserable feelings of self-pity and sorrow. It distracts him from the real issue, which is a basic error in his thinking.

With depression, a deep psychic wound throbs in the left brain. Some simple, logical, unacceptable fact is hidden and crusted-over in there, festering. The ego is trying to hide that wound from the outside world, even from its own conscious attention.

Meanwhile, across the corpus callosum on the other side, that loyal partner called the right brain is busily acting like an decoy bird trying to lure attention away from logic to itself. It goes into a song and dance of emotional symptoms. It is loyally trying to distract the ego's attention away from the traumatized left brain with its nasty hidden wound. The feeling function works to keeps things focused on itself by chirping out all kinds of woe-is-me noises and morbid attention-getters that declaim its sorrowful symptoms of failed relationships, despair, and so forth—trying to entice everybody's attention away from the real issue.

Don't be deceived. It's a noble sacrifice on the part of the right brain, but don't be misled. That moaning and fluttering you hear is just an anxious brain-mate desperate to lead you away from its deeply traumatized logical partner over there on the left-brain side, which is immobilized with the wound of some nasty fact it doesn't want to accept.

What happens if you're fooled? What if you buy into supposing that feeling is the cause of the problem? Then the mate has enticed you away by fluttering and trailing its fake broken wing and trilling its throb of despair. You go leaping after it while offering ineffectual first aid, saying nice words like "Cheer up" and "You haven't really got it so bad" and "Things will look brighter tomorrow" and "Here's a nice bracelet to plait"… and you never even notice that it is drawing you away from the nitty-gritty sliver of some sharp logical fact that is so deeply embedded and so festered-over that it cannot be recognized. Feeling's hoopla is luring you away from the logical fact-wound. So what is Mitch's wound in logic? Some simple truth relating to his partner. Not a feeling issue, a fact. Perhaps it's just human limits—people die, people make mistakes, etcetera.

My husband comes in and says that today he'll buy the ingredients for the dressing. And he'll cook it tomorrow. Davis is in charge of buying wine; Alton, of buying the turkeys and farming them out to local ovens for baking. Every family will bring a potluck dish to fill out the menu—yams, cranberry sauce, fruit salad, and at least fifty other items, for they'll be seventy people or so, it now seems, at Thanksgiving dinner this year.

Capable Annie is taking charge of the biggest load: organizing the eating arrangements—the tables and chairs, decorations, plates, napkins, glasses, forks, knives, spoons. I couldn't afford to get sick this week if it weren't for her. But as it is, I even decide to go downtown for an appointment of sandplay, which is a therapy technique I'm learning about.

And then I'll return home, throw in a third and final tub baby and go back to bed for a long sleep.

Tub Baby 3: Okay, what does your brain do? It takes in stimuli through your eyes, ears, nose, taste, skin…and from inside you too for that matter. It even registers your dreams and fantasies. That's data too.

The psyche takes all this data and goes to work on it. Using two different styles on the same data, it first perceives the information and then makes decisions on it. And through the corpus callosum, the captain can repeatedly switch from the indigo logical suit into the red analog suit, or vice versa, emphasizing one style or the other as needed.

The way it happens is this. The captain divides the brain into left/right complements—as linear and analog modes of data processing. It's sort of like splitting twenty-four hours into day and night. You can subdivide them again into four segments of about six hours each—as morning and afternoon—and before midnight and after midnight. By the same token, you can split the logical and analog modes each in twain. This makes the four functions of sensing and thinking on the logical side, and intuiting and feeling on the holistic side.

The two brain hemispheres are of course not really partitioned into four neat walnut-like lobes with Sensing and Thinking on the left and Intuiting and Feeling on the right. Instead, this chart merely represents the linear and analog modes subdivided into four functions of psyche. It shows the 4-in-1 unity that orients the psyche in life. Remember that the archetype of the number 4 gives balanced orienteering to stabilize one's world view—as in a compass with its four directions, or the four years that are traditionally needed for a college diploma, or the four seasons that make up the year, or the four moon phases that make up a month.

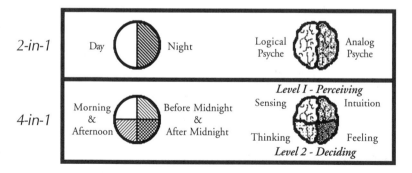

Note: the lobes are not really a brain (nor walnut kernels) but a metaphorical image of the psyche's data processing.

What are these four functions? The vertical cut is familiar enough. It shows the left and right hemispheres that divide logic from holism, or the cool blue-violet suit from the warm red suit. But the horizontal cut splits all the processing into two levels. At the first stage, Level 1, the psyche takes in data—either as linear details on the left side or as holistic networking on the right side. So this upper level is basically data intake. It takes in data by two kinds of perceiving—Sensing (logical and liner) and Intuiting (analog and holistic).

But it is at the second stage, Level 2, where your psyche makes decisions. It takes the data from Level 1 and evaluates it to form judgements about your own life circumstances. It uses two kinds of judgement—Thinking (which is logical and liner) and Feeling (which is analog and holistic).

Now the weird, wonderful thing is that you gets to mix-and-match between the two levels, since all data is processed in both modes on each level. At first, this may sound confusing—hmm, wow, two hemispheres working on two levels for any given problem? So which of the four messages do I accept? Do I blend them all into a unified approach, do I veto some as not relevant, do I even bury an occasional message in the unconscious because I don't like what it says?

Sure. That buried message is what's driving old Mitch into his depression. He has a buried message on the logical side of his mind. He doesn't want to accept his partner's death in the linear limits of ordinary time and space, in the real-world, material domain that is the left brain's bailiwick. You can suspect hidden damage to logic whenever a depression keeps cycling instead of thought being able to find its linear release in a product or goal. All the four major psychoses—mania, schizophrenia, obsessive-compulsion, and depression—can be seen in this way, as decoy-tactics in one of the four functions of the mind. The book *Going Crazy, Going Sane* considers these four kinds of buried wounds.

But buried wounds don't heal. They generate the living dead that walk around in the landscape of the psyche. The badly buried not-at-rest have inspired mythology about vampires, zombies, and ghouls. They inspire suspense stories and horror movies. Oh, they exist all right, these terrors, but they're in the interior landscape and projected onto outer reality. They're conjured up by complexes. This buried tension rises into figures that haunt the landscape of Transylvania or Maine or Haiti, just as Mitch's dead partner won't quit spooking his memory. Psychic energy can even constellate the "magic" of synchronous events that reiterate an issue convulsively in self-similar patterns on scales big and small—as patterned chaos, in short. By learning to understand how his own feeling is decoying him away from facing an issue on the logical, linear side, Mitch could get a handle on himself.

I go downstairs and hang wet clothes in the basement. Back upstairs creakily from hanging up clothes, I'm going to—

Uh oh, disaster. Double disaster for me—inner and outer. I'll tell you the outer part first, where I do battle with the world, and then move to the inner part, where I do it with myself.

I just got a phone call from Davis. It's about the Thanksgiving dinner. He says that Alton hasn't bothered to go looking for turkeys until this morning and there are no more turkeys left in the stores. Probably the Americans have snapped them up to bake today, Thursday. So Alton bought chickens instead. Annoyed, Davis says he wants to eat *turkey* on Thanksgiving, so he's phoned around and finally found a supply of turkeys. Now, unable to dissuade Alton himself, he wants me to talk Alton into returning those chickens and buying turkeys instead.

What to do? I'm quite angry too that Alton has neglected to secure the turkeys earlier, but I also feel that it's just too late and too much trouble to switch now. After all, it's late in Thursday afternoon and I don't feel enough energy to talk Alton out of anything. I still feel drained. So I tell Davis that if he can persuade Alton by himself, go right ahead, but I'm not geared to ramrod the switch myself.

Finally, he agrees to accept the chickens and do nothing. But then Davis rather meanly remarks that he has finally taken out the old ballot box from nearly three years ago and counted the votes that people cast for Alton and me when we first came into this post. The balloted votes were never even counted at that time because people suddenly decided to elect both of us instead of just one.

I say to Davis "So? You counted the old ballots? Well, who won?"

"Now I can't tell you that, Katya. It wouldn't be fair."

"Oh?" Okay, I admit I was irritable, and I raised my voice at him in a way I seldom do: "So it's fair for you to know, and to announce that you know, but not for me to know?"

"I can tell you it was close. You came within two votes of each other."

I am annoyed by the turn that this conversation is taking. "Davis, why are you doing this? Why are you saying you know who won, but

I can't? Why are you teasing me this way?" I realize suddenly that maybe he's even trying to zing me for not fighting his turkey battle.

Is he hinting that I lost the election and took office only because people at the last minute chose both Alton and me? Or is he just getting in a devious lick because I won't back his turkey switch? Or is it something else? What's this power play about secret knowledge he won't divulge? What's the point, anyway? Why do I even care? Davis won't tell me more, just hints and preens, so after a sharp remark, I hang up the phone. Puzzled at my anger. Wondering what to do about it.

At 6:05 p.m. the lights abruptly go out. All the lights. All over this side of the lakeshore. Also my computer and the electric range and the dishwasher. Fortunately I'd just saved on the computer, so I don't lose much text at all. A couple of sentences.

But the electricity doesn't come back on. This is almost unheard of! We live in techno-proud Switzerland. It has fail-safe devices on everything, even potato peelers. My husband and I light candles. We talk awhile. Then I call a friend—the phone is still working—and we make arrangements for transporting the dressing by car tomorrow evening.

When I hang up. My husband, after a tiring day, has already gone to bed early. I'm restless. I feel abandoned by my sleeping husband, the electricity, the stormy weather. I'm plunging into the dark, all right.

Why not plunge into more of it then with Mitch? I take the *Wax Apple* into the living room and read about Mitch's depression by the light of ten candles and a reflecting mirror. It's an ingenious arrangement, but not all that effective. How did Abraham Lincoln ever manage? It's barely possible for me to read.

I think of my *Darkening of the Light* hexagram. Yep, it's here, all right. This has been a day of reading about, hearing about, writing about darkness in various forms. The lights out. This aggravation I feel over those missed turkeys. Davis's nasty teasing about the vote count.

I decide that I'm hungry and go to the refrigerator. You know what? The light bulb shuts off in the refrigerator when the electricity goes out. I can't see what's inside, and besides the electric range is off too, so I can't cook anything I might find there.

Another phone call and I talk awhile. Alton's wife has called to notify me that he's bought chickens instead of turkeys. "Yes, I know." The jerk—he can't even tell me himself—he volunteers his wife to take the flak.

The lights come back on! Okay! I'll finish this chapter quickly. But first, maybe I'll just get something from the kitchen to eat. I'm hungry.

So I open the refrigerator. What do I spy? *A chocolate bar!* Lindt, 100 grams of dark squares filled with a lighter runny chocolate. My whole body goes—zong! on point—but I'm not realizing this consciously. My mind just says chummily, Oh hey there, Katya, you deserve a treat. It's been such a dark day and night full of depression and lights going out and rising anger. Now, dear little Katya doll, you don't want to take time to cook anything this late. You want to sit right down at the computer and finish up that chapter. So just grab this handy chocolate bar, carry it back to the desk with you, and you can efficiently eat it right at the computer as you do your work.

Ho ho ho. How convenient. How full of sugar and caffeine and seductive artificial endorphins that my brain can't tell from its own, so that chocolate's promise to lift me out of a dumpy mood is fulfilled—right before it plunges me back down far, far deeper. So I ate it all, whee and whomp!

Well…that's what happened last night. I can't believe it even as I write it. I almost *didn't* write it, I'm so embarrassed after telling you a few chapters back how bad sweets and caffeine are for me, especially on a body so stressed out with flu. Perhaps the reason I *am* telling you this is so you'll see my limits. Wow, I did go deeper and deeper.

I did eat that chocolate. Delicious. For five minutes. And within two hours my animus had become that sad dream man looking at his daughters, inspecting them one after another, each worse off than the last. And why did my animus turn so sad? Because I couldn't write anything. Oh, I tried, of course, but it just got more labored and artificial and strained and patched over, the harder I worked. I worked a long time. All night. I was so keyed up by sugar and caffeine and endorphins in the chocolate bar and my annoyance that I couldn't even sleep.

So I stayed up all night and tried to finish this chapter. Version after version limped by, all labored and crappy. Strange! When it had gone so easily before. Each time I inspected another daughter…I mean draft…it seemed worse than the previous one. I went deeper and deeper.

All because I decided to treat myself to the quick lift of a candy bar. Yeah. I went wacko for about twenty-four hours. I'm not habituated to sugar and caffeine and artificial endorphin rushes anymore. Used to be, though. I thought this terrible feeling was normal. Used to be I ran—sort of—on coffee and sugar and so forth.

But nowadays if a waitress brings me caffeinated coffee instead of decaffeinated, it takes only couple of sips before I start reacting to it.

My nerves start trilling in my flesh; they expect better treatment nowadays. They're not used to getting beaten up anymore.

Finally my husband woke up around 6:00 a.m.—Friday morning— to find me still at the computer, still in the dark about how to handle this damnable chapter.

"You're still up? I thought you were going to take care of yourself till you got your strength back. And we have that Thanksgiving dinner to attend tonight. Can you make it?"

"I was. I know. I will," I said bitterly. I was totally out of whack, inside and out. Oh, I could still walk, talk, make noises like a human, but my inner harmony was gone. It was the old familiar feeling that I had all the time back in those sugar-fix days—but back then I lived with the horribly accrued consequences of it piling up year after year.

For just a single day, though, I could pass it off as delayed flu symptoms. Tiredness. Woolly-headedness. Grouchiness. If I wasn't tracking so good at the Thanksgiving dinner, well, no doubt people would overlook it, consider it just flu aftereffects and remember the *me* they know instead. Meanwhile I can get back in touch with my calm, stable self in a day or two.

Because I felt truly fragmented. So much so that I couldn't even write about it at the time—well, I tried, but all those old versions had to be scrapped. Each was worse than the last. Poor daughters.

Since I couldn't write, I decided to go take a sandplay lesson. Whacked out as I felt, it might even teach me something about my weird situation.

When I came into her office, my teacher exclaimed, "Are you okay?"

"Why? Don't I look okay?"

"Well—" she said tactfully, "—rather exhausted."

"I am." And since it was so obvious anyway, I told her about the candy bar and what it had entrained. "I'm bushed," I finished up.

We went into the sandtray room and she gave me a nice low, comfortable chair to work in instead of the high stool that I normally perch on over the sandtray.

The way you do sandplay is to let your hands go where they will, do what they will with the sand and the hundreds of tiny figures and furniture and trees and rocks and castles that are lined up on shelves beside the sandtray. You mold the sand however you want it. You choose any figures that strike your fancy and put them into any settings that suit you on the sand.

All this is not consciously planned. You do it by impulse, "at random." Ha ha. The scene metamorphoses gradually into a little story that all unawares will recount your inner condition and conflicts. I mean mine.

Sandplay put my inner life out there on the landscape so I could see it.

After a bit I found myself pulling together this melange. Can you tell what it's about? I couldn't myself, for awhile. But when I got through assembling it, I began to realize.

I started telling my teacher that the little white elephant is magical, with a mandala on its back...and abruptly I *felt* the mandala as a symbol of my struggling for psychic order, trying to pull myself into a balanced harmony. This little elephant is trying to get to the top of the hill, I said, to complete the task. It is small but it's adequate for the job. When it gets up there, the rabbit will make beautiful music on the concert piano under the evergreen tree.

Look. A fish is buried in the sand hill. Its sacrifice will fertilize everything, I said. And this wise old man who is wearing the dhoti waits in the background; he will help me if I just give him enough time.

The main trouble, though, is that big hairy spider on the left—made of crepey rubber—which my fingers kept covering and uncovering as I talked. It was my problem with addiction, see, this big hairy black network of false friends like sugar and chocolate and coffee, those clutching substances that my system overreacts to and sends me reeling out of kilter.

Now you may think this reaction sounds impossibly overstated. All I did was eat a big chocolate bar. Uh-huh. The trouble is, it knocked me for a loop. It's not a matter of morals or nicety or propriety so that I can tut-tut, "Oh, too bad I broke my resolve."

It's simpler and deeper than that. I know the road up the Big Rock Candy Mountain, how it begins and how it ends. And I don't want to walk off that cliff again.

I said to the sandplay therapist, "When I got off the train at the station today, I looked around and the very air held a dissonant quality. I used to feel it as a child. People were walking around, buildings were there, but nothing connected somehow. Nothing related to anything else or to me. It was a sensation I used to have continually."

As I looked at that spider, I knew it was the key. Somewhere back in there, the benign archetype of analog connection had turned into Spider Woman. I was experiencing the normally nurturing holistic domain as an ensnaring force that held me captive in a web and drained me of energy.

Complexes are webs. They are networks of energy in the analog brain. They make up connective patterns that resonate and cling together without logic, only by association. The webby structure around eating, eliminating, and reproducing make for oral, anal, or sexual complexes. Sorrowful young Werther groaned it this way under the pen of Goethe: " Surrounded by the heavens and the earth and the powerful web they weave between them, I reel with dread. I can see nothing but an eternally devouring, eternally regurgitating monster." In that remark we can see the sandtray spider, its web of endless cycle without point or meaning spinning the whole world's pain.

But Weltschmerz or world pain really comes from this getting trapped in cycling. Eugene d'Aquili studied Weltschmerz in various patients and found that a huge and numbing despair is projected on the universe. It is grander than mere personal depression. It is depression on the cosmic scale: "The entire Universe is perceived as negative.... A person feels sadness, futility and a sense of man's incredible insignificance in the Universe, the pain of the world and the suffering of the human condition. In *Weltschmerz* the whole Universe is one vast pointless, purposeless machine."

I would call it the seventh chakra experience of perceiving the vastness of god—but negatively. But D'Aquili also worked with people who experienced god positively. Those people said things like "I think the world is good. I'm no longer afraid to die."

Yet there is a third state, far more spectacular, that combines the negative and positive poles into unity. D'Aquili calls it Absolute Unitary Being: "Time stands still…. A person sees only the totality of a given situation or psychological reality. There is a sense of absolute and complete unity—of self, of cosmos…. Those with a religious background think it's a direct experience of God…. But everyone who goes through this is absolutely certain that the transcendent, absolute realm of things does exist."

I have been in this place. In the negative vision first, then years later in the positive, and finally in the unity. And I've thought about it long afterward, for it isn't to be pondered at the time, only experienced. It is above everything I have ever known. Superb sex pales in comparison, addictions are unsatisfying surrogates, the tenderest human love is less than enough because it is merely human. This unity embraces the biggest and the tiniest, and it holds us all as one.

Sometimes I've tried to verbalize it. Mostly I cannot. But this spider seems to me a symbol of the analog function of number weaving its endless recycling Weltschmerz, that helpless world pain. In this same despair Chronos in his black robe cuts down lives with his scythe.

The sandplay teacher started talking with me about how I'd felt at the Stadelhofen train station, of the associations that go with feeling psychically drained and dismembered. Spiders suck your juice out and eat you up. A spider's got you in its power, trapping and disjointing you in its malign web. No exit. Existential angst. It had been triggered by flu stress, by unresolved anger, by the unexpected dark hours without electricity, by sitting irritably trying to read instead of going with the dark flow—all those things and more triggered me into eating that candy. And I flipped out. The candy bar was not the cause, but the last straw. It tipped the balance that sent me plunging deeper and deeper.

Remember? One side of me tricked the other, so that my left brain didn't notice the booby trap my right brain was setting up. That flimflam drained my psyche and set up physical flak that wobbled me even more.

Yep, that's what addictions do. I talked to my husband about it. He said, "I'd never believe this, not just from a lousy chocolate bar. If I didn't know you, I'd just think you were acting odd."

I don't mind acting odd. What I mind is being at odds. And then overcompensating for it. Often the addict who slips off the wagon does a *mea culpa* shtick, seeking forgiveness from the outside since she can't forgive herself. Well, I forgive myself. I know my right brain fooled my left brain into the slip. It didn't let my logic think about the limits that I face regarding chocolate and sugar. It didn't want me to be logical. Instead it hypnotized my attention with a rosy glow that let me slide my hand right into that refrigerator for the chocolate bar. I went into a trance, addiction-provoked, so I wouldn't be conscious of what I was doing. It was the old analog, association-oriented right brain getting its way by slipping logic out of gear and just running on immediate impulse.

Left-brain logic would have told me that the temporary lift caused by the chocolate bar was only going to plunge me deeper afterward, just like yesterday's dream promised. But I'm most vulnerable exactly when I'm already feeling down or ill. Addiction doesn't play fair; it robs my body of yet more vitamins and energy reserve. Its shortcuts turn out to be dead ends.

I went to the Thanksgiving dinner but left early, with my husband staying on. People were bemused at my uncharacteristic behavior but supportive nevertheless. Thank goodness for the goodness of people. As I moved around the big dining room, I had one response to the observations that I seemed tired, jittery, had just ruined somebody's involved story by fidgeting: "I'll be better soon." I spent most of my time fooling around in the near-empty kitchen because my nerves couldn't take the noise and commotion of the huge dining room. Davis said at one point, "You're not yourself tonight, Katya"—little did he know.

I thought of all those years I'd lived in a nervous anxiety continually, not knowing what caused it or how to stop it. I thought of the decades of frayed nerves and flayed self-worth and betrayed friendships.

No, it isn't silly or funny, that big chocolate bar.

I thought of how my first husband said when I was eighteen—yes, I married that young, it was my way of escaping home—he said, "When I think about you, I think of yellow and purple. Beautiful contrasts barely holding together. You're like that sometimes, but it's just too fragile, it breaks apart too easily."

I didn't answer. I knew he was right about the fragility part, this man whom I loved and yet couldn't get right for. I didn't know how to become myself. I could do it only for me, and only later. Too late for him.

It's taken me so many years to become myself. And he is long dead. But I think of him, and of that remark. And he was right, I was too fragile. A question: How can the peace that passeth understanding hinge on avoiding candy bars and Cokes and coffee and Baskin-Robbins ice cream? It's too absurd, ignominious, incongruous, ridiculous.

Well, it's taken me the whole next *two* days, Saturday and Sunday, to rest up and write this down. So I've spent four days on this chapter, all told. I'll tell you what I've dreamed in the last hours of sleep-wake haze. Three different times I woke with vague dream images of group activity going on, of many people doing things, busy at various events.

The first time, my immediate reaction was annoyance. I wanted a big juicy technicolor dream, not some social fuzz. I wrote in my log, "I don't want to dream about social units, people like bees or something."

The second dream was puzzling. It was about the same people doing the same things again, but somehow now with a realization that the social units don't have to be driven by empty rules.

It reminded me of something I read in the *Wax Apple*. I consumed that whole *Wax Apple* in bed during the last two days and I found it rather indigestible. At the end, yes, Mitch does discover who done it at the halfway house, but he never gets any better himself. He goes back to building his wall in utter solitude, for even his wife and son have left him now on an extended holiday that just might last forever. With a broken right arm, he works himself into utter exhaustion building that wall. (Note: right side of the body/left brain. His logic-side is hurt. These are the unconscious clues that the author and life itself hand us.) Mitch lays brick after brick left-handed, building that wall to keep from thinking, hoping in the final line he's tired enough that, "I'd sleep without dreams tonight."

Poor Mitch, afraid of his dreams. Poor Mitch with that bite out of the left side of his apple brain, as it's so aptly pictured on the cover. His depression is hiding a deep wound in his logical side. It knows a bitter truth about human limitations that his conscious mind can't face. Now Mitch is hiding from the truth by working himself into a dreamless exhaustion. Now he's constructed a solid wall inside too.

So my second dream reminds me of Mitch saying there's no point in trying to explain to the authorities what's going on at the halfway house. He used to be a cop himself, and he knows cops don't listen to reason or explanation. They fit you into legal categories with word formulas and lock you away.

Mitch even goes on to say that everything he and the doctor have done to uncover the crime could be construed as illegal and accessory to a murder: "'That's what the law is all about,' I told him. 'Getting the infinite variety of which human beings are capable broken down into a finite number of lowest common denominators. No defendant in the history of man ever recognized himself in court.'" So my second dream was about reversing this hopeless injustice that Mitch sees with a new society that does not break individuals with roles and rules.

But now this third dream, the one I woke up joyfully to this morning, was of a happy, busy society, active and various. They were individuals working within the whole, yet still themselves.

Perhaps I'm getting back in balance now. Remember the hive-like quality of that first dream? Societies can fit people into categories like that, reduce them to the lowest common denominator of the good, the bad, and the ugly. Collective rules lock people into a bee hive rigidity.

Then the second dream. The sense that people don't have to operate in that way. Societies don't have to be so rigid.

Then the third dream. A dream where people are truly individual, yet truly productive in the collective society too. What a lovely thought. Shocking. But somehow I think it might be possible.

Well, for instance—what if we all listened to our own dreams? People did it a long time ago, back before human consciousness developed so much. What if listening to our dreams and applying their messages would weave us into a busy, harmonious collection of individuals? Each going by one's own individual instinct trigger that, taken together, weave the bigger design within apparent chaos. Still fallible, of course, but with a touch of the divine guidance that bees allow themselves in their lower collective without question. Maybe we are far enough along now that we can even allow ourselves to partake of that old way again. Maybe we can regain guidance from instinct, but at the individual level this time. Unique for each, guiding each, helping each for all.

I think of that symbol on the dollar bill. That triangle-sided pyramid with the divine eye shining out of its peak. What if we let ourselves be guided by god moving within our individual dreams? What if we looked inside for our morality instead of outside to the collective dogmas taken on faith from somebody else's conviction, from legalities that dare us to see just how far we can stretch them and how much we can get away with?

Someone said to me today— "Do you know what the eleventh commandment is? Thou shalt not get caught." Yes, it's the motto of our outer-directed society. Could a Tao-directed society be possible, balancing the analog and linear forces to bring a united analinear way?

Such a way of living would offer us diversity in a community not directed primarily by a supreme court or dictator or horrific bloodthirsty spiritual leader. I am reminded of V.S. Naipaul's account of the holy hanging ayatollah in *Among the Believers: an Islamic Journey.* In god's name, he terrorized a society by banning alcohol and playing cards and high heels and cosmetics and free speech and press. Hey! No belief is plausible if it cannot withstand the onslaught of free choice.

Yes, I too find that alcohol puts me out of touch with the god within. But I don't force my own psychic setup on you under the guise of holy dogma. I only tell you what happens to my addiction-prone body when I use alcohol, and further suggest that you look empirically at what happens to you.

But Naipaul talks of people in Iran being beaten for eating in the daytime during Ramadan, the holy fasting month. Of a man being sentenced to death for a two-month love affair. Of people's eyes being gouged out and teeth extracted, of "…men shown before they were killed, and then shown dead, naked, on the sliding mortuary slabs."

And what is the role of women in such a society? A society that sees only the male-image god-father and not the mother? Woman's role is to go silent and veiled and banned from business and education and the public media, becoming truly the repressed feminine. But the devalued feminine is unconsciously portrayed in the fantastical art sold by the pavement peddlers in this desert country: "They offered blown-up color photographs of Swiss lakes and German forests; they offered dream landscapes of rivers and trees. They also offered paintings of children and beautiful women. But the women were weeping, and the children were weeping. Big, gelatinous tears, lovingly rendered, ran half-way down the cheeks."

In the Iranian mindset they were weeping tears for the sake of tears because "Those tears are *beautiful.*" Beautiful? Well, sorrow needs tears if nothing else can ease it.

But I want to get to the top of that hill in the sandtray where the evergreen tree of life grows, where my rabbit plays concerts on the grand piano. This rabbit. I have discovered it is the ancient symbol of synchronicity, of events that are not chance or accident, but move together with the sure-footed hop of analog connection.

The rabbit woman in Egyptian mythology was a divine figure who led humans into relationship with the unconscious. Even today the rabbit's foot symbolizes good luck.

Yes, that's what I want: I want my rabbit at the piano to play me back into the majestic major and minor harmonies. I *don't* want that hairy big black spider to get me. That nasty old complex snares me sometimes into imagining that I'm giving myself a treat with a candy bar. Hah!—it's more like a Halloween trick or treat with a psychic razor blades in it. So I'm swearing off. Again.

Bad as any alcoholic climbing back on the wagon, aren't I? Listen, I empathize with the addicts, the addictions. They fill up the empty space inside with ersatz hope. But I know too that the way to fill my empty space is with god, to find god in the all-connective pattern of my dreams and the synchronicities of life.

So this has been a Darkening of the Light, and then eventually its reversal, a Lightening of the Dark. I did go deeper and deeper into the dark, just like my dream promised. Four days of it, in fact, jumping through Ring 2's squares full of sharp limits.

But I found a rather quick way through this time. I'll lose my way again, no doubt. But I'm getting a little wiser over the years. Shortcuts to a phoney lift of spirits don't snare me quite so easily. My inner guide knows the territory now, reminds me to take the longcut and enjoy it, whispers that how you travel makes the whole trip worthwhile in life. I'll meet my guide again tonight when my dreams lighten up the dark of my sleep and carry me toward harmony.

This afternoon I napped and had only a fleeting dream impression: I kept going over this chapter and moving sentences around, smoothing things out. When I awoke, I thought, odd, because I've finished that chapter already.

But then I went back to look at it again, and my dream was right. The pages were still rough with awkward joinings—I've somehow lost Sunday's hexagrams during this haze—so I spent this afternoon sloughing away rough spots and rearranging sentences. Now it's finally winding down. How much more work this chapter has been than most! Oh well, that's how it is whenever things go out of balance. Everything is more work.

But I'm letting the way find me again. If my dream says to repair this chapter instead of resting now, who am I to argue? I can see, actually, that it's right. Today I feel happy with the rich abundance and shock of a rainbow appearing after the storm. I feel renewed after the flu and after that sugar bust. Mostly I'm happy, though, because I finally feel whole and receptive to the unconscious again, instead of lost in it. What a relief!

CHAPTER 19

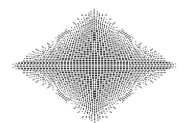

3D Heart

Dream Log—Monday, November 28:

Dream: A man and a woman. Each is collecting and carrying 3D images. They put the images in an art gallery. The woman is dressed in a neat silk uniform. Tailored, button-down-the-front jacket with a Chinese collar. Slim trousers. She puts a bunch of dots in order to make an image. Each art piece she picks up is an image sculpture, each is hand-molded, not made from molds.

I waken as my husband gets up. Almost 7:00 a.m. I lie in bed a bit longer, liking this dream, trying to see if I can remember any more by staying in exactly the same position and letting it drift back.

No, not really. The man and woman seem to be carrying 3D images, sort of like holograms, and they're setting them in order to display them in a sort of gallery. Wait—I also remember that each one has a different way of going about it. Somehow I identify with the woman. It's a peaceful dream, an aesthetic dream. It is calming after the disorder of the last few days. I'm glad.

Today begins a new week. I hope it's not just more lying in bed with flu-cold. I have clients, a lecture series to attend this week, appointments of all sorts to make up from the cancellations of last week. I'm glad this dream seems so active and creative in its tone.

As I think about it, maybe the last chapter has completed another ring of the dream circus. That first movement, in Ring 1, was nine chapters long—**3 x 3**. The **3** transcends polarity; thus, the **9** triply so. That ring held ego death and meeting the divine.

Then came the intermission of Chapter 10 before Ring 2 lolluped up in eight chapters—**2 x 2 x 2**, or polarity cubed. Apt enough, since it showcased material limits. And yes, it feels like the action in Ring 2 is now over. There's a new calm and ease. So maybe I don't need an intermission. Instead I'll just move on into the last ring. Ring 3, I recall, is full of Stuff. I wonder what stuff?

I sit down to breakfast, all showered and dressed, as my husband returns from his morning stroll to the Munz Cafe. He says he just finished reading yesterday's chapter over there and "found it fascinating, as usual." Well, he's a fond audience. "It's interesting to me," he says, "that you generated all that from a one-line dream."

His remark brings me to tell him (and you too), "Oh, I don't think I generated it from one line. It was already there. I just pulled it up into consciousness." The network of associations exists for each of us. We live in it daily. Attending our dreams just makes the network resonate more loudly, amplifies it enough so that we can hear its tenor. Mostly we drift along unconscious of this connectivity in our lives.

Today's dream…is it about collecting dream images and looking at them as holographic art? This guy may be my animus, helping to put them on display in the art gallery of my memories. The dream woman—who is partly me, partly a collective woman—walks along in her Chinese silk suit, turning a bunch of shimmering dots into an image. It reminds me of the quantum particles in earlier chapters. Also of pontillism and Seurat, but with a vital difference: this art is more like sculpture because these are 3D images she's holding.

Each piece is a sculpture, each is hand-done, not made from molds. Well, a dream is custom-made by the psyche. It is not an assembly-line product. It doesn't come out of a mold. Instead it is shaped uniquely. Picking it up to study reveals something to the *me*. A series of such images carries my soul through the gallery of events.

Now I know why this dream is so calming, so peaceful. It allows me to distance myself from the emotion of an event enough to study it. Art de-emphasizes the personal level enough so that we can see the form that the greater whole is taking. For example, we don't know Virginia personally when we go to see *Who's Afraid of Virginia Woolf?* We just watch. We don't go up onstage to stop the fight or egg on Virginia or her husband George. We can sit back and identify with all the parts at various times. We can see the whole process in action, in a way that we never do when we're caught in the longterm run of our own archetypal plays.

You know, when I got fascinated by that chocolate bar hologram, enthralled by it, I could have beaten myself over the head with that giant, monstrous, fascinating Lindt bar, absolutely overwhelmed by it until I was a gooey, sodden, possessed mess, a failure lying at the bottom of that chocolate bar sculpture dramatically backlit by the *Darkening of the Light* hexagram, worshipping such power and defeated by it: "I'm a failure, so why resist? I give up. I resign from hope. Or caring. Or life. Whatever." Insert your addiction and the defeat of choice.

Or I could step back and say, "What the hell is this? Oh, I see. The chocolate bar complex. Look at the way it controls me until I step back and possess it instead." So I pick up the dots of connective events and turn them into a piece of holographic art, a dynamic sculpture. It is intricate yet ultimately finite. It doesn't really deserve the obsession that it's demanding of me. Good art, yes, but I've seen better. Interesting and clever, ingenious in its own way, yes. But this fearfully intricate little piece should stay in its space, limited by truth: "I can't fool my body and psyche with trick food, not really." This attitude allows the sculpture to shrink back to its proper niche in the gallery.

Sure, it is a dramatically seductive hologram for me—I admit that. It makes a statement. But I want to move on past this theatrical hairy black spider chocolate bar sculpture. There's more to the art of life.

Oh. It's time for my seminar. While I'm gone, consider the last dream you had. Turn it like an art object and look for ways to access its holographic meaning. Note any special figures or colors or angles of intent that show its import.

Well. I'm back. Guess what that two hours was about? Creativity. People discussed painting and writing and dance, but I sat there and thought, "Today's dream said events are the true art form."

Of course, in the old days, dreams were revered. A dream could even energize a whole society with its power because we weren't all that conscious and individual. Egos weren't developed to such a fever pitch. Nowadays, we blot out dream memory and message by ignoring it, demeaning it, drowning it out with wakeup news. We never talk about it and allow no time for reverie. If only we realized what a great treasure dreams are. The Chinese used to revere their dreams, saying we move ahead only while asleep. Hmm. I wonder what that huge sleeping giant of China is learning right now. I think I can see it rousing.

Most old cultures suggest that some universal transcendent state exists behind the ordinary visible world. Plato called it the Ideal forms,

Jung the archetypes, Sheldrake the morphogenetic fields, Popper the World 3 of objective knowledge. Other people have drawn their boundaries a bit differently here or there. But Leibniz in the 17th century called it the perennial philosophy, and indeed it does seem perennial. Basically it goes like this: everything is interconnected and has a transcendent meaning.

This is what dreaming taps into. I think the way it works is this. Dreams show qualitative meaning in the holistic world of patternings. A cueing image comes into your brain as a dream during sleep, which can then be accessed by the ego when you're awake. This image is part of the stimulus-response mechanism built into the brain over aeons, which at a simple level, for example, lets the wolf and bear know when to put on especially heavy woolly coats for a hard winter coming.

In terms of evolution, we actually have three brains in layers.

1. The Reptile Brain—stream of movement—body-oriented—holds instinctive stimulus/response repertories such as a lizard turning sideways & displaying its dewlap as a threat.
2. The Old Mammal Brain—stream of feeling—limbic centers for feelings like rage & pleasure & balancing systems for desires like sex & thirst.
3. The New Mammal Brain—stream of thought—the convoluted gray matter allowing complex cognition & fine perception.

The Triune Brain

3. New Mammal Brain
Frontal Lobe
2. Old Mammal Brain
Parietal Lobe
1. Reptile Brain

3. Stream of Thought
2. Stream of Feeling
1. Stream of Movement

These brain layers work together. For example, Konner said "intimate connections between the frontal lobes and the limbic system" allow "foresight and concern for the consequences and meaning of events." D'Aquili said altered states of consciousness come from "a finely tuned interplay between the limbic system and the inferior parietal lobe of the right brain, which…have unusually rich limbic connections."

But for our purposes here, the physiology is not so important as the effect of dreaming. Dreaming is an altered state. It is not just sleeping; it is sleeping with activity. This activity goes on not in the material plane that the body is used to inhabiting as a construct of 3D matter trudging along the arrow of 1D time. Instead this dream activity goes on in the mind, which is formed in the brain along the ribboning tape called RNA. This RNA contains a string of data along a 1D line of space. So in the dream state, the mind moves in 1D space through 3D time—past, present, and future, while in the waking state, the body moves in 3D space through 1D time.

Asleep, the curbless dreamways of time are open. But space, now experienced as one-dimensional, provides an effective barrier to the conscious movement of your matter. The sleeping person does not move purposefully in space, but rather in time. In dreams, one can zoom back and get an overview of one's whole past—as I did standing at that dream window with my dog Happy. Or a dream can give a quick forecast of the internal weather coming up, like: "After dinner you're going deeper and deeper." Or it can even offer a whole lifetime-forecasting dream, which indeed most of us actually do have stored way back in our earliest memories, and we just don't notice it.

It is a complex activity that delivers a dream. Hobson and McCarley have called the brain a dream state generator. Generating a dream involves the cooperation of every part of the triune brain, from brain stem on up through forebrain. The limbic system sandwiched in the middle has an especially important role. It is sometimes called the pontine brain or bridge brain, and its little group of organs liaison your dream from bottom to top. It connects with the two hemispheres of the New Brain uptop, but in a more primitive, instinctual way—at a much deeper resonance than does that fibrous mass of the corpus callosum. The limbic system can deliver messages straight to the right brain without the intermediary of the corpus callosum, which is a good thing, because that big c-c bundle of fibers would just route the dream data also to the left brain for logical processing.

But the canny dream generator knows that to deliver its message with visceral punch, it must avoid the left brain's ego's judgments during the dreaming process itself. So what happens when you wake up and your ego comes online? "That dream doesn't make sense! Forget it."

A dream image can instinctively cue us with a "felt sense" only because it is allowed to go through the right brain without the analytical hairsplitting that is so characteristic of left brain consciousness. This image makes a communication link from brain stem to limbic system to right brain that bypasses the switching center of the corpus callosum. It offers us a cueing by the image *before* the message gets routed into the left brain's logical cause-and-effect, verbal-style analysis. In "Senses of Reality in Science and Religion: A Neuroepistemological Perspective" Eugene d'Aquili says, "Thus the right hemisphere can produce a rush of emotion and communicate a powerful sense of the validity of a gestalt perception without the gestalt itself being broken down via a left-hemispheric analytic process.... Obviously the ability of the right hemisphere to generate such powerful emotions must depend on connections between that hemisphere and the limbic system."

Thus I think the dream image and its symbolic message arise from a deeply planted individual-specific instinct trigger, or I-SIT, for short. This built-in mechanism can cue you to take appropriate instinctive action in your life. It has been developing finesse and power over the aeons. It speaks to you on a personalized basis, every night. For example, in this dream log, you can see my dreams cueing me nightly to help keep me going properly on my daily path—*if* I'll attend their emotional content and meaning, not just scan their hard data with cause-and effect rationality. Logic scoffs at all those weird dream details that seem so silly, like the hieroglyphic pants on a Chinese man or a witchy woman who turns into steaks that cook themselves.

Dreams don't *make* me go properly; they only offer a guide. I may ignore that guide. Why? Because the waking brain can split in its intentions through the corpus callosum in a way that the dreaming mind's deeper connections do not. I *do* have free will; I always have choice. But the more conscious I am, the more choices I have. Then I can even consciously recognize and willingly choose my guide.

Over the years I've collected many examples of this cueing attribute of dreams. A night's dream series, no matter how silly and pointless-seeming, can show the proper attitude to carry into the upcoming day—if it is amplified in a way that reveals the message. Dreams try to stimulate an affect, an emotional tone, an attitude that brings out the appropriate response for your upcoming events. For example, the dream that said, "After dinner you're going deeper and deeper" was warning me to expect a falling emotional barometer, a storm, and not be too frightened to lose sight of the calmer long range forecast.

Who knows—maybe life gave me that chocolate bar so I could *show* you a psyche divided and struggling, not just talk about it. I certainly didn't enjoy it, but maybe it was an important circus act in that ring of limits. And the dream of walking with a sad man who found each daughter worse than the last? It forecast my all-night battle to finish a chapter, and scrapping each effort. It was a one-night microcosm of Mitch's journey on the depressive treadmill to oblivion. My animus, the active male energy in me, experienced this failure. He was stymied and saddened as he found each daughter worse than the one before.

Well, by now I know that my ego will trip, but when it falls, dream time can help me stand up again and walk on. It helps me find some way to turn my experiences into meaning. Dreams—these emotion-resonant images—trigger messages now as I stroll back through my lifelong image gallery. The sad man checking his daughters...how poignant an art piece. That sorrow of fragmented creation.

But dreams are not always just personal. They also have a collective function. Tribal societies have spokesmen who dream or interpret for the collective. Joseph in the *Bible* said the pharaoh's dream was a warning of seven years of plenty and seven years of drought; it forecast the collective need. Eskimos often had a "dreamer" to dream where the hunters should travel to find a seal or walrus to keep the group alive. American Indian tribes had tribal dreamers and interpreters in their medicine men. In fact, one Indian chief of the 19th century said that his people didn't have big dreams any more after the white man came, only little dreams, and he conjectured that white men had taken over the big dreaming. Martin Luther King tapped into the collective level of dreaming for a race with his stirring speech, "I have a Dream."

Ancient societies used to accept this dream life as worthy of attention by a shaman or chief or pharaoh. But nowadays, no one is singled out as tribal dreamer. Yet we can still dream for the collective. As we move into a global tribe, perhaps it will become more evident in the culture. I see traces of it in various places.

We must learn how to be individual and yet also part of the collective. I think it is the task of the next two thousand years, the age of Aquarius.

Our test is to balance the individual with the collective, the unique with the traditional, the flash of holistic insight with the constructs of linear science, even metaphysics with physics. All this and more is symbolized by the paired planets of Uranus and Saturn in the sign of Aquarius. Hopefully, this polarity will not just play against itself, but rise to a unified transcendent third position.

Can the human ego rise above left and right brain to an overview including both? I hope so. We've made a lot of progress in the ego state already. Once our rulers were considered gods. They eventually became human. It became the duty of a king or queen or emperor to portray an ego on display for the collective to admire and honor and identify with, as embodying the grandest in themselves. Kings and queens helped us understand and internalize the ego model. They acted as the central focus in an undifferentiated kingdom—they symbolized its point of honor, pride, gratification—much as the individual ego nowadays acts as the central focus point in an unconscious psyche. These rulers revered by society have helped us learn how to have egos and to value this center of self-esteem and control. It is a job that Elizabeth II still takes seriously and does well. But most people nowadays have a unique ego identity as one's castlekeep, and makes it as honorable or unworthy a domain as the ruling ego dictates.

As king and queen were the ego model for society, so gurus and sages and saints were the model for connection with unseen wisdom. A guru tapped into deep mystery for devotees who gathered at his feet. Gurus acted as the spot of awareness for the less developed throng of followers who did not know how to reach such a state of grace.

But I think we all can be gurus. With dreams, each of us can tap into this wisdom daily for ourselves. The dream network is already fine-tuned to each individual's need and stage of development. Your dreams will accept you wherever you start, and work with your consciousness…if you let it. You can ignore your dream messages and life's synchronicities and other cues coming from the unconscious borders of "reality." But if you override the analog truth of your right brain with left brain rationality too long, then you move out of psychic balance and lose harmony in your days.

A book flipped open today in my hands by accident. The passage it revealed is rather long, but it holds in capsule this issue of learning from image clues. It comes from Jung, about a patient of his, a young woman whom he found to be "…psychologically inaccessible:

"The difficulty lay in the fact that she always knew better about everything. Her excellent education had provided her with a weapon ideally suited to this purpose, namely a highly polished Cartesian rationalism with an impeccably 'geometrical' idea of reality. After several fruitless attempts to sweeten her rationalism with a somewhat more human understanding, I had to confine myself to the hope that something unexpected and irrational would turn up, something that would burst the intellectual retort into which she had sealed herself. Well, I was sitting opposite her one day, with my back to the window, listening to her flow of rhetoric. She had an impressive dream the night before, in which someone had given her a golden scarab—a costly piece of jewellry. While she was still telling me this dream, I heard something behind me gently tapping on the window. I turned round and saw that it was a fairly large flying insect that was knocking against he window-pane from outside in the obvious effort to get into the dark room. This seemed to me very strange. I opened the window immediately and caught the insect in the air as it flew in. It was a scarabaeid beetle, or common rose-chafer (*Cetonia aurata*), whose gold-green colour most nearly resembles that of a golden scarab. I handed the beetle to my patient with the words, 'Here is your scarab.' This experience punctured the desired hole in her rationalism and broke the ice of her intellectual resistance. The treatment could now be continued with satisfactory results."

Amusing, don't you think? That scarab flew right out of her dream and in through the window, and at just the right moment. Events continually fly out of our dreams and into our lives, if we but look for them. They form a collection of images in your life's art gallery. These dreams occur in sleep, sure, but they're not just head trips. In a larger sense, they come from your heart. In fact you might call them—are you ready for this?—objets d'heart.

CHAPTER 20

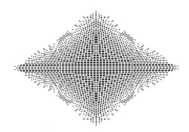

Do-It-Yourself Wiring

Dream Log—Tuesday, November 29:

Dream: I am drawing a picture of the brain on my computer. It is lying on its right hemisphere. I decide to lift out the right-brain section of fibrous connections in the corpus callosum. I go around it with my lasso tool to excise it and replace it for the owner. I plan to replace it with connections more modern and updated. But every time I try to put in the new fibers and improve things for the owner, I destroy the connections. The owner has to reach over to the keyboard and do it. Each owner has to attach the new connections personally.

Okay, this is *not* a hamburger, but a brain on its side. It's in for repairs. And that lassoed object is *not* a meat patty about to enter a double-meat burger. Instead, it's new improved right brain connections ready to replace the old.

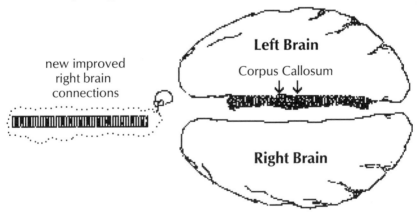

new improved
right brain
connections

Left Brain

Corpus Callosum

Right Brain

Leave it to dreams to express the inexpressible. For the first time since this book started, I tell my husband about my dream before I've even written about it. And he laughs too. It's funny, this notion of lassoing the brain connections to replace them.

I chuckle even as I'm drawing the cartoon because it's so inadequate to reveal what happened in the dream. But it's true that I can't rope in a new mindset for somebody, using my own version of improved right brain connections. Each owner has to reach over and do it personally. Each owner has to hit the keyboard and lasso and drag it in for oneself.

This reminds me of a talk I had on the phone with a client Sunday. She phoned to make an appointment for today. She said, "During this last vacation, I've had so much time to think about my dreams. I believe I'm beginning to understand them better. I'll show you."

"That sounds good to me. Do it. And I won't say much in the way of interpretation, but let you do it. I've been feeling lately that you're really sensing the messages of your dreams. And they've been changing character because of it. Even if you don't understand much about a dream, the attention that you give it creates change."

"But I see a lot more now, after this vacation. It's all this unaccustomed time I've had to spend on them. Normally I don't see all this, but now I can tell it's really there. It' has a lot to say about me. To me."

I'm glad she had this time to spend on her dreams…gladder still that she took the time to do it. A dream yields up its richest meaning to the owner. I learned this quite dramatically many years ago on a week-long dream quest with a small group. It was in true wilderness; we didn't see an outsider for six days. The leader was a woman who was a brilliant dream interpreter. She knew symbolism inside out and had an excellent intuitive feel for dream amplification and for its overall structure too. I saw her interpret dreams for various people so sensitively that the result was amazing.

But there was one woman—I will call her Connie—who immediately set up an obscure competitive game to put down the leader…who responded by refusing to notice it. Consciously. Yet her determinedly oblivious good cheer became its own signal that Connie was getting to her.

The game was played like this. Each morning in our camp we would get up, sit around the fire as the first order of the day, and tell our dreams and interpret them. And each morning Connie would hand over her night's dreams to our leader like a stack of unread mail to be deciphered. The leader, whom I will call Swifty, would immediately spew forth a slew of sharp, concise dream interpretations that always seemed right on, considering what I'd observed about Connie's life. But Connie never responded with any recognition. In effect, she never owned her dreams. The were just odd phenomena in the night, unaccountable, as the flocks of ducks passing overhead or the discovery that her new boots didn't fit or the sharp change in the weather.

Connie was saying nonverbally, "No matter how great you think you are at this, Swifty, it's just water rolling off my back. I'm a duck and I can duck anything. You think you're smart? You're not smart enough to trap me into owning my dreams. I'll never look at my dreams and see myself, no matter how hard you work at it. Fuck you."

Meanwhile Swifty was saying nonverbally, "Look, Connie, I can see right through you. You want to con me. You say you came along on this trip to learn about dreams, but actually, you're resisting it mightily. Admit it. Admit how smart I am to see right through you. All this shows up in your dreams. They show you're a con artist." Because the dreams kept saying in one form or another that Connie's life was in a turmoil from cheating, withholding, conning, being so tricky that she finally tricked herself. No wonder Connie didn't want to pay attention. Her ego floated above her turbulent unconscious, as impervious as a sleeping duck in a storm.

The pace of the game accelerated. Each morning, Connie presented more and more dreams. Four, five, seven. Swifty would spew out the interpretations like a Madame Oracle machine fed with coins.

Finally, the last day Connie came to the morning campfire with nine long, intricate dreams. How could she even recall it all, I wondered? She'd managed to turn the dreams themselves into a weapon against Swifty. By producing such an extravagant quantity of dreams, she was deriding Swifty's skill while at the same time she was taking up most of the time around the campfire. She served up to Swifty an incredible psychic banquet...vomited up. Again Swifty read the mess of symbols for interpretations. Again Connie didn't hear. It didn't seem to register.

Over the last several days I'd been thinking, "This isn't working at all. Swifty is not involving Connie in *working* with her dreams, in caring for them, in caring about them, these dream children of her psyche. Connie just turns them over to the babysitter and never comes back for them."

Finally on this last morning, after another session of futile dream regurgitation and poking through the ingredients for meanings that didn't connect, Connie suddenly rose from the fire, cursing and yelling in a huge temper tantrum! Shouting that she'd been rooked on this dream trip, that it had done her no good, that Swifty was a charlatan and liar, that she'd never recommend anyone taking this dream quest because it was worthless. She stomped off, packed her things in a huff, and walked away down the dirt road…after switching from her new hiking boots into old tennis shoes, I noticed. Ah yes, the comfortable old shoes do call us, don't they? All the old stances of the body and psyche. Even when they are worn out and don't offer much protection for the trek coming up.

Because remember, we were camping in true wilderness—mountains, evergreen forest, logging trails but no roads, the whole bit—and we hadn't seen an outsider in six days. We at first started to follow and coax her to remain with us. But Connie refused to come back to camp because she wasn't going to stay any longer with such trickery! We couldn't really stop her. She was an adult, and she refused to listen to any alternative.

Actually, I think that was the first good move she'd made on the whole trip. At least she quit faking a dependence on Swifty's leadership. And once you refuse to be led, then you have to start leading yourself.

Now, this was the morning we were going to break camp and leave anyway. So the rest of us packed slowly, taking down the tent and so on—for after all, Connie had left us to do all the work without her—and generally feeling uncomfortable over this unexpected end to our trip. Driving out on the dirt logging road, we watched carefully, hoping to see her waiting somewhere along the way, ready to rejoin us. But no Connie. Maybe she hid from us, maybe she'd hitched a lift somehow.

When we finally got back down the mountain, Swifty stopped at the ranger station and asked if anyone had seen Connie or given her a ride. No news. Several days later, the leader called me to report that Connie had turned up back home safely.

I thought about this a lot and decided that it does no good to spout out dream interpretations to another person who will not, perhaps cannot for ego reasons, make a felt connection to the dream. Better that one or two points of connection are hesitantly suggested by the dreamer herself, than to hand her a whole fancy layout of the dream's archetypal structure that the dreamer can't connect to. Always the dream must be seen and felt by the dream owner, within the context of that life, to be understood.

And this is why I've spent so much time laying in the background surrounding these dreams. It's the only way you're going to see them in context. Analyzing a dream out of context is like hooking a sailfish for its luminescent sheen and still expecting it to live.

And this is just one soul's record. Each person's is different. I can only show you night letters of one soul in its native environment. But you may not even want new connections to your dreams in your brain. I don't blame Connie for being afraid of what her dreams said. Her ego was very thin and brittle. It supposed that the only way to cope with such "chaotic and malicious" messages was not to notice them.

Dreams often reveal where we need to adapt or change some behavior, but a weak ego is threatened by all this. Yes, it takes a strong, flexible ego to allow itself to be permeable to the unconscious. Allowing this permeability will filter the unconscious message and give its turbulent flow some structure. The ego can derive great strength from channeling this rich power of the unconscious. Actually, the permeable ego has a sort of wicking action that draws relevant matter up from the unconscious realm and into the more orderly, linear light of day.

Once I heard a Japanese Jungian analyst say, "I think the oriental ego is more permeable to the unconscious than is the Western ego. The Western ego is more rigid and impervious and often resists the unconscious as an enemy. But a strong ego knows to quit resisting the power of the unconscious and instead greet it as a friend."

Yes, it does take a strong ego to allow a dream to teach it a new path. Only a healthy ego can relinquish control willingly to the greater self. Ultra-logical types can find clever ways not to let the unconscious have its due. They even deny their fear about it. "Pay attention to that idiot dream? Garble like that? Never! How pointless. How silly."

Egos have a blind spot…including mine. Other people's dreams can help me see where I'm going wrong. For example, a couple of years ago, while organizing a dinner for sixty people, I tipped over a case of wine in the street and broke two bottles, along with a bottle of juice. The night before, I'd lost seven hours of work on the computer. These accidents were enough to suggest that something was going wrong with my timing. Simple scrutiny didn't tell me what, for I was looking at it with my blind spot, staring right through the heavy workload I had been doing!

When I mentioned my accidents to a friend, she said, "Now I see I should have told you a dream I had a couple of days ago. I dreamed you were playing basketball and I was watching from the stands. You were moving around fast, very fast, but you were scooting on your bottom on the floor to do it. As you played, you kept patting the heads of all the little children around you. I admired how well you played even with this self-imposed handicap, but I thought, "Katya will never win if she keeps on playing like this."

Oh. I realized what it said. I'd been assuming a workload for others in an "I'll take care of it for you, folks" attitude, cutting them down to the height of children by doing the work myself, instead of standing up, insisting they stand up too and play like adults or get out of the game. I should have formed a committee to share this workload so that I could finish my own projects before getting dog-tired and careless at night, losing my computer work. Why play a game by self-diminishing rules?

So I thanked my friend and said, "Now I'm going to stand up and play with adults and make some points." That's how my friend's dream eased me into a new stance before I got an even harder boot from more "accidents" in an escalating roar. And sometimes I don't get the message this quick.

So what happens if my ego refuses to notice? Jung once discussed oblivious egos, saying, "It was formerly assumed that patients were ready to cope with normal life as soon as they had acquired enough practical self-knowledge to understand their own dreams. Experience has shown, however, that even professional analysts, who might be expected to have mastered the art of dream interpretation, often capitulate before their own dreams and have to call in the help of a colleague."

Sometimes an ego just will not see some point that the unconscious is making. Once a well-educated older woman, sensitive and considerate, spent nearly a year in analysis with me. Meanwhile her ego sidestepped carefully around the issue of a debilitating physical problem that had developed in the last couple of years. She did mention once that several friends suggested she consult a certain doctor of repute who was uniquely schooled in just this odd health condition, and who belonged to the same club. But she added that due to difference of opinion between the two of them about organizational procedures, she refused to consult the doctor. I then discovered that the illness had begun at the very time of the quarrel, growing slowly worse, and it was of such a particularly specialized nature that literally no other doctor could treat it quite so well as this one. Talk about a tailor-made semaphore trying to get her ego's attention!

Actually, I'd already suspected that some buried complex lay behind the illness because of various odd synchronicities that kept recurring in her life. They were all variations on the same basic theme. Again and again she was attacked by the "underworld"—by Mafia jewel thieves during a trip to Italy, by a bruising fall downstairs into a underground train passage, by subterranean gossip in the club that inflicted on her pride and status yet another penalty. Plutonic forces, she began to call them as each new accident occurred, and she asked me what I knew of the old Greek god Pluto, ruler of the underworld. How did this archetype operate?

The Greeks called him Pluto, but other cultures know this force by other names. Pluto ruled the underworld. He possessed not only the vast riches of buried treasure and minerals in the dark earth, but also the bodies and souls buried there. He caused earthquakes and volcanic eruptions. Through his hidden power, he energized vast upheaval and change in the status quo.

The archetype symbolized by Plutonic force works in hiding, deep underground—like the Mafia or gossip or unconscious complexes—so that you cannot not clearly see the extent of such power, only sense it. Another modern analog is the buried radioactive waste and chemicals of this society whose pollution routes we have only begun to guess.

But this subterranean force can also be positive, for it symbolizes the collective unconscious that is slowly forcing necessary adjustments, at whatever the cost to the cultural powers—like a volcano erupting and redressing an imbalance in the earth's crust, at whatever toll it takes on the structures perched there. Plutonic change works for renewal on a vast scale. You can see this collective force for good in the twenty thousand people who herd together to run in a marathon in San Diego, or in the international multitudes who give to stave off famine in a land they've never seen.

In the case of this particular woman, synchronicity was trying to get her attention with cues emphasizing the hidden collective. I thought a touchpoint was her club—it needed regeneration. A longtime member, this woman saw that it was fossilizing. Symptoms in her illness suggested that she couldn't bear to see what was happening to it, a certain rigidity and pomposity developing that was not in the original membership. Actually I thought she was correct in her assessment. But instead of facing the issue boldly and fighting those tedious bureaucrats into retreat, she had herself retreated at each crucial juncture, grumbling rather than confronting them directly. She even likened herself to a hedgehog, a timid antisocial creature that is all prickles and yet backs away from confrontation. So the problem only worsened, both in the club and in herself.

The illness offered a wonderful way, actually, to meet that doctor (a ringleader for the other side) on a neutral ground. It's very possible that the doctor could cure her illness, which oddly enough, was also a great way to get the doctor kindly and favorably disposed toward her.

But I didn't know how to encourage and strengthen her to do this fearful thing. Many of us quail and fail at facing the shadow side of the collective. And so it gains even more power through our fear to oppose it.

During her recital of a dream, it became evident to me that facing the doctor meant letting go of her own habitual martyr stance. She would have to cease retreating into the familiar role of being weak and misunderstood. She would have to confront the very club member who had humiliated her. She would speak of how desperate she was to shake off her illness. She would do anything! Anything but go see this doctor! She just couldn't take that! It was an insuperable task that her ego couldn't manage.

On hearing her life story, it became apparent that from childhood this woman had a trait of retreating into the isolation of wounded pride. Her complex was so strong that it had throughout her whole life engineered situations of wounding, in which she retreated like an bristly but ineffectual hedgehog at the threat of yet another heedless superior force. For her this illness was just part of a long-established pattern, another custom-made crisis that was trying to bring her attention to this lifelong penchant for retreating stubbornly into the burrow of wounded ego. And the club, ever-voracious as the shadowy collective unconscious is on scenting a victim, fed on her martyrdom. Each side polarized the other into stereotyped oppositional roles in this archetypal play. Fat with success, the organization grew even more smug and pompous in its rigid values.

Yes, it is hard to fight a stultifying organization. She chose to deal with it by a wounded retreat into poor health, never going to the club anymore. She hid in hurt pride, in illness, in isolation rather than face the opposition head-on, laugh and spit in its eye, and demand breathing room. Her retreat just emboldened the club to show its ugly shadow and even begin a purge of nonconformist members rather than tolerate them. The club declared that she among others should resign. But long before this happened, I had suggested that seeing this doctor might confront the issue in microcosm, while it still had a chance of being healed.

In fact, one day the woman asked me to consult the I Ching for her to see how her illness could be helped. So at home I did, following up a list of various alternatives. Nothing was encouraging until I asked if seeing the medical doctor in question would help. Then the hexagram answer was quite affirmative. On the next visit, when I showed the woman this answer, saying I really thought she ought to go see the doctor, at least to give it a try…her reply was that she didn't actually think anyone else could get answers for her from the I Ching. I said astounded, "But you asked me to! And you paid me for my time to do it!"

During several more months, the woman worried about her health, yet she began challenging my commitment to work with her. She said I wasn't really trying to relate to her. But on the contrary, I felt that she was no longer trying to relate to me.

Then two things occurred during a session. The woman said she wanted to terminate the analysis. She said it wasn't getting anywhere. I said I thought that important material was just beginning to come out and it needed more time to become evident. She said, oh no, nothing at all was happening and I was uninvolved and bored with it. I said I didn't feel bored, but perhaps she sensed that I still held an opinion she'd already rejected earlier. What opinion was that, she asked? Whatever could I be talking about?

So once more I said clearly that I felt it important that she at least consult this medical doctor once, as a matter of basic regard for her health, just to see what might come of it.

Then she actually said, "But don't you see? I can't! I can't go and have Dr. — tell me it's just a matter of—whatever it might be!—and cure it just like that! Not after I've spent these years and all this pain and suffering on my illness!" I was dumbfounded. She was declaring outright that she'd rather keep her illness and chronically hurt pride than give them up on the altar of good health. I stared at her amazed. I wondered if she even heard herself speaking this way and wished I had a tape recorder going.

I talked her into trying analysis a bit longer, and she said she'd ask the unconscious for a dream to help her. Next session, she reported a dream in which a voice told her that I was Joseph, the one in the Bible with the coat of many colors, who in her words "was beloved by his father and prophesied correctly and was sold down the river."

Yep, that's how I felt. I said, "What does this dream suggest to you?"

"Nothing! It makes no sense to me! Does it mean anything to you?"

After fishing awhile for her associations and getting no response, reluctantly I suggested that the Bible said that Joseph interpreted dreams correctly. But his prophetic ability hadn't kept him from being sold down the river by his ego-bruised brothers. If her dream called me Joseph, then perhaps it suggested that I too was being sold down the river, perhaps by her refusal to consider my advice about seeing the medical doctor. I really did think that doing it would change the situation for the better.

But she just shook her head. "No. It's impossible. It can't mean that."

"Then what does the dream mean to you?"

She said, "Nothing. Nothing at all. I asked for a dream but not this one!"

Indeed I did feel sold down the river by her, prophesy rightly though I might, because within the month, she insisted on terminating the analysis. I was sorry I hadn't found a way to help her better.

Often I've meditated on this intelligent, solitary, woman who was beset by the shadowy Plutonic forces. But the fact is that nobody else can make you change your right brain connections. Others—friend, family or counselor—can talk and reason and argue and cry and despair, but none of that will necessarily change you. The ego is entrenched in the status quo. This woman had an ego with blinders on, an ego resisting the paradoxical teaching of the higher Self. Synchronicity put her ego into a relentless vise when it ignored the subtle messages wrought in mute timing. A vise pinches the ego ever tighter until—hopefully—it gets the nonverbal lesson, wrenches free, and moves on to further growth. Regretfully, sometimes it lurches in the other direction.

And this afternoon came the client who said she feels more in touch with her dreams. She told me several dreams and her interpretations of them. Her basic sense of the gist was strong, although various symbols sometimes eluded her. She and I both felt that the dreams were basically telling her to wait on a certain issue, not to make a decision yet. It seemed that she would force a crisis if she decided prematurely. Near the end of the hour she said she felt such relief to realize this.

I told her that this session had given me something special too. It confirmed yet again that it is right for me to be doing this dream book as show, not tell. People can benefit from honoring their dreams without understanding everything in them. Of course we never do really understand them completely anyway. And that's okay.

CHAPTER 21

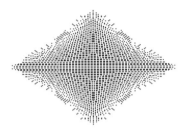

Evil as a Life Force

Dream Log—Wednesday, November 30:

Dream: I see it being made right before my eyes. It is not good, but harmful. What is this conglomeration? How to account for it? Finally I just have to say that it is evil.

I wake in the dark shuddering from this dream. Evil. So here it is finally. It's been showing its thin edge already during the previous twelve hours before emerging full-blown in this dream

Yesterday I picked up the next book off the stack, *The Fifth Child*, by Doris Lessing, and laid it beside my bed lamp to start at bedtime. But I did open it long enough to skim the front and back jacket blurbs: Hmm, it's about an unaccountably evil child who is born into a loving family. Unsettling concept, that. Am I up for this? Oh well. Doris Lessing is a good writer and I always enjoy her. I'll read it.

Then I went to the seminar on creativity that I'm attending all this week. Here again the topic of evil cropped up. A man brought up a question that for the first time slowed the lecturer down into a contemplative tone. His question was about libido energy and why it is often used in destructive rather than creative ways.

The lecturer, who is visiting this week from France, said, "I don't know. This is one of the big unanswered questions for me. Take cancer, for example. It is a kind of life energy. Yet it destroys the host. So you might say that cancer is evil. But I have seen cancer cause people to change their values and develop their sense of inner worth, as though the cancer with its looming death triggers a drive to nourish and deepen the psyche. All this comes at the cost of the life itself. So I don't know. I don't know what evil is. Good comes from evil and vice versa. It is the great puzzle."

Now this short time spent talking about evil changed the whole tenor of the seminar. No longer did the questions and answers flow so easily or cheerfully. It was as though the group was slowing down to consider evil. Faces turned somber, while a few people became contentious and even a bit malicious in their remarks. I felt the archetype of evil constellating in the room. That's what happens, you know. When you pursue a topic, its energy begins to flavor the room. So the audience got a bit devilish. Finally the lecturer said, "I'm not being very inspiring for you today."

But indeed, I think she was. She'd led us to dip a toe into the nature of evil. I can't say exactly what it is either. This dream today gives me no handy explanation, no diagram for coping with it.

So I went back to sleep without writing the dream down. And woke up this morning with a *second* dream that was a reprise of the first (as though to ensure that I wouldn't forget it), but with this addendum:

> Dream: Conglomeration of stuff all mixed together. What is all this? Is it some noodle concoction? I draw a balloon above it and put a caption, "These noodles are evil."

Yeah, sure. Evil noodles. Ohhh, I get it! Yes, some noodles do concoct really evil things. Gross evil. Take Hitler's plan to elevate the Aryan race above the rest of the world. It just involved killing off anybody who didn't submit. Such a noodle he had on his shoulders, that Hitler. Downright evil.

And here maybe I need to apologize for my psyche's outrageous puns. Don't think that it's taking this matter of evil lightly. It's just that the unconscious, resting in the broad base of humanity as it does, seems to be populist in approach. Anyway, getting back to last night, when I first saw the slivered edge of evil rising over the horizon, I drew some I Ching hexagrams that sounded to me like rather a hard day upcoming. So I also drew a card for the day ahead from an image deck I've developed that I call Kairos Cards (kairos being Greek for right timing in life). And what did its image show me? A fire-spotting tower burning in a forest fire, and I'd read that the spotter's dog was trapped in there. More evil?

And then along came last night's dreams about the evil noodle concoction. My god. How do I write about evil noodles? Maybe with a little cartoon caption that says, "Warning. Noodle concoctions may be hazardous to your health."

We all know of evil. We know of events that epitomize evil to us. But what is evil itself? I go back to that image of the hidden dog dying in the burning watch tower, of the destruction of the forest. Dog…that's god spelled backwards in my dreamtime shorthand…is evil just a form of god reversed into destruction?

Destruction. I think about entropy. For the human body, entropy itself becomes evil. It tolls the end of physical life.

I have seen evil. I have lived through a devastating earthquake in Turkey, where many people died in horror and misery. Once I was held in a French jail without bail and counsel and "encouraged" to confess to a student plot that I'd never even heard of. I've been given PCP in a Caribbean infirmary as an anesthetic while the drunken doctor was sewing up a hundred stitches in my leg—with football lacing-sized stitches—and let me tell you, hallucinations from the anesthetic were far worse than the accident. I've taught Vietnam veterans so psychically damaged that their daily preoccupation was figuring out the best way to hold a rifle in the mouth while lying on the bed to pull the trigger with a toe. They want to do it right and not mess up when they've seen too many fuck-up suicides.

I have lived through so much mundane evil that it's tedious to relate. But right now I'm thinking of *The Fifth Child*. The mother decides to put her brutish son away in an institution. Then after months of newfound peace in the family, she finally can no longer ignore the thought of that hidden-away son. So she goes to find him in the children's home: "In the cots were—monsters…every bed or cot held an infant or small child in whom the human template had been wrenched out of pattern, sometimes horribly, sometimes slightly. A baby like a comma, great lolling head on a stalk of a body…then something like a stick insect, enormous bulging eyes among stiff fragilities that were limbs…a small girl blurred, her flesh guttering and melting…a doll with chalky swollen limbs, its eyes wide and blank, like blue ponds, and its mouth open, showing a swollen little tongue. A lanky boy was skewed, one half of his body sliding from the other. A child seemed at first glance normal, but then Harriet saw there was no back to its head; it was all face, which seemed to scream at her. Rows of freaks, nearly all asleep, and all silent. They were literally drugged out of their minds." Is this evil? Or so-called acts of god?

As a teenager, I understood evil. It was the meaningless painful existence of human life. I lived beyond hope for myself. Or for any of us. I saw existential angst as the only honorable life in a godless universe.

No kidding. At the age of fifteen, I spent one summer vacation reading Schopenhauer, Sartre, and Camus—a serious child, what? I was trying to figure out why we exist. I remember putting down Camus' *The Stranger,* on the bed and realizing that this so-called fiction was describing the futility, sadness, insignificance of all human life. I recognized it in my own life. *Weltschmerz,* world pain. So humanity was noble and pointless.

I had a vision of the universe as a meaningless mechanism that is slowly grinding our lives up without even noticing us. This vision seized me like a black hole, holding me lost in it for several hours. At the end I cried myself into exhaustion and went to sleep, waking into a world that had lost its sheen.

In that summer I lost my reason to exist. More specifically, I looked hard for it, and found instead, nothing. Not for twenty years did I realize what damage that despairing vision had done to me. It set me on a path of hopeless futility. It voided my being for a long time.

And only recently did I finally find a description of that condition in the writing of Eugene d'Aquili: "…the basic affective valence toward the perceived universe is profoundly negative….and consists of a sense of exquisite sadness and futility, as well as the sense of the incredible smallness of man in the universe, the inevitable existential pain of the world, and the suffering inherent in the human condition. Often there is the perception of the whole universe as one vast pointless machine without purpose or meaning. A mild form of this often occurs with high school or college students and other young adults. In its full-blown form, however, it…occurs with a suddenness that leaves the individual totally perplexed. Usually the individual wakes up with a profound sense of loss and meaninglessness to the world which never leaves. It is the basic sense of reality which appears to underlie much existentialist thought, particularly in French existentialist literature. It is the sort of perception in which the universe is apprehended not in any way as neutral but as essentially absurd, and often suicide is thought to be the only truly human response."

Yes, it used to be easy for me to explain evil. Easy and cheap. Evil was just a fucked-up universe without god. As a mechanical universe, it just is.

Only I no longer believe the universe is just mechanical. It is organic. Alive and intelligent. But I think this cosmic consciousness is greater than we can imagine or explain.

And a part of the very force that keeps it evolving is what we call evil, destruction, death. After all, nothing alive is perfected, since perfection is static. I think some quirk is built into the very numbers of archetypal organization that keeps life going by keeping destruction going too. Personally, I think the odds are 3 to 2 in favor of creation.

Odd to get a firm number on that? Well, to put it another way, life is three steps forward and two steps back. I think failure is built into the system as part of its dynamic. For example, in working with the I Ching, I know that what people normally classify as "bad hexagrams" have their uses and indeed become difficulty in the service of good, if they're lived through properly. And here I take "properly" to mean proper to one's own true path, not a social definition of propriety.

So I get up, shower, have breakfast and sit down to write on evil. I know in my bones there's more evil coming today. Perhaps living through a manifestation of it in some form. Because a dream is a harbinger. I hope I can handle whatever's looming today.

So what's on the docket for today? I get up and wash clothes and consider evil. Is the blood on the sheet that I have to wash out beforehand so it doesn't leave a spot a minor form of evil? Is the car accident on the next block evil? Is the Swiss cleaning frenzy a form of evil?

People use such strong cleansers that I sneeze in the hallway every Friday when the maintenance man mops down the stairs. I open the basement windows of the laundry room when I go down there, because so much soap powder dust wafts in the air from the hanging over-soaped clothes and the disinfectant fumes of the scrubbed-down room. The apartment tenants put so much highly perfumed soap in their laundry that the smell never washes out. And these washers cycle longer and cleaner than the average American machine. A normal load takes over an hour. Then you can also do "cook-wash" which takes an hour and a half, and gets the water within two degrees of boiling.

Likewise, the dishwasher takes an hour and a half to do a load of dishes, and it uses the strongest concentrate I've ever smelled. I put in only a third of the recommended amount (just as I do for the biodegradable laundry detergent) and then I run the dishes and clothes through an extra rinse.

Today I walk by people's lines of hanging clothes and smell the "clean" chemicals. They weaken the autoimmune system, you know, over time. Living in, wearing, imbibing, breathing chemicals that the body isn't adapted for. As I hang up our clothes, I think of the statistics on the modern fumes and dust in sealed office buildings and how debilitating it is to the respiratory and immune system. Switzerland is the cleanest country I've ever been in. But it suffers from wash pollution. Their very cleanliness is overdone into a form of evil.

So what is evil? Is it the psychic equivalent of dirt—matter in the wrong place? Is evil action taken in the wrong place? Not in the right?

Nothing evil has happened so far. Unless you count too many jalapeno peppers in the cornbread my husband made, and I don't. Somehow things need a little hotting up today. He talks about how drab it looks outside—grizzly gray and "depressing"—an adjective he almost never uses, and I get the feeling that we are avoiding each other slightly in the apartment today not to rub each other wrong.

Seminar time. At the start, the lecturer mentions how oddly tired she felt last night. "The seminar was so intense in here yesterday," she said. In fact, she even "blacked out around nine o'clock," she said, and eventually came to. "It was like I went into a black hole," she said. I stared at her, pondering the archetype of evil and how I'd felt it constellating in the room yesterday, a slightly contentious, malignant opposition that soured the group. I suspected that was what she'd blacked out from last night.

Then the seminar began. Soon it was back to evil and at increasing intensity. Someone got hostile with the lecturer. Words became weapons and shields, not idea bearers. The rest of us looked askance. Several times other people tried to break in with questions that pointed in new directions. But nothing clicked, nothing led away from the conflict.

The lecturer looked drained half way through the two-hour session. The arguing student had a set jaw. And both of them, "good people," were narrow-eyed at each other, rough-voiced, hard-hearted.

After two hours we finally ended on a note that was heavy and unresolved. The teacher said, "See you tomorrow. If I'm still living tomorrow." A joke of course, but not really.

Afterward I had a dinner date with a woman sitting in the session. As we walked the block and a half over to her hotel—the Sonne on the lake front—and then later to the restaurant, we talked about what had gone on in there. She said, "The atmosphere was not at all friendly. It was heavy. Uncomfortable."

We discussed how the lecturer and heckler had refused to accommodate each other. Defusing hadn't worked. The archetype of evil had got hold of them and neither could pull free of it.

I admitted how uneasy I'd felt sitting there, and yet another part of me was fascinated to watch this psychic war. Even as I disliked it, I wanted to see what happened next. A shadowy part of me was chanting, "Hit 'em again, harder, harder." A psychic prize fight. Fights are fascinating. Ask Joyce Carol Oates, who's a fool for boxing. Ask a street gang. It's is the stuff of which movies are made. And divorces. And disinheritances. And G.I. Joe.

There's one good thing to be said about that weird, bitter confict today. Afterward, they both stayed and talked together. Tacitly they were trying to understand what dreadful dynamic had been activated. They did *not* walk away from each other yelling "Bitch!" "Bastard!"

It's not much, you may say, but I think it's enough to change the world. Trying to understand can keep people close enough to talk and argue and negotiate and allow each other's silly, unaccountable points of view. It is better than moving back into polarized rage and disgust and the longer-reach retaliation of swords, guns, and missiles.

Encompassing the tension and not capitulating to the polarity is hard. It's much easier to dismiss the other person along with his argument. "He's a fool, why talk to him?" "They're barbarians and I will never understand such people, not as long as I live." "My father and I never talked, we just argue." All this said with a certain grim satisfaction, of course.

Disagreement used to be hard on me. But instead of dismissing the other person, I tended to feel his stance was somehow more valid than mine. Remember, my ego was weak from all those invasions of the chaotic unconscious back in my fake food days. And so instead of crystallizing into a polarized stand, I would dissolve into no stand at all. After all, I was bent over backwards trying to accept and love and see the other person's view and not push my own. Why should walking around so carefully bent over backwards hurt so much?

Because there was no real me. But gradually I developed a sense of myself. Fallible though I still am, I am me, and these days I'm glad of it.

I think evil is just darkness perverted. I think that in the balance of things darkness must exist, but not evil. Evil is just darkness gone wrong. Darkness, depth, hidden connection are part of the eternal universal number generator, and it is powerful. But darkness can be useful if it is examined and reconciled and transformed instead of just projected outward into evil over there beyond me. Projection makes black hats versus white hats, good versus evil, you versus me.

I'm going to tell you a little story about some good coming from evil. This story popped out one weekend as I finally was allowing myself to un-backbend and straighten up and be me.

A Skinny Myth

There was a woman. She felt no age. She felt no beginning, no end—and so it was hard to tell much about her, and to know her. She was so clear that she was transparent and you could see through her to the other side. You could see the trees and the stars and the grass.

But where was she?

If you could see through her to everything else, who and where was she? What was her name? Her uniqueness? Where did she end and something else, someone else, begin?

She did not know, so she began searching through the world to find herself. She walked by someone who was sitting on a rock staring at himself in the water's smooth surface. He was saying, "Oh, you are so beautiful, you are so beautiful!"

She thought, "I will look in the water too and maybe I will find myself too, and maybe I will find myself beautiful." She bent over and looked in the water's surface, but since she was transparent, she could not see herself and so it seemed she was not there. She got up and went on, thinking, "Ahah! Mere reflection cannot tell me what I am."

She came to a town with people going about in it. "Ah. Here are some people. Perhaps they can tell me what I am, my nature, my dimensions, my purpose."

She walked up to a group of people who were busy talking, all telling each other who they were. "Oh, you always act this way." "You always say this to me." "You act just like that every time."

So they must be seeing each other perfectly, she thought. They can look at me and tell me what I am, who I am. But as she walked among them, it was as though the people were yelling at each other through her—and it hurt very much—and they were not really seeing what she was.

So she went off to search in books to find out who and what she was. The books told about her genus and species, her chemical makeup, heritage of civilizing laws and backlog of knowledge. And she thought, "But this is not me—not really me, the essence of me."

So she got quiet and went inside to God. She asked God what she was.

And God said, "Oh, you're a good idea of mine. I make you in lots of different forms and colors and I even make you in two sexes, so you can go around complementing each other. That is why you are now imagining me as male, in complement to you. But underneath you're all the same—all parts of the same good idea of mine.

"And right now you can't see yourself because you keep looking through yourself at me, at all the parts of me that are in the world. For all the world is me. And you are me.

"Your skin has been so thin that you could see right through it to everything else, to everyone else—it has all mattered so much that you haven't been able to find your own matter, what defines you and makes you a unique celebration of me. Thus, I think I will make your skin a little bit thicker—" and God turned a dial, saying "—so that you can notice better where you begin and something else ends."

As God turned the dial, her skin thickened up, and the woman saw who she was and what she was, and where she was, and why she was, and she said, "Oh, how wonderful! This world is wonderful! I am so glad to be in it, in this very skin situated in this very spot, at this very time—in this very life!"

And God said, "Good! Because part of your purpose is to know what you uniquely are, and to bring that knowledge back to me. Through you, woman, I create myself. I know myself and I grow more full through you and all of my creations. Through each separate identity, I explore a new facet of this world I have created. And underneath each separate identity is the connection that binds all the parts of me together into one.

"You, woman, and you, man, in all your separate forms and names, are an idea of mine made manifest. So remember to look down and treasure your own skin, your uniqueness, as well as the connection that goes beneath—the bond between these separate forms. See your skin, live in it, enjoy it, treasure it. "

And she said, "I do see, God. I will live, God. And I will take delight in it."

He said, "Then from now on I will call you Delight. Now, Delight, you may stay here in this very skin until it's time for you to take it off and go home in *de dark*." And he slapped his knee and laughed, because there's nothing God likes so much as a good joke, even when it's one he plays on himself—as we can plainly see by looking around at our own pasts and futures in the skins where we live. But when we get down beneath our skins to what unites us, we can all enjoy the joke together. And in unity we all have the last laugh.

CHAPTER 22

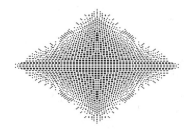

A Necklace
for the Subtle Body

Dream Log—*Thursday, December 1:*

Dream: A lot of work is going on to build this structure. I see this detail and that. It makes a gridwork of rods and connections. It's drawing toward completion. At last I recognize the woman standing over there—she's my daughter, watching and supervising. She is so happy.

I decide to give her a necklace. It is made of bronze metal globes—the fat centers are burnished, but the poles of the spheres are darker. I put it around my daughter's neck and realize that it is very much like a necklace of my own, except hers has a graduated row of globes, while mine has globes that are even all the way along.

My Daughter's Necklace

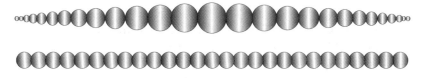

My Necklace

It's almost 7:00 a.m. when I wake up. I like this dream. It makes me happy. Who is the woman that I call my daughter? She doesn't look like my real, fleshly daughter, child of my body. It must be a child of my psyche...and she's grown now. Look, she's standing over there supervising the finishing details on a gridwork of rods and connections. It feels like this very dream book in your hands—I think it is what's being finished. And my dream daughter is directing its completion.

Hmm. I suppose this is really finishing up, if the dream says so. I'd been planning to spend a month on it, but exactly what *kind* of month I didn't know. Would it be a month of days? A month of chapters? Or maybe the cycle would be a lunar month—four weeks. There's a little leeway in all this, so I thought I'd just watch for the signs, letting it take its natural course. And now it is.

Look, my daughter is happy with the result. Then I am, too.

This necklace that I decide to give her, what is this about? What does it mean for her? Immediately I think of an African folk tale. Maybe this dream necklace means the same thing it did in that folk tale, since folk tales are the oral dreams of the collective.

Here's the African story:

The Girl Who Found her Own Necklace
The maiden happily put on the necklace she'd just made and went out to meet her friends. They were all wearing necklaces too, but theirs were made by the old man who made tribal necklaces—all just alike and not so pretty—and so her friends were jealous. While the girl went picking flowers along the edge of the river, they hid their necklaces under rocks. When she turned around, she said, "Oh, where are your necklaces?"

The girls all answered with solemn voices, "We sacrificed them to the river god."

"Then I will too," the girl declared, and taking off her necklace, she threw it into the river.

"Ha-ha-ha!" the others laughed as they pulled out their hidden necklaces and put them on. "You're so stupid, Girl, throwing your necklace into the river for nothing. Now you don't have a necklace at all. Ha-ha-ha!"

The girl felt sad. She walked away slowly long the river. "I am stupid," she thought. "I didn't want a necklace like everybody else's, but now I have none at all," and she began to cry.

"What's the matter with you, Girl?" She looked up and saw an old woman sitting on the river bank.

"My friends tricked me into sacrificing my necklace to the river god, and now I have no necklace at all."

"Yes, you do! If you will help me, I will help you. What you must do is lick the sores on my feet and heal them."

"Ugh! Is that the only way they can be healed?" the girl said, looking down at the old woman's wounded feet.

"Yes. The only way."

"Poor old woman. Then I will lick them." And she did. Just like a dog cleaning its young, she licked the old woman's bruised feet covered with sores. And abruptly, they were healed.

"Thank you, Dear. Now in return, I will help you. Here is a black stone. Hold it in your left hand and dive into the middle of the river. Go to the very bottom and ask the river god for your necklace. Show him the stone in your hand. He will give your necklace back without hurting you. Then rise up and get out of the river. Throw the black stone into the river without looking back at it, and the river god will never hurt you during your whole life long."

So the girl did all this, and it was just as the woman said...but with one big difference! The river god smiled and gave the girl a necklace that was much more beautiful! It was a wonderful necklace, like no other necklace in the world.

The girl came out of the river and threw in the black stone without a backward glance. Then as she was walking away from the river, the other girls came along. "Oh, what a wonderful necklace!" they gasped. "Where did you get it?"

"From the river god. He gave it to me."

"How? How? Tell us quick!"

"I jumped into the river and asked him for it."

Without hearing any more, the girls rushed off toward the river. But on the river bank they met an old woman. "Where are you going in such a hurry?"

"We're going to get new necklaces from the river god."

"Then you will surely need my help. I will help you if you will help me. Lick the sores on my feet and heal them, and I will help you get new necklaces."

They stared at her wounded feet and laughed. "Are you crazy, Old Woman? We don't need your help!"

And they all jumped into the river and guess what? The river god ate them all up.

Weird little story, isn't it, on the rational level. Like those Grimm's fairy tales where the little man stomps with anger until he rips himself right in two, or the wolf is cooked by falling down the chimney into the third little pig's pot of boiling water, or the Gingerbread Man gets eaten all up. But fairy tales operate like dreams. They don't work logically but symbolically, and that is why children love them so, blood, guts and all.

They understand it on an instinctive level. They sense what's being conveyed. That's why it's a shame to take the guts out of a fairy tale by cutting out the "nasty" parts and making it just chummy mice dressed in pastel clothes and plump shoes walking around in twinkle dust.

In this story, the girl is tricked into giving up her unique necklace. Why? Because her peers are jealous of what she's made for herself. A necklace is a tribal ornament. But this necklace goes beyond the tribal identity to state her own individual identity. It makes a statement about her personally. It shows that she is a separate entity over and above the tribal definition. This girl has carefully made her own necklace. But instead of designing their own, her friends just trick her into giving up hers.

That's what happened to me when I was younger. Early on, I had some sense of my identity, my uniqueness. I remember at three years old or so, staring down at the blonde hairs on my right arm in a shaft of sunlight and being amazed. Those shining hairs were mine! And this arm. This was me!

But then I threw my identity into the river of the unconscious when I was about five. I remember doing it. To be like the others and sacrifice to the tribal values, I threw my individuality away into the river. I wore the same tribal necklace that all little girls wore, the communal one designed by some old man of the tribe, not an old woman. You know that necklace, the strangulating one? It has several strands—the *be seen and not heard* strand, the *you're not good at math* strand, the *she must be riding the rag* strand, the *Barbie doll* strand where we wish for shoulders twice as wide as our hips?

But then I realized I had nothing. I walked along and cried until finally, much more slowly than in this African story, I met a wise old woman within me who said, "Look, Girl, I'll help you go into the unconscious and deal with the dangerous power there. You can regain your lost identity—but on one condition."

"What? Anything, anything!"

"You must humble yourself to help the long-abused feminine values—you must lick the sores on these old feet that have trod so long and far without attention. You must clean this weary stance with living water, with saliva—for I am the primordial feminine in you that is damaged. By accepting and healing me, you heal yourself. Then I will give you a philosopher's stone to protect you whenever you dip into the channeled unconscious. Demonstrate to this force your left-handed wisdom. Then it will give back your identity, and never hurt you again."

And I got my identity back, but with a bonus. It was fuller, richer than before. It allowed me an individual identity like no other in the world. And it will keep me from drowning in the river of the unconscious, even if it swallows up everyone else—like in Nazi Germany, for example. That's a wonderful necklace to wear.

The only thing is, I must throw my philosopher's stone back into the river so that it will always keep a solid, mute wisdom for me. And I must do it without a backward glance, without a doubting countermand of logic that denies my having met the river god. Logic wants to devalue and deny the mystical experience, but I mustn't let that bullying logic dismiss as just foolishness all the dreams and somatic messages and sudden gestalts and synchronicities arising from the subliminal edge. A black stone in black water is invisible to the logical eye, but it gives a solid place for me to stand in the amorphous currents of life.

But what happens if you leap rambunctiously into the unconscious, without any humility or wisdom, demanding what life owes you?

It eats you up. Really. That's no fairy tale. In mental institutions and crack houses and jails, these lives are sacrificed up to the chaotic unconscious—they are the Guayana slaughter victims and the Las Vegas slot machine addicts and the blithely-overspending dupes of mass advertising who have maxed-out credit cards.

This necklace in the story is about learning to find and appreciate one's own unique identity. So it is a wonderful necklace for my dream daughter to wear. For this book to wear. It is a necklace for the subtle body.

But why is it made of bronze? I hardly even wanted to write down that word *bronze* when I first woke up, because it did not convey the numinous sense of this necklace. *Bronze,* a metal less valuable than gold or silver—it made no logical sense to me. Bronze? That's a third place metal.

Ah! I smile. "The third place" is what the seminar teacher has been discussing for the last two days. The third position, the *tertium quid,* the transcendent third eye. So is it a transcendent necklace?

Okay, I get it now. You remember the three-ring circus back there? The first ring held triangles of ascension. The second held squares of limits. And the third held "stuff"—I couldn't see what. I guess this is stuff whose nature is only now becoming evident.

I guess this final stuff is about combining the reach toward god of the first ring along with the material limitations of the second ring, and from them, developing a new position for the psyche. Hmm. This third position wants to live in the real, material world, yet be linked to the divine. That's why this necklace is made of third-place bronze. Now I'm glad I stayed true to the dream and wrote down *bronze*, even if my waking ego balked.

This soul necklace actually does resemble one I own. Well, after all, I have been trying to describe my psyche for the past twenty-seven days. But there is surely some difference between what I say and what I am, no matter how carefully I work. So this dream daughter has her own necklace. And identity. Notice too that it is composed of graduated sizes, her necklace...but my real necklace is not.

I feel a meaning in this. This dream book has graduated spheres—

—because its momentum starts off small, gets bigger and more heavy in the middle, and now it's tapering off again. Seeing this taper is a relief to me, somehow. I guess I'd automatically thought, oh dear, I must end this book in some big crescendo of a finale. But how? But I can see from this necklace's shape that it will taper off naturally. Good. It is important to know how to stop.

So this dream today is cueing not only the end, but even how to end. Not with a big finale. Just tapering off, like a jazzy *String of Pearls*...that aural mandala is composed of globes of cycling notes strung along a thread of continuity. And that's what this book is too. Each chapter is one bead, and the center chapters get bigger and heavier. Each is accreted around a grain of dreaming, strung one after the other along the calendar of days. Only a couple remain. Time enough to put on a clasp, I suppose.

As for its burnish and tarnish, I've tried to show you both—in my days and on my soul. But the dark plays up the gleam, don't you think, and both are necessary for the whole picture.

About those even beads in my necklace. Yes, it's true, my days are all even somehow—sometimes I get the flu and once in a while I go off the deep end with a chocolate bar, but not often. I see and feel and be evil sometimes, but I sniff it out and do something about it. Sometimes I have a luminous day, too. Yet stronger than the ups and downs, something holds a continuity that I maintain by trusting my dreams to guide my days. Dreamtime is the string that holds all these daily beads together in evenness. Otherwise my ego might fray things to drop and start the beads rolling around and getting lost. I never have a lost day anymore, not even on flu days. Not even on chocolate bar day. Not even when shadow walks loomingly into the room and tries to find a home. Even shadow has its function in the rhythm.

Today while talking with a Jungian analyst, I told him about my dream necklace. "But I don't understand this about bronze. What's in bronze? How do you manufacture it?"

"Let's look it up in the encyclopedia. 'Bronze—a metal formed of copper and tin, sometimes with other trace metals added. It was usually mixed in the proportions of one weight of copper to two weights of tin. This alloying makes copper more fusible, harder, less malleable.'"

He said, "Bronze is made of copper and tin. Hmm. Copper, mythologically speaking, is the metal of Venus."

Of loving relationship, I thought. Writing this book has been a labor of love. It's easy to see why my dream child has a necklace with copper in it. But the tin? I asked, "Why tin? What about tin?"

"Jupiter. It's Jupiter's metal."

Jupiter. Good fortune and generosity. Yes. Two measures of fortune to one of love. I love to share with you my good fortune in dreams. I want to be generous with what I've learned, because it's changed my life for the better. I give my time and effort this month, so that you can see how the dream world and the waking world mesh together.

You know, it is not a matter of faith with me. It's experience. I don't expect you to take it on faith, either. I just hope you'll explore and see for yourself. It means discovering from experience that your dreams signal events in your reality. You'll feel a connection with inner meaning that nothing can fake. So pay attention, turn up the volume on the symbols, amply dreams till you get the message. To amplify a symbol, make associations to increase the dream resonance. Turn up the feeling tone, clarify and fine-tune it until you hear the message vibrating loud and clear.

The great religions once made this felt connection with many people. Unfortunately, dogma has made it a dead experience for many now. Organized religion often lacks the personal impact of deep meaning, a felt connection. But god didn't die, you know. It's just that our experience of god died. It was our projection that god grew weak and petty and indifferent to our modern times. But the symbols for god, like everything else in this finite world, suffer entropy and have to be revitalized occasionally.

"Bronze. It is a union of male god and female god. Venus and Jupiter. A divine *coniunctio*."

"Oh. I hadn't thought of that. But look, it's in my hexagram for today. *Harmony*, 11. To the Chinese, that's a union between heaven and earth."

"You do hexagrams every day?"

"Yes."

"Carl Jung stopped using the I Ching eventually. He said he already knew what it was going to say."

"Well, I'm not Carl Jung. I don't know the right way to go lots of times. Maybe he did. Or maybe he just got lazy and quit. I don't know."

He looked at me, almost…shocked. I was reminded of Jung's remark in old age: "Thank god I am Jung and not a Jungian." So I merely said, "I'm just a human being. This helps me when I get puzzled or angry or scared. Tired or confused. It helps me grasp some continuity behind the random-seeming events."

"You get a lot of information each day."

"Yes. It helps me stay in tune."

"So this how your psyche stays at its best. Like not drinking caffeine. When some might wonder why you're not indulging yourself in a nice treat." He meant himself. He thought I was I odd for drinking herbal teal when he ordered us a treat from the cafe downstairs.

"Yes. It helps me pick up the rhythm of some music beyond my understanding. And it only goes so long as I move in service of it."

Yes, harmony has constellated for me today. I feel it in this dream of the bronze necklace. I feel it in today's events. There isn't much left to say. Harmony becomes wordless after a certain point. Of course if you don't know the words, you can just hum along.

CHAPTER 23

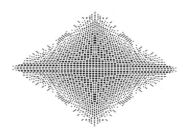

The Left-Brain Handle

Dream Log—Friday, December 2:
Dream: I am moving around it and looking at the name. I lasso and pull it out of the text and consider it. Is it too American? I put in another name. But what?...I can't see it.

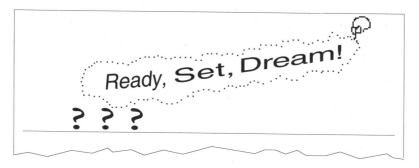

I wake up to church bells. Almost morning. I keep my eyes closed, trying to see my dream still, and that new title atop the page. The old lassoed-out one I can see clearly enough: *Ready, Set, Dream!* That's the name I gave this book on the first day. It was a working title of course, but I assumed it wouldn't change.

However, about—what, three days ago?—something shifted inside. Now the book wants a new name. You can see it questing in this dream...all the question marks. Hey, this handy lasso tool comes right out of a computer program. It roped out the old name, but I can't see the new one yet.

So I'm dreaming about the dream book? Dream and reality are drawing together like the narrowing end of a funnel. Inner and outer worlds are merging into one.

Up pops a bubble of memory. Yesterday that Jungian analyst was asking me about this dream book. So I related my necklace dream. He said, "But how does the necklace relate to the gridwork—how do these two things work together? Do they come to the same thing finally?"

"I don't know. Do they have to?"

"I don't know. I don't understand the purpose of this gridwork structure. Can you say in one sentence what this dream book is about?"

"In one sentence!"

"Or in one sentence for each chapter?"

"I haven't tried. I don't know." I felt puzzled by this. "Um, I guess I could write a sentence summary of each chapter. Maybe put it at the end of the book, along with the I Ching hexagrams for each day, to show how it all fits together. That's a sort of gridwork, isn't it. Wow, " I said softly. I was amazed.

"Another thing. You know, a necklace to me suggests a stone, a jewel. You've described this necklace as being bronze, but somehow I wonder about a stone, a jewel in it somewhere. Is there a stone of great price hidden in it somewhere? Perhaps a philosopher's stone?"

I gazed at him. I hadn't mentioned the African fairy tale and the black stone of wisdom. "Yes, there's a stone. But it's carried in the hand. In the water—it involves an African folk tale. You want to hear it?"

"Not now. But do this gridwork and necklace become the same thing?"

"I hardly know what you're saying."

"I don't either, it's just a feeling." Yeah. Great help.

So today, along comes this dream about a title. Hmm. A title makes an even shorter summary of a book than a sentence would. And look, I'm removing the old title with a lasso. Why? Because…well, because it's too hard-sell. Our extraverted American culture, with its hands-on, can-do, material-manipulating approach to life—it deals with matter instead of soul. Why, in America, even soul food is matter—collard greens, cornbread, grits and gravy.

How do you nourish your subtle body? This book is for that. It's not a how-to, can-do manual for cracking dreams into components and charting them like chemical compounds. So this title—*Ready, Set, Dream!*—is too hard-sell in its approach. It almost pulls the starting trigger on a subliminal race against others. But dreaming is an entirely personal event—more than sex, defecation, all the other things we closet ourselves away for. We closet ourselves so completely for dreaming that we closet our eyes and shut out sound. Tune out reality.

And it is noncompetitive. A dream that looks tiny and meaningless to you can be full of significance for me, and as Connie showed me with her campfire banquet vomited up each morning, you can also be starving at a feast. So this book touts no feat of extraversion—instead it discusses introversion at its most profound. It looks inward to communicate with soul.

Yes, indeed. I need another title. But what? Well, this book shows how to work with dreams, but more than that, what comes of it, of talking with a source that actually answers. When I ask for help on a problem before I go to sleep, it's no despairing prayer thrown up to the stone arches of an empty cathedral. Instead I usually get a night letter, and all I need is the patience to read it.

I need a title to capture this essence. But what? Can I go back to sleep and find out? See it in my dream? It's too close to morning. And I can't dream on demand and set up its exact conditions. But I can ask.

I drowse for awhile in a never-never land between wakefulness and sleep. My husband gets up. He turns on the overhead light, and I cover my head with a pillow. I don't want to wake up yet. I fuzz off into…

Dream : I'm sitting and looking critically at the computer screen showing a page, a blank space in the header. I type in a title: *Autobiography of a Soul*.

I wake up. Was I really asleep? Then I remember that fade-out zone where I dropped off. Yes, I was asleep. Busy trying titles. Do I like this one? *Autobiography of a Soul?* Well. It is the nature of these night letters. But too long a title.

A title is a handle. Names are how we get a grasp on an idea, a person, a book. John Wayne asked the stranger in town, "What's your handle, pardner?" I need to attach a good strong handle to this book so that you can pick it up and hold it more easily. And use it.

A name takes you into identity, the American Indians thought. An adolescent went out to find his own true name, by means of a dream or vision or quest. Initiation of some sort.

This week a woman named Catherine said to me, "My name means pure in body, mind and spirit. But I don't know the meaning of my proper name." What is a "proper name," anyway? In the old days, when people started getting their own last names, one proper to themselves and no longer just serfs and property of the fiefdom, it was a proper name. When I lived in Turkey, my landlord said Turks chose their last names in the early 20th century and his father chose Star.

Regarding names, a friend said to me recently, "You can't get away from yourself. My sister thought she'd change her name completely, from Gail to Alana. Then she found out they mean the same thing in different languages. She was just coming at herself from another angle."

Okay. I need a new name for this book. I must come at it from another angle. I get up and have breakfast while my husband talks with me. Not eating. He's already gone to the Munz Cafe for coffee and a croissant and his morning paper. So I eat brown rice and a chopped apple and almonds with a bit of yogurt on top. Big breakfast, but I'm hungry today.

Eventually I ask my husband what he thinks about dreaming.

"I think it works—for you. Also, I never realized you were so unhappy when you were young. But you're not unhappy now. And it seems to be all this work you've done that's changed you. But for me, I don't know."

"What do you mean?"

"Well, I've never been very unhappy. I've enjoyed my life a lot. I had two good parents who loved me and admired what I did. They were so proud of me, and I was proud of myself. I was a happy child, and grew up into a happy man."

"I know. You're a lucky man."

"Oh, I admit there was a bad time when I went through that divorce with the mother of my children, but even then, I somehow persuaded myself that we'd all be happier in the long run. I've enjoyed my whole life. I was successful enough that I didn't even have to work very hard at my career. Not as hard as I could have, I saw that from the other people around me. But I got as high as I wanted. Well, I was even national president of my professional society for awhile. I was content enough to be a little lazy, and I enjoyed it.

"So nothing ever pushed me very hard to change myself. Not like with you. I was happy enough from the beginning. For instance, I never doubted that my parents loved me or that I loved myself. It never occurred to me to want to kill myself, not like you wrote back there when you tell about trying to commit suicide. I never even thought of it. I never realized you were so unhappy."

"But I told you about it. I described it all before."

"Yes, but somehow I never really understood what you meant until I saw it written down in those chapters. So now I can see you found the means to change yourself. You had to, it was the misery that forced you... But with me, well, my dreams are just dreams. I'm satisfied enough with myself. I don't see much reason to change. I doubt that at my age it would even make much difference anyway. So why bother with trying to make sense out of my dreams? They're just dreams. I wouldn't know where to begin."

"The way to begin is simple. You just notice them. You don't even have to write them down. Just start telling them to someone else in the morning, so the dreams get noticed. Play with them a little bit, getting associations and feelings. Mainly just notice what starts to rise in you—feelings, memories, fantasies. You notice what makes a felt connection."

"What if there's nothing?" he said impishly. "Nothing?"

"Could be your ego may resist it and not want to recognize it."

"Yes," he said eventually. "I do have dreams sometimes."

"You want to try it? We could do it tomorrow morning and see what your dreams say to you."

"My dreams don't say anything to me. They're just weird little stories, not even stories sometimes."

"What did you think of that African story?"

"Oh, I thought that chapter was fascinating. I'm finding out things about you I never knew before. And that African thing—is that a real African folk tale?—" I nodded—"Well, it reminded me of those books I've read by Laurens van der Post."

My husband met van der Post in Zurich a couple of years ago and was impressed by him. Later he even asked me to find all of van der Post's books. I think what particularly impressed him about this frail, shrunken old gentleman was the aura that he carried as he spoke of his eighty-five years in trekking over Africa, and internment in a Malaysian prisoner of war camp, and finding beauty in the Kalahari Desert and in human nature.

As van der Post spoke, an owl kept calling from a tree outside the open window. My husband looked over and raised his eyebrow, oddly excited. "Do you hear that?" he whispered. "Is it an owl? What's an owl doing here in town?"

Wisdom, I was thinking. Wisdom sits here with us. Afterward, a woman told me that she was playing a tape of the talk and she could hear the owl calling in the background. To me, it showed event and symbol weaving together, and my husband noticed it and I believe got the message on a subliminal level, if not a conscious one.

I said, "In that African story, what did you think of the old woman with the sores on her feet? Of her asking the little girl to lick them."

"To tell the truth, it reminded me of an old joke. The man goes out into the wilds. He pulls down his pants and starts to take a shit. A snake bites him on his butt. He rushes back to town to get help. Now, the only way you can treat a snakebite is to suck out the poison. So after awhile he says, 'By golly, this is a time when you find out who your friends really are.'"

Isn't that the truth! It's the old lady and her feet all over again."

And now it's time to stop and see a client.

So guess what happened. Yes. You've got it. Somehow the session was about the client following the path of dreams to her true identity, not a composite mask imposed by society. In one dream, she tried on three different noses, hoping to find the correct nose. But they were all masks that hid and distorted her real face. She needed a true nose, not a false one. Developing a nose for things means you're training your intuition. Yes, she is. This will lead her into her true way.

Just as I need a true title for this book, not a false one. That earlier title—*Ready, Set, Dream!*—I can tell now, was imposed by my notion of what the buying public wants—another how-to, can-do, get-up-and-go-gettum book.

But my dreamtime said, "Uh-uh." Okay. It knows about the collective. After all, it's based there. I've got to reach out now to clasp the true handle. It should be something about getting and reading nightly letters.... I'll ponder that.

So perhaps this chapter provides half of the clasp on the dream necklace. The yang plug, maybe, or what electricians and plumbers call the male connector. A yang clasp will put a handle on the book's true identity and name it. But that yang rod needs to enter a yin socket for closure. Maybe that's what's coming tomorrow, the last chapter. This closure of this necklace, I mean.

CHAPTER 24

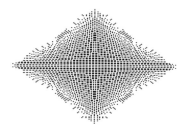

Full Circle

Dream Log—Saturday, December 3:

Dream: A boy, my son, but not my real son. He's standing in front of it all and looking at it. He's eager to begin.

In the dark I start emerging from sleep, and I'm losing all the rich detail. It eludes me even as I try to go back in after it. And then my husband starts coughing. I recoil from the sound because it's ripping me out of my dream.

But John keeps on coughing, more and more. This is not normal. Part of me is fighting to rise up out of the dream and see what's wrong with him; part of me wants to submerge and dive into my dream again.

He keeps coughing, though—it sounds almost like choking now—and I wake up, worried. "Are you all right? What's the matter?"

"I don't know." He props up on one elbow, keeps clearing his throat and coughing. I imagine a horde of dancing tiny feathers inside his breathing passages, tickling his throat and nostrils. I wonder if it's something he's breathed in during the night, fluff or whatever.

Still he's coughing, as if once the mechanism's been triggered, now it can't stop. Finally he puts his feet over the side of the bed. Turns on his light. "Guess I might as well get up."

"Not me," I groan, knowing it's close to morning. I'm sleepy and also I've lost my dream. I need it, or another. Otherwise, how do I finish this book?

I go to sleep again, but no more dreams. Eventually I get up and encounter my husband in the hall. He's all dressed. I guess he's been up awhile. I don't remember hearing him dress. "What time is it?"

"Six-thirty."

"What was wrong earlier? Why were you coughing so?"

"I don't know. Some crud in my throat, I guess."

"What time did you get up, anyway?"

"5:30. But I went back to bed after I peed. I just got up again."

"You did?" I don't remember any of this, not him coming back to bed, nor getting up, nor dressing. I must have been out.

I return to bed—after all, it's 6:30 a.m. on a dark Saturday to sleep for another hour. When I wake up, still no more dreams. What am I to do? Here I am ready to bring this log to a close, but with no closing dream to end it. Just a gobbet where my son stands in front of things, looking at it, eager to begin.

Hmm. Earlier my daughter was in a dream. She was supervising this book structure, enjoying her creation, happy with it. So I gave her the necklace for her subtle body.

And now here comes my son, eager to begin...what? Working with dreams, I suppose. I open my dream log to today's hexagrams:

How Will Today Be?	*Help Me Go Properly Today*	**My Feeling Today?**
1 59	10 6	56 23

Hmm. *Creative Action*, 1, has three changing lines, so I have to hold the creative energy and not act on it yet. The movement then changes to *Dissolving the Blocks*, 59. That sounds good. But how? Can I go back to sleep and dream up something? Well, the I Ching says it will turn out okay if I'll just hold onto the creative energy.

So how can I go properly today? *Tread Carefully*, 10—I'll be stepping on a tiger's tail today, but I won't get bitten. Then it changes to *Conflict*, 6. Sounds ominous, doesn't it, yet this is the proper path today. So I must allow for conflict, both in myself and with others. Conflict can be constructive, after all, if it's handled well.

Finally, how will I feel today? I start out as a *Traveler in a New Land*, 56, where I do not know the territory. Yep, I don't know how the layout for this chapter. Yet my psyche son stands looking things over and he's eager to begin. But there's more; it changes into *Breaking Away From the Old Condition*. This is a hexagram that I often see mishandled in the I Ching books. Generally, it is interpreted as negative, as some form of breaking apart. But I've found it means splitting away from an old condition, and that can sometimes be very good.

I mull this over till my husband comes back from drinking coffee at the Munz. Then I get up, still in pajamas, and mix some brown rice with milk and chopped banana. I take it to the breakfast table and sit down across from him.

"I don't know what to write about today. I lost my dream this morning while you were coughing. I tried to get it back, and then I let it go to see about you. I don't know how to end this chapter."

He looks at me oddly. It almost sounds like if I'm blaming him for the lost dream. Well, I don't mean that, actually, but I feel stymied.

Why do I have such a feeling of loss, anyway? For that matter, this fragment is no shorter than several I've worked with in the last month. What's the big deal? But still, my dream son was looking forward with eager anticipation. Looking forward to what?

My husband says diffidently, "Well, I had a dream today. I had it after I went back to bed this morning."

"You mean after your coughing?"

Suddenly I'm beginning to figure out—right now—what my dream son is looking forward to. Is it jumping into my husband's dream?

"Yes, after you lost yours. But you didn't say that till just now. I had mine—I don't know—sometime between 5:40 and when I got up."

I eat my rice and consider this. Dreamtime bonds us all. We go into the unknown together when we sleep. I suspect that my dream son, this explorer born of my psyche, is now anticipating a new adventure in the territory of my husband's dream. I am excited by what I see, the thin edge of it coming. This dream of my husband's sounds like maybe it's for the both of us. Maybe that's the way to end this book.

If my husband agrees, of course. After all, it's his dream, not mine. Would he want to share it with others?

I smile to myself, remembering the hexagrams about today. Yep, here it is. I need to tread carefully about his dream and not get bitten. And I am conflicted about it. I don't want to snatch his dream out from under him. Yet somehow I know he's going to share it. For many reasons. Because of his tone. Because of how this day has been laying itself out so far. And because it dissolves the block. It also explains the travel—I'll be traveling in the new land of his dream instead of my own, breaking away from my old way of working. That must be what *Breaking Away* means.

So this is the feminine part of the clasp. It will be holding someone else's symbolic meaning in the last chapter, connecting it with the rest.

I say tentatively, "Yesterday we said we'd talk about your dreams today. Do you want to?"

"I guess so. Why not? But this dream doesn't mean anything at all."

"Well, let's talk about it and see."

He starts telling it to me: "It's you and me and my ex-wife. I was with you, and she was several yards away, sort of separate from us the whole time. She didn't talk, but she looked serious. We all did. We weren't laughing and joking. You were kind of in charge of the whole thing, I do remember that. We were taking all these children...taking them on a hike. Kind of an exploratory hike. Not *our* children. That's the only way I know how to put it. There were quite a few of them.

"Most of them were walking up ahead, exploring sort of, but you were carrying one on your shoulder, and I was too sometimes. We wandered through a kind of land with a lot of scrubby vegetation on it. Really, they were young saplings. They were about one and a half or two inches in diameter and eight or ten feet tall—not much foliage on them. We got down to a low area where there was a grassy...kind of a swampy area. You could see a little water in spots every once in a while.

"And about that time I noticed a kind of electrical phenomenon happening right on the ground, hovering just a few inches off the ground, like lightning. It looked like current or thin electrical wire maybe, thick as a big pencil lead—like lightning a few inches off the ground and making a shape sort of like this when you look down at it." He drew a sketch of it.

"This would be a picture of one instant looking down—but it was not static, it kept moving. It was white lightning tinged with pink and blue. It looked interesting to me."

"And I remember that I saw off to the right, up the hill a bit, this young girl maybe twelve years old sitting on the front porch of a shack-like cottage. She was staring out at the ground and looking disconsolate. Not much expression on her face, really, but she wasn't very happy.

"Then we were walking along, just starting up the hill, and we came to these young guys, teenagers, fourteen or fifteen years old. They were teasing us or harassing us. But we kind of brushed them aside, at any rate.

"We set off up this slope. Some of the children were running on up ahead of us, going fast. And we were carrying a couple. I remember feeling that this expedition wasn't going quite like we'd planned. It was supposed to be a lot of fun, but I was feeling some apprehension too."

He thought a minute as if checking to see if he'd said everything.

"And I remember that part of the time you were carrying a kid on your shoulder, and when we were going through the thicket, I was apprehensive that it would get lashed by the branches.

"I do remember that my ex-wife was off to one side the whole time, but she was there. We weren't talking, but I remember her facial expressions as serious. None of us were really laughing and smiling.

"I remember too that the ground going along in that marshy area was not smooth. There were angular places like the grass was covering over slabs of rock.

"And I remember feeling that it was a good thing, what we were doing. We were being nice people to take these kids on this hike." He chuckled.

"Then I woke up, and got up. I remembered this dream. And then I thought of you and your book of dreams. I thought of how different my dreams are from yours. My dreams always involve people. They are real people—usually people I know—like in this case you and me and my ex-wife."

"John, do you know these children?"

"No, not any of them. They're just children. This morning I asked myself if maybe one of those children was Sibbeth." She's a three-year-old he'd babysat a couple of hours last week for her parents. "But no, it wasn't Sibbeth. I didn't know any of those children. It occurred to me—isn't it odd, here I've been reading your dreams for a month now, and I can't remember many that involved real people. Seems like your dreams are a lot simpler—sometimes they involve just a kind of abstraction. But mine, they involve my sons and daughters, my friends, coworkers. My brother."

"Well, dreams go in phases. You get different motifs at different periods. Like Picasso's blue period and his pink period. And I used to have a lot more people I know in them. They're more abstract these days—I don't know why. Maybe I'll start getting more people back in my dreams later. Dreams flux and flow."

"But my dream doesn't make any sense to me. Does it to you?"

"Well, maybe." I didn't want to push it, though, because he's not used to analyzing dreams. It takes time to start seeing the symbols and feeling the associations and delving for the meaning. And as Swifty taught me, it does no good to analyze a person's dream up, down, sideways, and backwards and hand it over printed on a card. Not if the person doesn't make a felt connection with it. The meaning has to resonate within the dreamer or it's just academic conjecture.

"What does this dream remind you of?"

"Not anything. Taking some children on an expedition."

"And what did you think about after you woke up?"

"I started thinking about you and your dream book."

"Could this dream have something to do with the dream book, then? Notice whatever pops up in your train of thought right after dreaming. Because it's related somehow."

"I don't see how. What? Do you think it's about the book?"

"Well, it's the first thing you thought of, me and the book. I doubt it's only that, though. You can look at a dream from lots of different angles. And they all work. It's a hologram. Probably this dream has a whole raft of things for me and another whole raft for you. Dreams are that rich."

"What does it mean for you?"

Better to be truthful, I guess, than coy. "I'm wondering if maybe this is how the dream book could end. Not with my dream, but yours. With starting to work on someone else's dream. You can see, it is spreading it to another person."

What I'm thinking, but not saying, is this: it feels like a dream for the collective. If that's the case, those children could be dream novices. Together he and I are taking them up the mountain to explore the dreamscape.

What I said was, "Well, I lost my dream today. It left me weirdly stymied. All I had left was this son eager to begin. Begin what? I wonder now if maybe he is beginning to look into your dream? To find out what it means for both of us. And for the readers too."

He thought it over, started smiling.

"See, you had your dream after I lost mine. So maybe my dream son knew I was going to lose my dream and would be walking into yours.

Sure enough, here I am right now, appearing in your dream with you. We're taking a bunch of unknown kids on a exploratory hike."

"But how did I know? You didn't tell me you'd lost your dream. How could I know to dream up a final chapter for you?"

"Hey, here we sit at the breakfast table, just human beings limited to moving in space. But god isn't limited to that. God can also travel in time. Back and forth and in the moment. Knitting things together. We just don't realize it because we can't do it. But god can do it. And so god can rework the future infinitely, depending on our choices along the way. It matters what we do. And are. And because of that, god resets the timing of the future for us as we change. Constantly."

He was looking odd.

I said, "Well, don't you think so? Even the timing of your dream suggests that. Dreaming is not just a private act. It is also a collective act that ties us together. So…look, would it be okay if I finish the dream book with your dream? If I'll write it down exactly, and we talk about it and so forth?"

"Sure. If you think it's worth it. Doesn't matter to me."

"Yes. It's a wonderful dream, and it feels like the right way to end. Come sit beside me at the computer, so I can get your words exactly. It's a long dream. I want you to tell it all again, starting from the top."

So we did. Then I printed out a copy, gave it to him, and said, "Think about this as you go around this morning. We'll talk about it later. Okay?"

"Yes. But what do I do?"

"Just notice what this dream reminds you of, what it makes you think about." Then I added, "And thanks."

"For—?" he said with a deprecating laugh.

"For sharing the dream. For helping me finish the book."

Then I sat down again, considering this dream. You do it too.

Later in the morning I asked my husband what the dream brought up in him. "Well, all these children. They're not my children. But I care about them. I'm concerned about them. I guess for the welfare of others." He says it rather tentatively, looking at me apparently to see if it sounded strange or oddball. "After all, I've spent a lot of years working with the younger generation." He used to teach school.

"Okay. Anything else?"

"And then this hike we take. It wasn't any easy pathway, you know. Going up the hill. Well, that's life, isn't it? That's the way it is."

"Yes. An uphill climb."

"And you're carrying a child mostly, but I am too sometimes. And you're sort of in charge—like with the dream book."

"What about your ex-wife? Do you know why she's there?"

"No. She's just helping out somehow. Although neither of us talks to her. She's just some kind of backup support, I guess." Anima figures, I'm thinking. I'm one and she's another. He loved her a lot, and she still means a great deal to him. And I guess he's projecting his soul image onto both us women. We carry the projection for him.

"What about this dream girl sitting on the porch?"

"Well, she's on the porch of this shanty-cottage…looking very sad."

"Disconsolate, you said earlier."

"Yes. She looks unhappy. She's left out of things. I didn't think much about her at the time. I just noticed her there."

"Why is she sad? Do you know?"

"Well, those boys are all together, those harassing boys. But she's all alone. She has no one to play with. I think she's lonely. She somehow or other got left out."

"And the boys?"

"I don't know. They're not my boys. Not my real sons, you know. They're making a nuisance of themselves. They're trying to harass us on this hike up the slope. I remember I can't to see to the top. I don't know where it ends." He stops. "That's all I can think of."

"Okay."

After lunch I said, "Look, I'm going over to see Katrine at 2:00. Would you mind if I take a copy of your dream along to show her?"

"Why? Why would she care about my dream?"

"Well, she knows you and she knows a lot about dreams. We can talk about it tomorrow when she comes over to dinner. Somehow I feel like it's a collective dream—all those little children—and I'd like to see what she says…but only if that's all right with you."

"Sure. Fine with me."

Printing out the dream, I discovered I needed to stop by the stationer's for computer paper before it closed at 4:00 p.m. for the weekend. So I bought computer paper and then walked over to Katrine's apartment and we walked on down a block to Fahnlibrunnen Restaurant, where we sat in a booth for over two hours. Nearby was a table of Swiss card players, drinking and playing and joking. Eventually, I got out my husband's dream and showed it to her.

"What a wonderful dream!"

"That's what I said too. I'm wondering what you see in it."

"Well, I see that this book has made a bridge between you and John. He didn't understand before, about this interest in dreams that he didn't share. But now he is perhaps beginning to suspect that it could be important to him. Now you are not alone in working with dreams, in understanding the meaning. Or in seeming like only you care to notice the meaning of things. Because it is not true. He also cares. He's just not familiar with these ways of reading the unconscious."

"Yes. Okay."

"It's interesting that his ex-wife is here. What does he think of her?"

"He loved her a lot. I'm sure he still does."

"But he's walking with you."

"Yes. She's in the background now—well, like in this dream. I think she helped him a lot, meant a lot to him. She left him, not vice versa. He cares about her still, and that won't ever change."

"An anima figure."

"Yes. She's an old anima figure, and I'm a newer one."

"But look at this young girl sitting alone on the porch."

"She's been left out of things. He told me that she is lonely."

"Oh? And she's twelve. I wonder what happened to him at that age? I wonder what happened to leave this aspect of his feminine side alone and sad on the porch as he grew up?"

"I don't know. I'll ask him."

"She needs to play, maybe."

"Maybe."

"And all these children coming here. You're going up the hill together with all this creative potential. It's a good thing you're doing for the children."

We made a date for her to join us for Sunday dinner at 1:00 tomorrow. My husband is cooking a leg of lamb, and I'm doing green beans and potatoes. When he found the meat in the market yesterday, we decided on asking company to help us enjoy it.

Back at home, I wondered how to pursue this with my husband. I felt conflicted. How much should I probe? Give it a rest, I decided, don't push, wait till tomorrow. This evening, we'll go out to see friends.

At 6:30 we walked a block to the train station. Rode twenty minutes up the lake. Entered our friends' apartment. And wonder of wonders, within thirty minutes my husband was bringing up his dream. It drew out reminiscences about being married, about his children, about his childhood. It was such an unusual tack for my husband to be taking that Brad and Carla kept asking him more questions, making comments, and voila!—before the evening was out, the three of them covered all the dream ground I'd wondered about and decided not to probe.

What of that solitary girl on the front porch of the shanty? It seems that my husband started high school at the age of twelve. A four-year high school—freshman, sophomore, junior, senior. He'd been double-promoted twice, and felt much younger than the others, and he held his own by being very smart in a scholarly, sensible way. He dropped his art interests because he didn't believe he excelled at them. Dropped painting, although he used to water color (now his son has oils and watercolors hanging in various galleries, and his daughter's witty acrylic above the living room couch is one of my favorite paintings). Dropped writing poetry, although he used to enjoy it (and he still makes up dirty limericks). Dropped short stories. "After all," he said, "I read Shakespeare and it made chills go up my spine at the words. The stuff I wrote looked pretty puny."

"Well, it's easy to put creativity on hold, set it on the porch of a shanty to languish alone." We turn art, symphonies, movies into public spectator events—and we're used to that. TV took even storytelling away. Where is there room left for the ordinary person to express creativity? Where is the ordinary family willing to audience it?

Sitting in the couch, my husband was nodding agreement.

Carla said, "What about that electrical energy dancing around? That's amazing! Maybe it's creative energy coming from the swampland."

"From the watery unconscious," I said, recalling my own dream at the first of this book. Yes, this final dream of John's does makes a circle. It connects the end with the beginning.

Brad said, "So you turned very rational. You had to hold your own with boys—that can mean very rational. The little twelve-year-old girl is left on the porch of the rundown shanty of your creative life. Hah!—that's about the age I stopped my painting too. What about those boys, John? Fourteen and fifteen-year-olds? The age of the boys you were facing when you started high school…they harassed you out of expressing your inner feminine side. So the twelve-year-old girl got left on the porch then."

My husband was nodding yes. Obviously this was striking home. Here's how others can help with dream work, I was thinking. They can express reactions and ideas, and either it clicks or it doesn't. Either way, okay. Either it's not so, or the dreamer denies it for some reason. If someone starts stonewalling, well, okay. You can't force revelation.

I remember the little boy who used to appear in my dreams. Once he was seven years old, wearing cowboy boots, and he took my hand in trust. He wanted to go up in a rocket. But I said we weren't ready to go up yet, we would just sit in it awhile first and practice. So it became more like a child's scooter, because braking involved dragging our feet alongside the scooter part.

My own fine analyst back then never said, "Oh, that's a woefully undeveloped animus figure, that little boy. Move more swiftly." Instead, he just carried me on through the process of inner nurturing and growth. The dream process works with or without the jargon, if you can get it going.

And now that kid's a man in my dreams and he helps me. His face changes often, and his professions—he's quite versatile. But always he's inside. Always. He is my soul image, my guide into the hidden world. If I am loyal and faithful to him, things work out. Perhaps not the way that I had in mind.

It was a good evening last night. At the door, my husband apologized for talking so much. Carla grinned. "Oh, don't apologize. I loved hearing that stuff. I thought I did very well not asking too terribly many questions, not as many as I wanted to."

At the train station on the way home, I said, "You know, I have a watercolor set. It's not expensive, but they're nice colors, over twenty of them. And a pad of paper. You can fool around with them if you want to."

"I might take you up on that."

Yes, I do think this dream completes the book. It puts the lefthand, feminine clasp on the necklace. It brings closure. We're full circle now and the chapters form a necklace. So I turn it over to you. In your hands you hold this necklace for your subtle body. Yes, even for you men too. Some part of you can wear it. And yes, I think it suits you. I hope you like it. Wear it in good health.

295

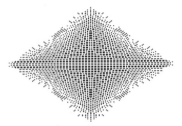

Dream Discovery Tips

Here are some tips to help your dreaming become a good, close friend.

Keep a dream log. Write down your dreams as soon as you can, even in the middle of the night. At the very least, write them down before getting out of bed. You're likely to lose them if you move around much. Hold the same position for a few moments after waking to help you remember the dream better. Another possibility is to use a voice-activated recorder and then write the dream down later.

Log your dream in the present tense. Act as if you're dreaming it even as you write or speak. For example, say "I am walking down the road" instead of "I walked down the road." In this way, the dream retains its immediacy and helps you to recall the details better.

Welcome each dream, even the troubling ones, and even the fragmentary bits. All can give information. Welcome and treat all dreams as your inner guide to psychic balance.

First, go for the affect—the feeling tone in the dream. This is the single most important clue. Don't judge a dream by how you feel about it *after* you wake up, but by how you feel *in* it. For example, if you walk around as an ax murderer in a dream and enjoy it immensely, don't censor and hate yourself for the dream act. Instead figure it out—what is it that you need to end in your life? Is it a destructive relationship, a job you hate, a stupid ego stance you've been posturing in? Learn *symbolically,* so you don't find yourself enacting it blindly in flesh! Your dreamtime theater is bigger than your ego. Don't mistake or equate its events and feelings with your waking behavior. Don't think that your dream must be lived out literally. It is only a symbolic show of changes to make.

Draw little diagrams of the seating at dinner or house layouts or whatever shows up in a dream that you can't quite get into words. Sometimes even as you draw it, you'll realize why something was positioned just *there.* Nonverbal imagery can tell you much.

When you finish writing down your dream and thinking about it, give that experience a title. Its very title will tell you much about what it wants you to learn from it.

Share your dreams with others when possible. Dreams like to be told. They want to relate and be related. You don't have to say much more than the bare dream sometimes. The meaning is often signalled and understood at an unconscious level. When you can say more, it will aid you in finding and becoming and liking your true self.

Talk your dreams over with someone to amplify the message and make it stronger, much like a speaker system amplifies music. If you have no partner who can willingly share dreams with you, then consider starting a small dream group or circle. Include four to six people who can meet once a week or twice a month and really share and discuss each other's dreams—with tact, honor, and discretion. Things uttered in this group belong only here; group members must count on each other's loyalty and ability to protect privileged information. Working in a dream group is a real exercise in insight and honesty; it develops kindness, tolerance and dependability among the group members. You learn to work with each person's brilliance and shadow in tolerant surroundings. A dream group is a real gift that you can slowly learn to be worthy of.

Comment on dreams by expressing your own feelings and associations. Do not judge or condemn yourself or others for the dream content. Dreams are the drawing board for life. Each night elaborates some old sketches and presents some new ones. Murdering your cousin in a dream does not mean that you will do it in real life, or even that you want to. Having sex with your boss in a dream does not mean you're about to do so in real life. Dying in a dream does not mean that you're about to die. Each event is a metaphor for a psychic situation that needs exploration. A dream is presenting this night letter with a little parable in it. Read it in the daylight of consciousness to understand the metaphor. One important reason for sharing dreams is that it helps you go beyond your own ego boundaries of interpretation. Others can present to you new aspects.

Bring dream work into your daily life. Dreams are the human heritage. They need not be reserved for a private office and an analyst's couch. They are our common link with humanity each night and our shared tool for evolving the group psyche. It is only in the truth of shared dreams merging into reality that we can learn to be individual within our common genetic and cultural heritage.

Realize that you won't see the whole message of a dream at once. Or ever. A dream is a hologram. You will not see it from every angle immediately. It will open symbolically over time, endlessly, giving new aspects and vistas. When I go over a decades-old dream, I still discover some unexpected new angle and continuity.

Sometimes details rise slowly to consciousness like in a developing photo. One client of mine wrote her dreams down at the end of the day instead of the beginning, because for her, the details continued to emerge at work through the day. Some might say that she was perhaps embroidering or rearranging her dreams. Perhaps, but I don't think so. I think that probably bits of the message came up in the day as she was ready to consider them, triggered by association.

It is known that sometimes people will tell a dream in a somewhat scrambled order when first awaking, and then rearrange the sequence or emphasis on later consideration. This has been taken by dream researchers to mean that the first version of the dream details was the correct one and the second version a mere distortion by consciousness. But it seems to me not necessarily so. The mind is subtler than that, and more profound, and later variations and sequences in the layers of meaning may have a more comprehensive import.

For example, after finishing writing this book, as I read back over the manuscript, I found a continuity of dreams and chapters that I sometimes hadn't noticed in the heat of the moment. The *Chronicle of Days* gives a one-sentence overview of the chapters on a symbolic level, along with the I Ching hexagrams for the day. Be sure to overview the record of your own dreams occasionally to find the threads of continuity.

Consider doing Dream Drama. Over time I have developed a way of enacting and studying dreams that I call Dream Drama, which nowadays I teach in workshops. It is a quicker, more accessible version of the psychodrama techniques that have been developed by a number of people. I urge you to explore this or some other enactment technique, because it makes the dream more immediate and tangible to the dreamer. Dreams have a secret language, full of verbal and visual puns. Much of it is hidden in the dumb show of symbol, gesture, setting, and stage props. Acting brings it alive.

If you can't remember your dreams, ask yourself why. Try to figure this out. Do you really want to bother with them? Do you keep a pen and pad or diary or recorder by your bed to log your dreams when you awake? Welcome each dream and it will open like a flower.

Have you explained to your mate that studying your dreams matters to you and why? The person you sleep with needs to understand this odd habit you are now trying to develop—turning on the light or talking into a recorder in the middle of the night—and why you're doing it. Perhaps it will even be possible to share your dreams in daylight with this person. On the other hand, a lack of empathy in your bed mate can stifle the dream-remembering. It can even become a sign that messages from the unconscious are being ignored and repressed in the relationship.

Everyone dreams; some folks just don't remember it. Are you suppressing the memory of your dreams because you don't really want to find out what they say and rock the boat of your unhappy but survivable (barely) present lifestyle? This is a common ego hedge against changes. If the waking life is trying to paper over an enormous unhappiness with a fragile facade of "let's pretend," it takes real courage to look into your dreams honestly.

The only good thing about dream repression is the relief that comes from quitting it. Let go and relax into your dreams. Once you start really facing your dreams, they become much less threatening than you'd expected. As you start cooperating, the figures become welcome, helpful friends instead of haunting monsters to flee from.

If you just can't remember your dreams, check out these aspects of your health—*stress, diet,* **and** *exercise.*

1. Stress—Some people get more stressed out than others by the "normal events of daily life." Are you thin-skinned? I mean this literally here—is your skin sensitive and fragile? Are you blonde? Red-haired? Blue-eyed? Significantly underweight and wispy, or maybe puffy and inclined to overweight? Are you a female in the last few days of your premenstrual phase? Do you smoke? Drink alcohol? Do drugs? Live in a polluted, noisy environment? Are you physically ill? Suffer from allergies or asthma? Do you lack the time for quiet periods for yourself? Do you live in a taxing environment or personal relationship? Is your work situation a chronic aggravation? Do you crave sugar and caffeine, especially in the late afternoon or evening? Does something sweet just make you crave more rather than sating your appetite? Are you depressed? Frantic? Often angry? As winter comes on, do you crave carbohydrates or alcohol and feel depressed?

Any of these characteristics can show a person who is quickly taxed by stress. You need to find ways to reduce it. Make time for yourself. Put more pleasure and satisfaction into your work, your personal relationships—somehow. If you frequently feel the need to escape into drugs or alcohol or adrenaline-based thrills, something is basically wrong with your lifestyle. Ask why you're stressing yourself out with dangerous distractions instead of moving to deal with the basic issues.

Realize that not all stress is bad, nor should all of it be removed from life. You need *moderate, resolvable stress* to keep you active and creative. But some people get so stressed that their B vitamins become depleted. Why? The water-soluble Bs are used up very quickly in stress. Also, some bodies don't utilize them as well as others. Workload and exterior events, a cold or flu can temporarily rob your body of the Bs. Asthma, skin rashes, and allergies are physical symptoms that also wave a red flag for stress on the psyche. A yeast infection can also be behind the stress. Allergies and hypoglycemia are often the signal of a massive systemic yeast infection. It can be treated with herbs and vitamins.

If you can't *ever* remember your dreams at all, this is a sign you're under too much stress. Cut down on stress and add more B vitamins, the natural nerve padder. One way to do it is to take acidophilus capsules to help your body manufacture its own Bs. Insufficient Bs, and especially B6 cause you to forget your dreams. Since taking vitamin C can energize the B vitamins, it's good to take them in combination.

2. Diet—The issue of what one can drink and eat with impunity is not a morality issue to me, but merely one of physical and psychic health. Some people may eat lots of fatty meat and refined carbohydrates and smoke and drink alcohol without unduly impairing the psyche and body—but a whole large class of us cannot. The task becomes finding out what your own unique psyche and body tolerate and need.

In times of stress, the body gets a craving for carbohydrates as comfort foods. Unrefined foods like oats and whole wheat bread really do comfort the nervous system. But *refined* carbohydrates just weaken it further! Since your body can't process refined carbohydrates without getting the lacking Bs from somewhere, it draws them from the store you already have inside. In consuming ice cream and candy and beer and whiskey, you wind up with a deficit rather than a bonus of Bs, and your nerves just suffer further from this fake form of comfort food.

Experience has shown that often anorectic/bulemics suffer from this very problem. They have such trouble because bad eating habits have put the blood sugar regulator out of whack. The worsening situation feeds back into its own escalating disaster program. Guilt, family pressure, and medical mismanagement further reinforce the negative feedback loop. This pattern is especially common in women because the female body is more susceptible to getting into this feedback loop. The woman can find a way out, but only by altering the loop itself—how?—by giving the body *healthy* food in moderation, and by indulging only in healthy sweets, not those bulemic-driving addictors like the refined sugars and salts and chocolate and weird diet additives in junk food.

Eating healthy whole foods is the best way to keep your psyche healthy *and also to remember your dreams.* Too old-fashioned to sound appealing? Then you've bought the fake-is-better mystique, to your own detriment. By the way, getting adequate B_6 can have an interesting side effect. It can greatly increase a woman's orgasmic potential. Many who do not easily come to orgasm will enjoy sex better with this supplement. I don't know if this applies to males too. I suspect it does.

3. Regular exercise, odd as it may seem, helps one dream more regularly. The stretching process of yoga, for instance, decompresses the vertebrae of the spinal cord—in yoga terms, it lets the coiled serpent of kundalini energy travel up through the chakras to the brain. From long experience, I have seen that this is not malarky! It really does unleash potent new energy, sometimes so abruptly that it is startling. Once I had a friend who trembled most of the time for six weeks as the kundalini was rising through her body. When it was over, she was far more insightful and balanced in her life course. It really enhanced her spiritual development. But any regular exercise will benefit your waking and dreaming body. Walk the dog for twenty minutes in the evening, if nothing more.

I hope you've enjoyed these dreams and days. But more than that, I hope this book becomes a springboard for diving into your own dreams. You needn't take my approach, of course, which is basically analinear. Other dream strategies work too—straight Freudian or Jungian or gestalt, for example—but I've found that combining analinear analysis with Dream Drama yields the most gold for me. It explores archetypal analogs and connects them with cause-and-effect logic. It emphasizes psychic growth and development throughout life rather than harping on childhood traumas in a guilt/blame-oriented way. It is positive rather than negative because it promotes the understanding and integration of shadow issues as a normal part of growth. It helps me dream my life and live my dream, and have them become one.

Good dreaming.

How to Do the I Ching

The *Chronicle of Days* in back gives a brief summary of this month. It includes the I Ching hexagrams that I derived each evening for the upcoming day. I used the I Ching stones that I developed after studying the I Ching and its many commentators, especially Richard Wilhelm, Hellmut Wilhelm, and Larry Schoenholtz. I like this method because it is faster than the coin method, yet as Schoenholtz, says, it retains the mathematical proportions of the ancient yarrow stick method. It has superior aesthetic harmony and smoothness.

Basically the stones method is this: find some small stones or beans or buttons *of the same size* in four different colors. Color-code them to represent the four different kinds of hexagram lines. Mix them in a container using the ratio of 7 yin to 5 yang to 3 changing yang to 1 changing yin—or 16 stones in all. Now you have your ongoing I Ching consulting kit. You can keep it in a tin or box or bag. I use a cloth pouch.

Here's how I made my own kit. First I color-coded the four I Ching lines according to the elements of black earth, clear air, red fire and blue water. Each color symbolizes a specific kind of line: *Stable Yin* is black, *Stable Yang* is clear, *Changing Yang* is red, and *Changing Yin* is blue. Then I bought some flat glass "stones" in these colors. (I call them stones, since they look like colored quartz). I decided on glass stones for several reasons. Glass is a natural substance—silica. With glass, I can get uniform weight and texture, as well as size. Its black mimics the opacity of Yang Earth, while for Yang Heaven, the transparency of clear glass offers a better symbolic representation of the sky's clear air, in my opinion, than does opaque white. The kit can also be purchased commercially, if you don't want to go to the bother of making your own kit.

Stable Lines		*Changing Lines*	
		changing	changing
yin	*yang*	*yang*	*yin*
7	5	3	1
Black Earth	**Clear Heaven**	**Red Fire**	**Blue Water**

*Use 7 **black** to 5 **clear** to 3 **red** to 1 **blue** stone.*

302

Notice, to show a changing line, I mark a dot after that line. Some people use Xs and 0s written over the lines, but I prefer the after-dot.

Before asking your question, meditate on it. Ask for the answer you need, not the answer you want to hear. Seek truth, and seek to be able to recognize and accept it. The I Ching can become an amazing therapist, if you can hear and heed. Write down your question to review and evaluate it later. Also jot down the date and any other info you may need later.

Now consult the I Ching to find your hexagram answer. Do this by taking one stone or bead out of the container without looking inside. Its color gives the bottom line of your hexagram. Write down this hexagram line keyed to its color. For instance, if it is a black stone, write down a bottom line of stable yin. Then replace it into the container in order to keep the proportions true. Next draw out a second stone to get your second line, which is again keyed to its color. For instance, if it is red, write down your second line is changing yang. Do this six times in all to get the six lines, which builds your hexagram from the bottom line up. Mark your changing lines, as shown in the graphic. If you have one or more changing lines, then also write down your changed hexagram. This second hexagram is also part of your answer.

For example, suppose you first get a red stone; second a white; third a red; fourth a white; fifth a red; and finally a red as your top and last line. The dots will show four changing lines. Looking at the hexagram key of any I Ching book will show that you've got Hexagram 1, ☰ Heaven, changing to Hexagram 40, ☷ Thus, the dots of Hexagram 1 show four changing lines, which turn it next into Hexagram 40.

These hexagrams provide the answer to your question. Look them up in your I Ching book and mediate on them. Consider the analogies for your own situation. Pay attention to your intuition and associations.

By the way, you may notice that some of the hexagram titles I use are not exactly like those in some of the best-known translations. From studying ancient Chinese and the sixty-four hexagrams correlated with their event patterns, I have come upon the titles you find here. When one consults with various sources, one finds a translation of the characters can be rendered with wide latitude, so it is understandable why I Ching versions vary so widely. Therefore I correlated each hexagram's dynamics with the recorded years of my own questions and events for each day, and thus came up with the titles you find here.

Good traveling. The I Ching is an organizational pattern deeper and higher than I can reach, and exploring it is an endless trip.

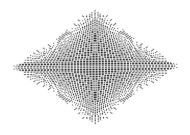

Chronicle of Days

Chapter 1: *Saturday, November 5*
Sawing Logs, Building Dreams
In which I find a book.

How Will Today Be?
Having Much changing to *Increase*

14   42

Help Me Go Properly Today:
Rich Abundance changing to
Bite Through the Task

55   21

My Feeling Today?
Synchronicity changing to *Easy Growth*

25   35

Chapter 2: *Friday, November 4*
God is Dog Spelled Backward
In which I find that happiness leads my life and god is disguised in ordinary ways.

How Will Today Be?
Breakthrough! changing to *Enthusiasm*

43   16

Help Me Go Properly Today:
Sprouting Upward changing to
Receptive Embrace

46   2

My Feeling Today?
Conflict changing to *Sprouting Upward*

6   46

Chapter 3: *Sunday, November 6*
Three Witches of Entropy
In which I voyage to a new collective feminine identity.

How Will Today Be?
Inner Truth changing to
Onward Through the Danger

61   29

Help Me Go Properly Today:
Tending Small Tasks Conscientiously

62

My Feeling Today?
Invisible Force

7

Chapter 4: *Monday, November 7*
Uncle Sam Meets His Other Half
In which the new woman appears in the society.

How Will Today Be?
Retire and Retreat changing to
Open Fellowship

3 3   **1 3**

Help Me Go Properly Today:
The Feminine Takes Action changing to
Traveling in a New Realm

4 4   **5 6**

My Feeling Today?
Following the Path changing to *Shock!*

1 7   **5 1**

No Chapter: *Tuesday, November 8*
In which I take a vacation.

Chapter 5: *Wednesday, November 9*
Our Scheduled Night Flight is Delayed;
Please Relax in the Lounge
In which I decide not to shorten my left leg and lose this book's
stance; so taking down a tool that seems to be made of *would* but
actually contains *mettle*, I update my computer to put the whole
picture before my friends.

How Will Today Be?
Human Family—Woman Must Go Properly
changing to *Synchronicity*

3 7   **2 5**

Help Me Go Properly Today:
Modesty changing to *Easy Growth*

1 5   **3 5**

My Feeling Today?
Sprouting Upward changing to *Modesty*

4 6   **1 5**

306

Chapter 6: *Thursday, November 10*
The Soul's Heaviside Layer

In which I discover that losing can be winning, at least on the shadow side of the soul.

How Will Today Be?
Taming Force of the Small changing to
Break Away From the Old

9   23

Help Me Go Properly Today:
Shock!

51

My Feeling Today?
Onward Through the Danger changing to
Penetrating Power of the Gentle

29   57

Chapter 7: *Friday, November 11*
Harvest in Shadow Land

In which my loathsome shadow undergoes cooking and becomes beautiful.

How Will Today Be?
Breakthrough! changing to *Attraction*

43   31

Help Me Go Properly Today:
Taming Force of the Great changing to
Peaceful Unity

26   11

My Feeling Today?
Easy Growth changing to *Enthusiasm*

35   16

Chapter 8: *Saturday, November 12*
Spaceship Universe
In which I decide that ego is not the center of the universe and soul is a light in the flesh.

How Will Today Be?
Having Much changing to
Traveling in a New Realm

14   56

Help Me Go Properly Today:
Waiting and Wanting changing to
Following the Path

5   17

My Feeling Today?
Power of the Great changing to *Modesty*

34   15

Chapter 9: *Sunday, November 13*
Rising Action—Ah!—Winding Down
In which I read a plot line, musing that the upward fall past physical death is not really so different from the downward fall past ego death.

How Will Today Be?
Gradual Growth changing to
Receptive Embrace

53   2

Help Me Go Properly Today:
Bite Through the Task changing to
Shared Clarity

21   30

My Feeling Today?
Traveling in a New Realm changing to
It's Not Over Yet

56   64

Chapter 10: *Monday, November 14*
You're on Your Own
In which you do it yourself.

How Will Today Be?
Grace Period

2 2

Help Me Go Properly Today:
Shock! changing to *Following the Path*

5 1   1 7

My Feeling Today?
Penetrating Influence of the Gentle
changing to *Learning*

5 7   4

Chapter 11: *Tuesday, November 15*
One, Two, Three Dream Circus
In which the spotlight moves from the ring of infinity to the ring
of limits, and indiscretion becomes the better part of valor with
you the audience.

How Will Today Be?
Revolution changing to
Onward Through the Danger

4 9   2 9

Help Me Go Properly Today:
Well of Renewal changing to
Peaceful Unity

4 8   1 1

My Feeling Today?
Inner Truth changing to *Starting Small*

6 1   4 1

Chapter 12: *Wednesday, November 16*
Oh, Mistress Mine
In which what goes around comes around, as wisdom reunites with knowledge.

How Will Today Be?
It's Not Over Yet changing to *Modesty*

64   15

Help Me Go Properly Today:
Peaceful Unity

11

My Feeling Today?
The Feminine Takes Action changing to
Tending Small Tasks Conscientiously

44   62

Chapter 13: *Thursday, November 17*
Grand Central Station
In which the male centers the gauge and rebalances the big picture.

How Will Today Be?
Holding Together changing to
Taming Force of the Great

8   26

Help Me Go Properly Today:
Retire and Retreat changing to
Break Away From the Old

33   23

My Feeling Today?
Following the Path changing to
Laboring Birth

17   3

Chapter 14: *November 18-20*
The 72-Hour Influ-Insight
In which for three days I see more asleep than awake, and find the diamond of myself in the trash.

Friday, November 18

How Will Today Be?
Inner Truth changing to *Starting Small*

6 1   4 1

Help Me Go Properly Today:
Critical Mass changing to *Enduring*

2 8   3 2

My Feeling Today?
Holding Together changing to
Sprouting Upward

8   4 6

↓

Saturday, November 19

How Will Today Be?
Creative Action

1

↓

Sunday, November 20

How Will Today Be?
Synchronicity changing to
Retire and Retreat

2 5   3 3

Help Me Go Properly Today:
Bite Through the Task

2 1

My Feeling Today?
Standstill changing to *Retire and Retreat*

1 2   3 3

DREAM MAIL

Chapter 15: *Monday, November 21*
The Pretty Poison
In which I find that fake food is dispiriting and nutritionally speaking, pretty is as pretty does.

How Will Today Be?
Shared Joy changing to *Enthusiasm*

58   16

Help Me Go Properly Today:
Attraction changing to *Obstruction*

31   39

My Feeling Today?
Back to Square One and a Half
changing to *Invisible Force*

40   7

Chapter 16: *Tuesday, November 22*
Two Into One
In which a chunk of data becomes twins, and after a shadowy sacrifice, finds its true home.

How Will Today Be?
Gradual Progress changing to
Removing Decay

53   18

Help Me Go Properly Today:
Shared Joy changing to *Peaceful Unity*

58   11

My Feeling Today?
Sprouting Upward changing to
Enthusiasm

46   16

Chapter 17: *Wednesday, November 23*
The Colorful Captain
In which it seems better not to do things by halves, especially when they fight each other.

How Will Today Be?
Bite Through the Task changing to
Following the Path

21   17

Help Me Go Properly Today:
Grace Period changing to *Obstruction*

22   39

My Feeling Today?
Receptive Embrace

2

Chapter 18: *November 24-27*
Darkening of the Light and Vice Versa
In which depression, anger, a power-down, and addiction darken my light—temporarily.

Thursday, November 24

How Will Today Be?
Penetrating Influence of the Gentle
changing to *Sprouting Upward*

57   46

Help Me Go Properly Today:
Receptive Embrace changing to
Invisible Force

2   7

My Feeling Today?
Darkening of the Light

36

↓

↓

Chapter 18, *continued*
Friday, November 25

>**How Will Today Be?**
>*The Feminine Takes Action* changing to *Retire and Retreat*
>
>44   33

>**Help Me Go Properly Today:**
>*Following the Path* changing to
>*Turning Point for the Better*
>
>17   24

>**My Feeling Today?**
>*Retire and Retreat* changing to *Obstruction*
>
>33   39

↓

Saturday, November 26

>**How Will Today Be?**
>*Rich Abundance* changing to *Shock!*
>
>55   51

>**Help Me Go Properly Today:**
>*Following the Path* changing to *Receptive Embrace*
>
>17   2

>**My Feeling Today?**
>*Removing Decay*
>
>18

↓

Sunday, November 27
>**No Hexagrams**

Chapter 19: *Monday, November 28*
3D Heart
In which the artful hologram holds the heart of the matter.

How Will Today Be?
Open Fellowship changing to
Bite Through the Task

13   21

Help Me Go Properly Today:
Contemplation changing to *Increase*

20   42

My Feeling Today?
Waiting and Wanting changing to
Well of Renewal

5   48

Chapter 20: *Tuesday, November 29*
Do-It-Yourself Wiring
In which nobody else can rewire your brain circuitry.

How Will Today Be?
Inner Truth changing to
Bottleneck Pressure

61   47

Help Me Go Properly Today:
Easy Progress

35

My Feeling Today?
Creative Action changing to
Walk This Way!

1   10

Chapter 21: *Wednesday, November 30,1988*
Evil as a Life Force
In which the spur of evil keeps good alive.

How Will Today Be?
Removing Decay changing to *Modesty*

18   15

Help Me Go Properly Today:
Bottleneck Pressure changing to
Obstruction

47   39

My Feeling Today?
Inner Truth changing to *Limitation*

61   60

Chapter 22: *Thursday, December 1*
A Necklace for the Subtle Body
In which dreams, linked by spirit, string the beading days into a
necklace of my soul's own nature.
How Will Today Be?
Peaceful Unity

11

Help Me Go Properly Today:
Bottleneck Pressure changing to
Dissolving the Blocks

47   59

My Feeling Today?
Waiting and Wanting changing to *Peaceful
Unity*

5   11

Chapter 23: *Friday, December 2*
The Left-Brain Handle
In which I seek a proper name for this book.

How Will Today Be?
Shared Clarity changing to
Rich Abundance

  30 55

Help Me Go Properly Today:
Taming Force of the Small changing to
Onward Through the Danger

  9 29

My Feeling Today?
Tending Small Tasks Conscientiously
changing to *Receptive Embrace*

  62 2

Chapter 24: *Saturday, December 3*
Full Circle
In which—without a dream to write about—I appear in the dream of another, and together with many children, we go exploring the dreamscape of the subtle body.

How Will Today Be?
Creative Action changing to
Dissolving the Blocks

  1 59

Help Me Go Properly Today:
Walk This Way! changing to *Conflict*

  10 6

My Feeling Today?
Traveling in a New Realm changing to
Break Away From the Old

  56 23

Bibliography

Abt, Theodore. *Number Symbolism*. Privately published. Zurich: 1989.

Alexander, Patrick. *Death of a Thin-Skinned Animal*. London: Futura Publications. 1985.

Bellow, Saul. *The Dean's December*. New York: Harper & Row. 1982.

Benson, Frank, editor. *The Dual Brain: Hemispheric Specialization in Humans*. New York: Guilford Press. 1985.

Coe, Tucker. *Wax Apple*. London: Sphere Books Ltd. 1975.

Da Liu. *I Ching Numerology: Plum Blossom Numerology*. New York: Harper & Row. 1950.

D'Aquili, Eugene G. "Senses of Reality in Science and Religion: a Neuro-epistemological Perspective" in *Zygon*, Vol. 17, No. 4, December 1982.

D'Aquili, Eugene G., Laughlin, C.D., and McManus, J. *The Spectrum of Ritual: A Biogenetic Structural Analysis*. New York; Columbia University Press, 1979.

Fromm, Erich. *The Forgotten Language; An Introduction to the Understanding of Dreams, Fairy Tales and Myths*. New York: Grove Press, 1951.

Goethe. *Young Werther*.

Gordon, Rosemary. "Reflections on Jung's Concept of Synchronicity," *Harvest*, Vol. 8, pp. 77-98. 1962.

Gopi Krishna. *Kundalini: The Evolutionary Energy in Man*. London: Stuart & Watkins. 1970.

Graves, Robert. *The Greek Myths*. London: Penguin Books. 1955.

Jung, C.G. *Collected Works of C.G. Jung*. Princeton: Bollingen Press. 1959.

...*Modern Man in Search of a Soul*. New York: Harcourt, Brace & World, 1933.

... "Four Lectures on the Chakra Symbolism of Tantric Yoga and the Kundalini System" (1932). New York: *Spring* Annuals of 1975 and 1976.

King, Stephen. *Stand by Me*. New York: Viking. 1970.

Kreutzer, Carolin S. "Archetypes, Synchronicity and the Theory of Formative Causation," *Journal of Analytical Psychology*, Vol. 27, pp. 255-262. 1982.

Legge, James, trans. *I Ching: Book of Changes*. First published in 1899.

Le Guin, Ursula K. "The Language of the Night," *The Language of the Night*. New York: Putnam, 1979.

Lepore, Franco; Ptito, Maurice; Jasper, Herbert, editors. *Two Hemispheres—One Brain: Functions of the Corpus Callosum*. New York: Alan R. Liss, Inc. 1984.

Levy, Jerry. "Interhemispheric Collaboration: Single-mindedness in the Asymmetric Brain" in *Developmental Neuropsychology and Education*. C.T. Best, ed. New York: Academic Press, 1980.

Mindell, Arnold. *City Shadows: Psychological Interventions in Psychiatry. London:* Routledge. 1988.

Morrison, Toni. *Beloved.* New York: Alfred A. Knopf. 1987.

Naipaul, V. S. *Among the Believers.*

Oates, Joyce Carol. *Marya: A Life.* New York: Berkley Publishing Group. 1988.

Prentky, Robert A. *Creativity and Psychopathology, a Neurocognitive Perspective.* New York: Praeger. 1980.

Saunders & Ross. *Hypoglycemia: the Disease Your Doctor Won't Treat.*

Schoenholtz, Larry. *New Directions in the I Ching.* Secaucus, N. J.: University Books. 1975.

Watson, George. *Nutrition and Your Mind: the psychochemical response.* New York: Harper & Row. 1972.

Werntz, D.A., Bickford, R.G., and Shannahoff-Khalsa, D. "Selective, Hemispheric Stimulation by Unilateral Forced Nostril Breathing," *Human Neurobiology,* Vol. 6, pp.165-171. 1987.

Wilhelm, Richard, trans. *The I Ching: Book of Changes.* Princeton: Princeton University. 1950.

Wilhelm, Hellmut. *Change: Eight Lectures on the I Ching.* Trans. C.F. Baynes. Princeton: Princeton University Press. 1972.

About the Author

Katya Walter received a Ph.D. with an interdisciplinary emphasis from the University of Texas in Austin. She spent five years of post-doctoral study at the Jung Institute in Zurich. She has taught in universities in the United States and China, and has published in the areas of cosmology, social analysis, fiction, and poetry. Her recent book *Tao of Chaos* has received wide critical acclaim.

These days Dr. Walter sees clients in analinear analysis, lectures, does workshops, and writes on life as an expression of chaos patterning, with an emphasis on spiritual growth. She has a special interest in conducting Dream Drama workshops that demonstrate how to understand the dramas in your dreams. She is married and has two grown children, two dogs and two cats.

About the Kairos Center

The Kairos Center was founded to explore the integration of body and soul. It is centrist and yet it investigates the edges of spiritual reality. It honors the best of old and new, left and right, East and West, physical and spiritual, linear and analog domains. Our members work for love as well as money, and our network taps a wide range of expertise from theory lecturers to experiential facilitators to body workers and Chinese medicine practitioners.

If you want to order a set of I Ching stones in a fabric pouch, call for current pricing. If you want to be on the Kairos Center mailing list for news about workshops, classes, or spiritual tools, call, write or FAX to:

Kairos Center

4608 Finley Drive
Austin, Texas 78731
Phone 1-800-624-4697
FAX: 512-453-8378